Not Stupid

Not Stupid

The Inspiring True Story
of One Mother's Fight to Give
Her Autistic Children the Quality
of Life They Deserve

Anna Kennedy
with Ivan Sage

JOHN BLAKE

Published by John Blake Publishing Ltd,
3 Bramber Court, 2 Bramber Road,
London W14 9PB, UK

www.johnblakepublishing.co.uk

First published in paperback in 2009

ISBN: 978-1-84454-784-5

British Library Cataloguing-in-Publication Data:
A catalogue record for this book is available from the British Library.

Design by www.envydesign.co.uk

Printed in Great Britain by CPI Bookmarque, Croydon, CR0 4TD

1 3 5 7 9 10 8 6 4 2

Papers used by John Blake Publishing are natural, recyclable products
made from wood grown in sustainable forests. The manufacturing processes
conform to the environmental regulations of the country of origin.

Every effort has been made to contact relevant copyright holders.
Any omission is inadvertent; we would be grateful if the appropriate
people could contact us.

I would like to dedicate this book to my sons Patrick and Angelo, since they have taught me anything is possible and they have given me the strength to make a difference.

I have learned a lot from you, Sean, and have achieved more than I thought I was capable of, because you were by my side. Thank you.

Has this ever happened to you?

Not getting a joke?

Feeling left out?

Not knowing what to say?

Saying the wrong thing?

Not being able to concentrate?

Interrupting someone?

Making a mistake?

Feeling confused?

Feeling frightened?

Being told off but you don't know why?

Not understanding something?

Doing your best but still getting it wrong?

Imagine this happening to you every day. This is what it can be like for children with Asperger Syndrome and autism.

Contents

Foreword
by Esther Rantzen

I used to take as my proverb the warning by Edmund Burke, 'For evil to triumph it is only necessary that good men do nothing'. But that was in my youth, and the young are inclined to be pessimistic.

Now in my maturity – as we old people call our sixth decade – I prefer to turn that saying upside down: 'For goodness to win through,' I say, 'it is only necessary that a good woman does something' – and you can't get a bigger, better example of that kind of victory than Anna Kennedy's story.

What a woman! Sometimes when you watch great athletes leaping over a hurdle you wonder if they really understand how high it is, how many ordinary mortals would give up at the sight of it, or crack their shins painfully at the first attempt, and never try again.

Anna has leapt over hurdles most of us would run from, barriers so high that you wonder how it is that she's not totally worn out. She is a slender, pretty brunette who doesn't look like an Olympic athlete, but then among her other huge talents Anna is a dancer, and dancers have a very special energy and grace.

She has needed those skills. To create the school her own sons, Angelo and Patrick, and hundreds of other autistic children in Hillingdon urgently needed, Anna begged, borrowed, persuaded and cajoled individuals, local councillors, companies, charities and the media.

She's not a rich woman; she's not a politician – all she originally had on her side were her two sons to inspire her, and her husband Sean to stand alongside her. But she is so eloquent, so committed, and her passion is so infectious that she soon attracted a powerful group of disciples who offered their skills and their money to make her dream a reality, and she attracted a terrific team to provide the skills and expertise she needed.

She didn't want much. Just an appropriate education for her sons, and for half a million other autistic children in Britain. And yet, given the fashion for inclusive education that all too often is an excuse for stinginess and neglect, and denies disabled children the care and attention they need, appropriate education is heartbreakingly difficult to find.

Special-needs schools have been brutally phased out, instead of being expanded and developed, and, in many places, as the Children's Commissioner has pointed out, for autistic children such schools simply don't exist. But now in Hillingdon there is the one that Anna and her team created: Hillingdon Manor, with its glowing Ofsted report, its waiting list, and, alongside it, pioneering provision they have created for older autistic students. Because, as with all parents of disabled children,

Anna's greatest fear is what will happen to them when she is no longer there to fight for them.

Where does Anna get her vision, and the strength to make it a reality? The answers are here in this book. I met Anna only when she was well on the way to creating her school as I was making a television programme about her. Reading about her teenage years, I am eternally grateful to her Italian father, who tried and failed to control her, to stop her going to college, and marrying the man she loved. Winning those early battles and proving she was right must have given Anna the confidence to believe that she could win other, tougher battles.

She and Sean persuaded Hillingdon Council to let her have disused school premises, and Barclays Bank to lend her the money she needed, and an army of volunteers to turn it into an attractive practical school. That was just the beginning, but all the while she was dealing with the dramas and dilemmas in her own family life, for autistic children have a different kind of logic, one that often sets them at odds with the rest of the world.

So there are plenty of moments in this book when you can laugh with Anna, while you are consumed with admiration for her stamina and resourcefulness. How would you like to be stuck on a motorway in the freezing fog in a broken-down car, with a mobile phone that has no signal, and two autistic children? She coped without panicking, just as she coped with all the other ordeals in her life.

This is not a textbook on how to bring up disabled children, nor the best way to teach them, or a toolkit you can use to set up your own school, although I'm sure many parents and communities will use it that way, because there is plenty of useful information for others who want to follow where she has led.

This is not a personal story of victory, either – Anna is far too modest to see it in those terms – but it is a remarkable testament to the fact that one woman can make a difference, if that woman is Anna Kennedy.

So let me rephrase my proverb again: 'For goodness to triumph, it is only necessary to have Anna Kennedy on your side'.

Introduction
by Ivan Sage

Thankfully, the vast majority of families rarely need to trouble themselves with thoughts of coping day by day with the complex needs of loved ones whose lives have been blighted by either physical or mental conditions. That's not to say these families go through life without any problems but, when you compare their lives with those who find each day and night a battle to get through, few of them really take the time to fully appreciate their good fortune. I count myself among that number. In fact, until I was invited to help write this book, I had little awareness of how devastating living with autism in its various forms could be.

The chances are, however, that, by picking up this book, you have been touched in some way by the condition. You may be a parent, relative or friend of someone diagnosed with autism or someone coping with it as a carer. Alternatively, you could be someone in the world of the teaching or caring professions whose contact with autism may be limited but you have a need to find out more about the condition in order to gain a better understanding of how to deal with it within your own field. Or, of course, you may be a person with autism yourself.

Whatever your reason for picking up this book, I truly hope it will enlighten you in the same way as Anna's story has enlightened me. Anna, I know, does not want to be put on a pedestal for what she has achieved, but it's so hard not to place her there, for she is a remarkable woman.

Faced with the challenge of finding appropriate educational provision for her two boys, Anna, and her husband Sean, decided upon a course of action that most people would never have contemplated: founding a specialist school dedicated to the care and education of young people with various forms of autism. It was a mammoth task that, on the face of it, was one of folly – but how they have proved everyone wrong!

There are several good reasons for writing *Not Stupid*. From a human-interest point of view, it is a remarkable story of a couple's love and dedication for their children and their determination to provide them with as good a chance of a happy and productive life as other, more fortunate youngsters.

On the other hand, their story highlights the barriers and misunderstandings placed in their path towards that goal by those who were either too ignorant or too inflexible in their ways to appreciate fully the scale of the problems faced by so many in society when it comes to autism.

Not Stupid highlights the depths of despair Anna and Sean endured in their quest to help their boys, and the boys' torment, which, particularly in their time in nursery and mainstream education, saw them subjected to ridicule and bullying.

That said, this is a story of hope. Anna and Sean have proved that mountains can be moved if you have the determination to focus on your goals, and that living with autism can be made easier when it is more fully and widely understood.

I trust this book will, in some small way, help towards that end.

Chapter One

Shattered Dreams

Looking at the psychotherapist's report, I felt a rush of blood from my feet going straight to my head. 'It says here my son's got Asperger Syndrome.'

'That's right, Mrs Kennedy.'

'Well, this report says it was diagnosed three years ago – this is the first time we've heard anything about it!' I was incredulous. How could this total lack of communication over such a vital diagnosis possibly have happened?

Ever since his traumatic birth, our son Patrick had endured poor health, and his experience of life in his nursery school and, later, in a mainstream school had resulted in copious tears and frantic tantrums since day one. Now at last we knew why.

'Why didn't anyone tell us this before?' I demanded.

'We just assumed you knew.'

My husband Sean and I were attending an annual review at Patrick's school in 1997, in Hillingdon, northwest London, to discuss his progress – or, should I say, his significant lack of it.

1

The head teacher, Patrick's teachers and the educational psychologist present at the meeting didn't know what to say to us when they realised no one had had the foresight to inform us of Patrick's condition.

To be honest, the rest of the meeting was just a blur and I was unable to concentrate on anything being discussed because I was selfishly thinking, Christ, both my boys have autism! This is terrible. What have I done wrong?

When we arrived home from the school it soon became obvious that Sean was reluctant to talk about Patrick's condition at all. Instead he preferred to discuss ways to get back litigiously at the doctor for failing to inform us when Patrick had been originally diagnosed.

All this was in the wake of learning, shortly earlier, that our younger son, Angelo, had autism. At the time we had known nothing of the condition. If I remember correctly, my first instinct was to wonder how long Angelo would live and I had immersed myself in a quest to find out as much as possible about the condition, with varying degrees of success, ever since. At least the literature I had recently read had given me some idea of what Asperger Syndrome was.

Nevertheless, the news that Patrick had it made me realise that my dreams of one day having children of my own and a carefree life were turning out to be a far cry from what I had hoped. Because my own childhood had been so regimented, I had been looking forward to a more relaxed way of life when, eventually, I would settle down and have a family of my own. I'd had dreams of days on the beach with my kids building sandcastles and having fun. Now all those aspirations seemed like a distant memory.

I decided to speak to the consultant paediatrician at Hillingdon Hospital to find out why we had not been informed of Patrick's diagnosis three years earlier. The paediatrician insisted he had, indeed, informed us of his diagnosis at the time. 'I think we would have remembered something like that if you had,' I replied angrily.

My only recollection of that particular meeting in 1994 was that the paediatrician had said, 'Your son has got very difficult behaviour' – and that he had recommended we send him away to a residential school, but there was no way Sean and I would even have considered that, particularly as Patrick was only 4 years old at the time.

Sean and I now found ourselves setting out on a new path in life that would, over the following years, see us embroiled in a long and drawn-out lobby with the civic and education authorities as we battled to provide our sons with the same rights to an appropriate education and way of life as other, more 'normal', children have.

There's no doubting that a diagnosis of any of the conditions in what is known as the autistic spectrum would plunge any family concerned into a deep sense of crisis – and we were certainly no different. As with most people, our knowledge of autism prior to Angelo's diagnosis had been practically nonexistent and we can now recognise that what many people can see only as a naughty child can be anything but the case. We had now entered a world where only those directly affected can truly appreciate the difficulties and barriers that need to be overcome.

Autism, we discovered, affects around 520,000 people in Britain. The condition, a brain disorder that impairs the ability to relate and communicate, is unrelated to intelligence. In fact, the autistic spectrum includes both highly intelligent individuals and others with severe learning needs. People with autism face difficulties in interacting socially. They have poor concentration and, in some cases, can display disruptive behaviour, which many observers unfamiliar with the condition often put down to naughtiness. Hopefully, this book will go some way to explaining what autism is all about, will reassure parents of children recently diagnosed with the condition, and hopefully, educate those who do not fully understand all the difficulties faced by sufferers and their carers.

There are several instances in my past that have had a profound bearing on my personality and that have shaped me into the type of person I am today. At the very least, the following few pages will illustrate why, to me, barriers are there only to be broken down.

It was back in 1984 that I first met my husband Sean. It was not long after my family had moved back to Middlesbrough from Italy – an unplanned return following the destruction of my parents' home by an earthquake in Monte Cassino.

The earthquake had been an extremely frightening experience. My mother had just persuaded me, a teetotaller, to try a glass of Cinzano. As I sipped it, the walls shook and saucepans and pots began falling onto the floor. My sister Maria Luisa began screaming, then jumped on top of me and flung her arms around my neck in blind panic. I could hardly breathe. Mum prised her off me and we all hurried down the stairs as they were splitting apart under our feet.

As our home shook even more violently and began to disintegrate, we rushed outside into the piazza. During a smaller, subsequent earthquake, I saw the nearby church become badly damaged and saw mannequins crashing through the windows of the shops.

I was 24 years old when we returned to the northeast of England. Given the chance, I would have loved to remain in Italy to continue running the successful dance school, Scuola de Danza de Anna, that I had set up on our arrival in Monte Cassino three years earlier, but my father, who is Italian, was having none of it. As far as he was concerned, the family – my mother, brother Tullio, Maria Luisa and I – would all return to Britain straightaway. I was gutted. My dance school had taken off really well and had the added selling point that I spoke English, so the kids coming to classes could improve their language skills at the same time.

Back in Middlesbrough, when I was 25, I found work in the office of the Whinney Banks Community Centre during the daytime and worked teaching dance to teenagers with special needs at the centre in the evenings.

One evening, as he rushed into the building, I noticed a young man wearing a Crombie coat, green socks and Dunlop trainers. He had what I would describe as a Jackson Five fuzzy haircut and a thick, bushy beard. He ran through the building and dashed up the stairs three or four at a time to where the yoga classes were being held.

He returned the next day as I was sitting in the lounge area during my lunch break. I must have been sitting very upright in my chair when Sean approached me. 'Have you got a rod up your back?' he asked. I just looked at him. What a strange guy! He sat down and stroked his beard.

'Do you like beards?'

'No,' I replied as I turned my head away and ignored him.

'OK,' he said as he got up and off he went.

He was back again the following day, minus his beard. He looked at me and was obviously waiting for me to say something, but I didn't. Then he started chatting to me. I have to admit, I really liked his eyes and the soft tone of his voice, which was surprising coming from such a big chap, who turned out to be a former rugby player – Sean was around six-foot-four tall and weighed around 18 stone.

After a while I got up to leave. I needed to be at Kirby College to attend a dance class to learn a new routine that I'd never tried before. Sean asked if he could walk me there and, on the way, he asked me for a date. I declined, concerned about what my father would say – even when I was 25 years old, my father strongly disapproved of me dating; the same went for my sister. Dad was so strict that if I was watching a film featuring a scene with a couple kissing I would be told to turn my head away. I was still doing so at 18 years of age because I'd been so conditioned by him. How crazy is that!

As a child, I hadn't been allowed to go to friends' houses to play. I'd been living such a sheltered life. From the ages of 13 to 16, I attended a convent school, where I took GCE O-levels and CSEs (Certificate of Secondary Education, which preceded the General Certificate of Secondary Education, or GCSE, in the UK) in French, English, needlework, domestic science, religious scriptures, maths and Italian. At the time I was incredibly naïve.

After leaving school, I had, at the age of 16, my first experience of death and feelings of loss and despair when my friend Karen, who was also 16, died from a brain tumour. I found her death very hard to handle and to come to terms with.

I never dated at all until I was in my early twenties. When it came to boyfriends I'd had to be sneaky in case Dad found out. I had to pretend I was going to run an errand for my mother in order to get out of the house because Dad had such a controlling influence on us all. I think he was scared that my sister and I would be taken advantage of.

On leaving school at 16 I had wanted to enrol at Kirby College in order to learn to become an interpreter, but Dad had ripped up my application form. 'Good girls stay at home,' he'd insisted. When I was 17 my mother had a word with Dad. She told him I shouldn't be hanging around at home all day. If I didn't go to college he should let me go out to work. He reluctantly agreed and, after an interview at the Binns department store, I was taken on in the lingerie department, which necessitated my attending Kirby College one day a week to undertake business studies, so I did get there in the end.

My only escape from such regimented order came in the form of dance. When I was a young child, my mother had taken me to the Mavis Percival Dance School and it was there that I felt truly free to express myself. In a way, I was like a free bird when I danced – even though Dad tried several times to stop me going. As I'd grown up I'd enjoyed preparing for dance competitions and shows. I loved tap dancing but I also had to do ballet, which, to be honest, I hated. I much preferred fast-tapping jazz routines – ones you had to attack. I'm not a smoothy, floaty person. That's just not me. But the ballet was a necessity if I was to improve my posture.

After working at Binns for 18 months I decided to open my own dance school. I'd studied for my teaching qualifications and was pleased to pass with 96 points from a possible 100. After helping my own dance teacher for a while, I began taking classes of my own in a church hall in Middlesbrough. At one time I had a hundred pupils. It was a very satisfying experience but, after I'd worked at Binns all day, dancing in the evenings meant I was always knackered! I had to choose between Binns and dance classes – so I chose the dancing.

It was only natural, bearing in mind Dad's strict manner, that, when Sean asked me out for a date, my main concern was of Dad's reaction, should he find out. But, when I declined Sean's offer, he refused to give up, even when I explained my reasons why. Sean told me he would meet me in the nearby Debenham's store and that I could use the excuse of running an errand for my mother as an excuse to get away.

It was absolutely pelting down with rain as I made my way to Debenham's. I was convinced Sean wouldn't be there, but there he was, wearing a smart suit and holding an umbrella. I was nervous. Although I'd already secretly seen a few boys in the short term, my first date with Sean was in the wake of a bad experience with one boy that had really scared me, mainly because I had been so naïve at the time. Sean, on the other hand, was quite forward and not shy at all. After chatting, we were surprised to find out that we had attended the same school in Middlesbrough and at the same time, although, to the best of our knowledge, we had never met.

Within three weeks Sean had asked me to marry him. At the time, we were in the house he shared with his mother, Coral, and his Aunt Pam. Sean had even cooked the meal for the occasion. A week later he took me into the town because he wanted to buy me a ring. It was now time to break the news to my family, but, when we got home, we discovered that Maria Luisa had been rushed to hospital with appendicitis, so it was obviously not the most appropriate of times to share our news. Instead I went straight to the hospital to see her.

However, the time eventually came when Sean was to be introduced to Dad. It was a complete nightmare. Everyone was nervous and Mum was baking for England. I'd already primed Sean to say all the things I thought Dad would want to hear, but it very soon became obvious that Sean was his own man. No one was going to tell him what he could or couldn't say!

I was cringing as Dad became angrier and angrier. There were long silences, interrupted only by Mum frequently asking if anyone wanted more strawberry cakes. The meeting was a disaster. Dad was completely unimpressed, declaring, 'He's not going out with my daughter!' Consequently, further meetings between Sean and me had to be clandestine.

I was heartbroken when Sean left Middlesbrough to attend Brunel University in Uxbridge, northwest London – and so was he. On arrival in London he rang me to say he'd get the first bus home to be with me again, but I persuaded him to stay. After four or five days, however, I was missing him so much. My Aunt Anita could see how low I was and said I should just pack up some things and go to him, that at my age I shouldn't still be under Dad's wing. Although I only had around £20 on me,

I took the train to King's Cross, where Sean was waiting for me on the platform. It was so good to see him again.

Sean had been sharing in a boys' bedsit, so he had to smuggle me in to his room, where we shared a single bed. Considering Sean weighed 18 stone, it was cramped but fun, and I had to hide my clothes so the cleaners wouldn't find them.

Moving in with Sean was a scary experience for me, bearing in mind my complete inexperience with boys, but things went quite well and, after a time, I found work, first in a Woolworth's store, which I hated, then at Sanderson's, a textiles manufacturer, as a supervisor in the orders office, where my language skills came in handy. I even managed to get my dance classes up and running again. Meanwhile, Sean, who was studying biochemistry during the day, found night work in a nearby Tesco supermarket to help make ends meet.

My move south to London angered Dad so much that he wouldn't speak to me for six months and even my sister wasn't best pleased with me for leaving her behind. Mum, apparently, had cried when she found out I had gone. Because I hadn't the heart to tell her I'd moved in with Sean, I told her I was sharing a bedsit with four other girls. The trouble with lying is that you need to remember what you tell someone, and this cover story meant I had to make up and remember the names I'd made up for my imaginary friends whenever I spoke to Mum.

It wasn't the best way to start a relationship, but Sean and I were happy together and, without telling our families, we married at Uxbridge Register Office in front of two witnesses we didn't know on 24 September 1986. We moved out of the bedsit into married quarters at Brunel University and, not long afterwards, moved again, this time into a shared-ownership house in Uxbridge. It may have had only one bedroom, but we were so excited when we moved in.

Then, in 1989, I fell pregnant. We were delighted. This was meant to be the start of a wonderful experience for us both, but little did we anticipate the heartache and traumas ahead of us that would have such a devastating effect on our family.

I had always hoped to have my first child before I reached the age of 30, but I endured a really bad pregnancy. I suffered from pre-eclampsia which, basically, meant my ankles became swollen and I had problems with my kidneys, which resulted in proteins leaving my body via my urine. It is an extremely dangerous condition for both the mother and her unborn child. There were fears that there could be deadly complications, one of the main concerns being my high blood pressure.

Toxaemia, which indicates toxins in the blood, was also diagnosed. My body was giving up on me and I knew I was really ill. It was really scary. For the first 12 weeks I couldn't stop vomiting, which meant I couldn't go to work. I thought, If this is pregnancy, you can keep it!

After a while, though, the vomiting became less frequent and I was able to return to my work at Sanderson's but, within weeks, my feet had swollen up like balloons. When I was 25 weeks' pregnant I was getting severe headaches and silver dots began appearing before my eyes. My colleagues were telling me that I didn't look well and that I should visit my doctor. I made an appointment but found I couldn't even get my shoes on.

After checking me over, my doctor wouldn't even let me get off the chair. She tested my urine and discovered that the sample contained three plusses of protein, which put my baby and me firmly in the danger zone, and my blood pressure was through the roof. She immediately telephoned for an ambulance.

I was taken to Hillingdon Hospital and there I remained for weeks and weeks in the maternity ward. It had been decided that I needed bed rest to bring my blood pressure down and I was placed in a room next door to the nurses' station because I could be more closely observed through a window in the dividing wall.

Despite all the care and attention I had been receiving and weeks of bed rest, at 28 weeks my blood pressure went through the roof again and, because the special-care baby unit did not have a suitable cot and the doctors had decided I might need to have an emergency Caesarean operation, the hunt was on for a hospital that could not only deliver my baby but would have a specialist cot to accommodate him or her after the birth.

When I was informed that the nearest hospital to meet these requirements was in Brighton, I panicked. I didn't want to go there. After all, there was no way Sean would have been able to get there and I really wanted him to be with me when our baby was born. The doctors and nurses tried to reassure me. If, they told me, my blood pressure could be reduced, I could stay where I was. Nurses came in to help me with relaxation exercises and, thankfully, my blood pressure responded accordingly.

Two weeks later, on 5 January 1990, a nurse came in and told me I would be OK to go on for another day. 'The longer you keep the baby in there, the better.' The next thing I knew, I was surrounded by medics telling me they needed to get the baby out straightaway after they had studied the results of some medical tests. I was to have an emergency Caesarean operation. There was just enough time to telephone Sean before I was put under a general anaesthetic.

For the next 48 hours I had to have a nurse by my side. My kidneys were packing up and I was continually being sick owing to an allergic reaction to the anaesthetic. When I came round, Sean was sitting next to me, stroking my hand, but because our son Patrick was so small, he had already been taken to the special-care baby unit.

Normally, under these circumstances, a picture is taken of the newborn baby to show the mother when she wakes up but, unfortunately, the camera was broken so all I knew about Patrick was what Sean had told me. 'He's really lovely,' he said, before explaining that Patrick was receiving special care owing to the fact that he weighed just 2 pounds 10 ounces (about 1.3 kilos). He also had pre-eclampsia and his body, like mine, had been filling with fluid. When it was drained from him, his weight dropped further to 2 pounds 4 ounces (just over a kilo).

It wasn't until Patrick was four days old that I was taken down to see him for the first time. There were lots of tubes and wires attached to him and, when I first saw him, I broke down and cried because it was so scary seeing him like that. He was such a tiny little thing, lying there with an oxygen box to help him breathe, and feet so small that the only way the nurses had found to keep his socks on was to tape them round his ankles to stop the skin rubbing off, because he was moving his legs around so much. From this point on I saw Patrick every day. Having our own child was exhilarating but scary at the same time, since we had little idea of whether he would survive or not.

I was kept in hospital for ten days after the birth. Bearing in mind all the stress I had been under, I was less than impressed as I walked through our front door. The house looked as though a bomb had hit it. There were piles of washing up and it was obvious Sean had not been coping at all with living alone. I ended up picking things up from the floor and, to be honest, I was fuming.

Each day afterwards I was taken to visit Patrick in the hospital by a voluntary helper since, because I'd had a Caesarean operation, I was not permitted to drive. Sean found fatherhood rather scary. He's such a big bloke and, of course, Patrick was so, so tiny. In fact we have a photograph of Sean holding Patrick and Sean's thumb is as big as Patrick's head.

Patrick's health gave us and the medics plenty of cause for concern. He wasn't responding well to treatment or tolerating his feeds and he became very seriously ill. Sean and I were informed that, unless Patrick had a successful blood transfusion, we might lose him. To say we were desperate and scared would probably be an understatement and I found myself praying all the time – the Hail Mary, one of my favourite prayers. Things became so serious that Sean and I agreed we would ask the hospital's Catholic priest to come to Patrick to baptise him and to administer the Last Rites. Patrick was given two sacraments. The first allowed him to be baptised and this allowed him to receive a further sacrament, the sacrament of the sick.

The decision to ask for the sacrament of the sick was born out of pure desperation. Patrick was, indeed, extremely ill. A successful blood transfusion was his only hope of survival. Thank God for people who so kindly give their blood! Had it not been for people like that, Patrick would not be with us today. Sean and I were overjoyed that he responded so well to the blood transfusion – in fact, he looked like a little tomato afterwards and, a couple of days later, his tolerance to feeds improved, he gained weight and became stronger and stronger.

However, there were still a few scares along the way, not least when workmen outside the hospital accidentally cut through an electricity cable and the emergency generator failed to kick in. As a result there were nurses running around the special-care baby unit, frantically handing out blankets for the babies and operating bellows-like equipment to help some of them breathe. Thankfully, after 20 minutes or so, the power supply was restored.

Patrick didn't get the all-clear until he was ten weeks old. We were on cloud nine when we were at last told we could bring him home, but we soon discovered life would be far from straightforward. For a start, sleeping was a problem. Having been in the special-care baby unit for the first ten weeks of his life, Patrick had become used to all the beeping noises of the equipment that had helped him to survive. At home, he began to make strange growling noises as he slept and, after a while, it was driving Sean and me round the bend. What was going on?

I telephoned the midwife, who came round to reassure us that Patrick was probably only compensating for the noises he had got used to hearing while lying in his incubator. She suggested we get a clock, wrap it in a towel and lay it next to Patrick as he slept. Thank God it worked!

After Patrick had been home for ten days, Sean's mother Coral came to stay and to offer support. That day, we put

Patrick down for a sleep but, after a while, I became concerned, particularly since he hadn't woken up as normal for a feed. When I went over to Patrick, my concerns were raised because he looked so very pale. I called Coral in to have a look at him.

Being a nurse, Coral knew instantly something was not right and noticed that Patrick was blue around the mouth. I telephoned our doctor, who suggested I make an appointment to bring him in, but Coral disagreed. 'We've got to get this baby to hospital right now!' she insisted. As I picked Patrick up he was limp and his head just flopped right back. We rushed outside and I handed him over to Coral, who, by now, was sitting in the back of our car.

I have to say, I drove like a lunatic en route to the hospital, mounting pavements and jumping red traffic lights and, on arrival, I just abandoned the car in the middle of the car park. I grabbed hold of Patrick and ran as fast as I could into the hospital. 'Someone's got to look at this baby right now!' I yelled and, fortunately, right in front of me, a consultant appeared who had tended to Patrick and me while we had been in hospital a few days earlier.

'Whatever's the matter?' he asked. He laid Patrick in his arms with his feet towards his chest and his head in his hands. Then he raised and lowered his arms. 'Come on, Patrick,' he said before slowly repeating the movement. By now I was frantic and holding tightly onto Coral's arm, but the consultant remained calm and raised and lowered his arms once more, at which point Patrick took a huge intake of breath. What a relief!

Patrick was treated for septicaemia and given a lumbar puncture – and it was a worrying 24 hours waiting for the results. He was diagnosed as suffering from apnoea, also known as sleep apnoea, a breathing-related sleep disorder that can cause the sufferer to stop breathing up to 400 times during the night. We were concerned to learn it was a potentially life-threatening condition but glad it had been diagnosed early as, untreated, it can be associated with heart attacks and strokes.

Patrick was kept in hospital for ten days. After such a scare I was afraid to take my eyes off him even for a moment, and I often had to pinch his earlobes to wake him up in order to remind him to breathe again. Thankfully, though, we were told he would eventually outgrow the condition.

Nevertheless, for the first three years of his life, Patrick was a sickly child and had to be given so many injections for his various ailments that he began to look like a junkie. Among the setbacks he encountered were a number of chest infections, glue ear, throat infections, vitamin D deficiency, severe croup, whooping cough and a disorder known as rickets, which causes poor development of the bones. I felt we could have had a permanent room at the hospital, since we seemed to be returning there on such a frequent basis. Sean and I often had to give Patrick nebulisers because it seemed he would pick up any bug that was going around at the time.

Because Sean was now working as a proofreader for Middlesex County Press, much of the day-to-day caring for Patrick was down to me and I would often find myself spending the night at the hospital while Patrick was being treated for one thing or another.

When he was two years old we all moved to nearby Acton because our one-bedroom home was no longer big enough for the three of us. Again, we purchased a shared-ownership home, but this time we had an extra bedroom and a garden. Not only that, the lady living next door was a childminder, which allowed me to return to work and, fortunately, despite my prolonged absences, Sanderson's had kept my job open for me.

Our neighbour got on really well with Patrick and, after working as his childminder for a while, soon got to know a lot about him. Patrick would play with her little daughter but, one day when I went to collect him, she told me that she had noticed Patrick playing inappropriately with the toys. For instance, rather than running a toy car along the floor like most children would, Patrick would turn it upside down and just spin the wheels with his fingers. Meanwhile he'd learned the alphabet really quickly and even knew it backwards.

One day, while sitting in the doctor's surgery with Patrick, I noticed other patients listening as he recited a *Thomas the Tank Engine* story, word perfect, from memory. He was only three years old at the time and he was just staring at the wall with no book in sight. What the other patients didn't realise was that, by now, Patrick had memorised all 25 of his *Thomas the Tank Engine* stories – each one word-perfect. Sean and I were convinced we had a little Einstein on our hands!

To our disappointment, our neighbour packed up childminding. We found another lady to take over but, after unexpectedly returning early to pick him up on a couple of occasions, we had not been impressed to discover that she had left Patrick outside the front door – which had been shut each time – and that he had been sick, unnoticed, in his buggy.

I took the decision to check Patrick in to an independent

nursery at St Mary's School in Hillingdon but, although I was convinced this would be the best move for him, he had other ideas. To say he hated the experience would be an understatement. Whenever I left him there in the mornings he would scream and scream and scream. He wouldn't play with the other children, preferring to sit by himself in a corner of the room. He wasn't getting on at all well. I was, naturally, worried but I put his behaviour down to the facts that he had been so poorly for so long, and that he had become so used to my being with him almost all of the time.

In 1992, when Patrick was three, I became pregnant again. Once again I was diagnosed with pre-eclampsia, this time after 31 weeks, and was not impressed when I was informed it was rare to suffer it twice unless I now had a different partner! My condition meant I had to stay in hospital for nine weeks.

Because of this, Patrick had to stay with my mum in Middlesbrough. At first he would speak to me on the telephone but, after a while, he refused to do so, probably because he thought I had deserted him.

Because of my history, the doctors wanted to keep a close eye on me but, after being in hospital for four weeks and seeing other mothers come in, having their babies and leaving, I soon became pretty fed up. Eventually, I was allowed to go home at the weekends, but only on the condition I return to sleep at the hospital each night. At least that gave me something to look forward to.

When I got to 40 weeks, the consultant informed me he was about to go on holiday and that he would see me in two weeks' time on his return. He told me my baby would be delivered by Caesarean section but he would like me to experience labour pains because I would feel 'cheated as a woman' if I didn't.

Only a man could say that!

After returning from his holiday the consultant was informed I had not experienced any labour pains at all. As a result, on 21 January 1993, he took the decision to deliver my baby by Caesarean section straightaway.

I'd had to have an epidural, which was a weird feeling. Sean was supposed to be present at the birth but he chickened out, claiming there wasn't a gown big enough for him. Instead, he stood outside, looking through one of the windows and giving me the occasional thumbs-up sign for encouragement.

There was no pain at the time of birth, just a tugging feeling as they pulled Angelo out from me. When he was born Angelo had the cord around his neck – and red hair! He also had an infection in one of his eyes, but at least he weighed 6 pounds (2.7 kilos), a much healthier birth weight than Patrick.

At first, Sean and I were pleased to believe everything would be more 'normal' with Angelo. After we brought him home, Patrick returned from my Mum's. He went to run towards me to give me a hug but then saw Angelo in the Moses basket and refused to come either to me or anywhere near his newborn brother. He also declined to go anywhere near Sean. I suppose, in Patrick's eyes, we'd replaced him with a new baby. However, I'm a very cuddly, kissy person and, over the next few days, I was able to reassure Patrick that we still loved him just as much as we ever had.

After a few months Coral and Sean's Aunt Pam came with me and the boys to spend a brief holiday in a Pontin's holiday camp in Jersey. Sean didn't come. He absolutely hates holidays, but at least it was a much-needed break – particularly as far as Patrick was concerned because it meant he didn't have to be dragged screaming into the nursery for a while.

Everything seemed to be going well during the holiday and I was pleased to note that Angelo was passing all the milestones any parent would expect from their child as he or she grows up. In fact, we have many photographs taken during this holiday showing Angelo smiling and looking at the camera with loads of eye contact. As far as I was concerned, Angelo was a particularly good little baby who was happy just as long as he was fed and kept comfortable.

When Angelo was 18 months old I took him to have his measles, mumps and rubella (MMR) injection. From this point on, his health would become a major concern to us. During his belated christening, history seemed to be repeating itself when he stopped breathing, as we stood by the altar in the church. Then, suddenly, there was a huge gasp as he got his breath back. I suspected he too was suffering from sleep apnoea.

Later, Angelo came down with a severe ear infection and a very high temperature – so high that we took him to the hospital to be checked out. The infection had become so acute that his ear had filled with green pus. He was given antibiotics but he was allergic to them. As a result his neck began to swell and he developed blotches all over his body. A different antibiotic was administered to correct the problem but he was allergic to that one too and became really ill.

Eventually, the infection subsided but Angelo was now noticeably beginning to act strangely. For a start, he didn't want me to touch him and he would stare, fixated, at the patterns on our wallpaper. He would frequently line up a variety of objects in perfectly straight lines across the room and, if you moved any of them even slightly, he would go completely berserk.

He developed a high-pitched scream and boundless energy, and would repeatedly run from one corner of a room to the other – sometimes for hours on end – or he would bash himself against the walls. Other times he would walk around on tiptoes or just stand in a corner for really long periods of time. Worst of all, he wouldn't let me cuddle him, which I found just heartbreaking. Although Angelo seemed to be a happier child than Patrick, his communication skills were extremely limited, usually no more than one-word demands.

Patrick's communication skills were difficult nonetheless. In his mind, he had to be in control of a conversation and would be most upset if it didn't go completely his way. We soon realised he had very little desire to listen to anybody else's point of view.

His screaming fits each time he was taken to the nursery added to the stress Sean and I were experiencing. In all, Patrick was at the nursery for three years and there wasn't a single day when he didn't protest on the way. One day, he even released himself from his car seat and grabbed the steering wheel in an effort to prevent me from taking him there. Distracted, I turned to tell him to get back into his seat, which resulted in my driving into the rear of the car ahead of us. I ended up with whiplash but, fortunately, both Patrick and Angelo were unharmed.

It wasn't the last time such an incident would occur. Later, on the way to the school, I was distracted by Angelo playing up in the back seat. It was only a momentary lapse in concentration but it was enough to cause our car to collide with the car in front of us. Our car was very badly damaged but, fortunately, no one was injured and the driver of the other car was very understanding as we exchanged our details.

Nevertheless, I was in quite a state. Once I got home I was nauseous and headachy and just could not stop crying, especially since Sean seemed to be so cross with me. As was, and is often the case, I was relieved that a two-hour keep-fit session that night made me feel a lot better and washed away some of the stress I'd been under.

By the time Patrick was five he had moved on to St Mary's School from the nursery but his behaviour was still giving cause for concern. He would constantly talk to himself and failed to understand even the most basic of instructions. He adopted a solitary manner of play, being particularly wary of large groups of children, and this became most apparent when he developed an obsession with jigsaws.

He hated it if I left him, whether at home or at the nursery, and, even if I was going to the toilet, he would want to come with me. Patrick didn't want me to go to work and, at night, he would get out of bed to check I was still in the house.

I had assumed that his behaviour had been down to all the problems associated with when he was a special-care baby, but we were eventually advised to take him to Hillingdon Hospital to meet with the consultant paediatrician who, unbeknown to us at the time, had already diagnosed him with Asperger Syndrome. The paediatrician then advised us to go as a family to see a psychotherapist, Mrs Porter, at the Child, Family and Adolescent Consultation Service, where children can get access to one-to-one or group therapy. We assumed this was because of Patrick's screaming sessions at school, but this was not the case: the wheels had been set in motion regarding Patrick's diagnosis of Asperger Syndrome. It's just that no one at the hospital had seen fit to tell us!

Mrs Porter noted that Patrick would benefit from individual psychotherapy and, as a result, we returned to see her on a weekly basis. Patrick made good use of these sessions, gradually becoming more talkative and expressing his ideas on paper, either through drawing or writing. He still reacted poorly when subjected to change or stress, but Mrs Porter reckoned he was responding well to clear limits placed before him.

In fact, Patrick's self-esteem benefited from these sessions. He felt more grown up when he was alone with Mrs Porter, although at times he was unsure who should be in charge of the sessions – an adult or himself. As time passed, she changed the sessions by moving into another room, a change that affected Patrick's progress quite significantly, as his play immediately regressed to become repetitive and stereotyped.

Mrs Porter pointed out that Patrick would continue to require psychotherapy in life to ensure he would be aware of clear and safe boundaries in all situations to enable him to function successfully. The psychotherapy sessions were clearly helpful to him but, one day, when Angelo was two-and-a-half years old, Mrs Porter said, 'I think you need to have Angelo diagnosed by the consultant paediatrician.'

'What do you mean?'

'I think he may possibly have autism.'

I gripped the sides of my chair. What a horrible-sounding word. 'What's that?' I asked. The only thing I vaguely thought I knew about the condition was what I had seen in the 1988 movie Rain Main, starring Dustin Hoffman. I noticed the shock on Sean's face and watched as his shoulders dropped. It was as if a hundred-pound weight had been placed on each of them. As for me, when the penny dropped, it was as if the world had exploded, but there was no noise.

On the way home, all I could think was, Oh, no, more barriers and hurdles to overcome. Autistic tendencies? What's that? Why us?

Nor was I looking forward to breaking the news to our family. Of course, we knew the boys were no different from the way they were before this bombshell, but we realised, given this knowledge, that our expectations for them would undoubtedly change.

We were not given any information other than that there may be a support group in our borough but, even then, no one at the Child, Family and Adolescent Consultation Service seemed too sure. Autism was hardly explained to us at all and we left after being told we would have another appointment in six months' time. I tried to find out about our local autism support group and was dismayed to discover it had folded because the lady running it could no longer find the time to continue.

After receiving such devastating and life-changing news, we were totally on our own, it seemed, to deal with our problems. After we had attended a specialist centre, Harper House in Radlett, and the Child Development Centre in Hillingdon, it was finally confirmed: Angelo was, indeed, autistic and the next few days in particular saw Sean and me trying our best to come to terms with the situation.

It really hit me when I rang my mother. I just cried and cried, but I knew it wasn't going to help anyone. With me crying and Sean burying his head in the sand, it seemed the kids were just going to carry on doing what they were doing. Of course, Coral and Mum were very supportive, but with them in Middlesbrough and us miles away in London, they could offer only emotional support and I felt very alone.

Thank God then for 'Aunty' Zita, who used to work with me at Sanderson's, the loveliest woman anyone could ever meet. She really stepped up to the plate and was a wonderful support to us all. She's a small lady whom I used to pass on the way to work and had ended up giving lifts to. Zita has no family of her own and I guess I became the daughter she never had.

Meanwhile, Angelo seemed to be in a world of his own. I really wished I could get inside his head, just to have some idea of what he was thinking. I remember mentioning this to our GP when I told him about Angelo's diagnosis but I'm sure he felt I was just being a fussy mother, particularly when he said, 'Oh, what do you think about that, then? I reckon you must feel your son's an alien, don't you? Every time your boys come here, they never sit still and they're always touching my things.' Needless to say, I didn't go back to him any more.

Five days after diagnosis, on Valentine's Day, we took Angelo to Hillingdon Hospital for a blood test to eliminate the fragile X syndrome, which is a chromosome deficiency. After we had waited for an hour and a half, a nurse attempted to take blood from Angelo, who, by now, had become quite hysterical. The nurse called two of her colleagues to assist her while I held onto Angelo, but even then it took five attempts before they eventually succeeded in getting the required blood sample. At least the blood test revealed that Angelo did not have the syndrome after all.

Later in the day, I visited Grangewood School in Eastcote, which had been recommended to us. This specialist school had a facility for autistic children but, in spite of that, after viewing the school I didn't think it would be an appropriate place for Angelo. Sean and I were convinced he would be better off going to a mainstream school with one-to-one tutoring. We felt he would have the added stimulus of other 'normal' children, which would help him integrate and progress more satisfactorily. I know this sounds cruel, but I did not want Angelo to go to a special school for children with learning difficulties and physical disabilities – I just couldn't help the way I felt at the time.

The following day a health visitor called round to see us but, surprisingly, she didn't have any information on autism for us. Instead she gave us an information sheet with names and addresses of help groups and voluntary societies. She remarked at how amazing Sean and I were, in that our marriage had not suffered in spite of all the problems we had already faced over the previous six years with Patrick. She told us she knew problems of such magnitude often split couples up and I remember desperately hoping that our marriage would be strong enough to withstand all the extra pressure it now faced.

After another depressing meeting with Mrs Porter, we learned that Angelo would need lots of help – at least two years of intense psychotherapy – and she stressed the need for us to prevent him from performing all his habitual rituals. By now, I was not feeling too good. I was beginning to feel like a wind-up toy, my brain filled to saturation point, but at least Sean and I had a nice romantic evening at a local pub that night, which made me feel a little better.

A couple of days later, though, the cracks began to appear between Sean and me, when he just stopped talking to me, even though the rest of the family were being supportive. I'd been finding it difficult to concentrate at work but the silence from Sean was even harder to deal with, because he was bottling up his emotions. To my mind, he was in denial, but I really wished we could talk it out between us, that we could work together, not only for our sakes but for Angelo's.

As a child, I would keep diaries but, after a while, I had stopped doing so. Now I just felt the urge to write my feelings down on paper once again. I began writing each day. I guess it was my way of sharing my problems with someone – even if it was just myself.

Fortunately, within a few days, the tension between Sean and me subsided and, after I'd made it clear to him that we would have to work together if he wanted to see an improvement in Angelo, he made more of an effort. Meanwhile, I'd spoken to Ingrid, a trainee social worker from Network 81, a support group of parents of children with special educational needs. She was very helpful and assisted me through the process of obtaining disability allowance.

After a couple more days Sean was in a much better mood, which was surprising, especially since Angelo had had a very disturbed night, not having slept until around 4 a.m. I was absolutely shattered. Unfortunately, the following night he wouldn't settle again. I found myself getting increasingly tired and cross with him, even though I knew I shouldn't. Sean eventually snapped, 'Shut up!' at Angelo and went up to bed, unable to cope with his laughing loudly and constant running around the room. Angelo eventually went to sleep at 2 a.m. – a sleep pattern that would become all too familiar to us in the years to come.

The less Angelo would sleep, the more hyper he would become. With his seemingly boundless energy and night waking, it was rare to get any decent sleep and often I found myself sleeping on the sofa downstairs. I even took to doing my housework in the early hours, reckoning I may just as well be doing something useful if I was awake anyway. Sean and I were becoming exhausted. Both Angelo's and Patrick's disturbed sleeping patterns were having a detrimental effect on us and the resultant levels of stress often made us irritable with each other – even to the point that I wondered whether our relationship could survive.

Jocelyn Phillips worked for Portage – a service that supports parents with strategies in the home – and she turned out to be a great support to our family in the months to come. However, she disagreed with my views on not having Angelo attend Grangewood School and considered that his going to a mainstream school would not do him justice. Jocelyn felt that Angelo needed a specialised way of teaching and that Grangewood School was particularly appropriate to his needs.

What a dilemma!

When Angelo's diagnosis was confirmed, an appointment was made at the Central Middlesex Hospital for a brain scan and, it goes without saying, there was little chance Angelo would be too happy about it. When a nurse attempted to put glue on the side of his temples in order to attach at least 20 wires, Angelo became very distressed and refused to co-operate – even when I held down his hands and someone else held down his legs he was too strong. It broke my heart to see him so distressed.

In the end it was decided to return to the hospital another time and to complete the scan under sedation in the children's ward. I was asked if Angelo had been tested for epilepsy, since it was believed up to 50 per cent of autistic children either have or can develop it.

All this uncertainty, the lack of sleep, the worry and strain that we found ourselves subjected to meant that every day resulted in a roller coaster of emotions for Sean and me. It all boiled over a few weeks after Angelo's diagnosis and resulted in a major argument between us during which I even threatened to leave home.

Don't let anyone tell you that living with autism is easy. It is testament to our relationship that it has survived so strongly over the past few years in spite of all the heartache and challenges we've had to face along the way.

Chapter Two
What is Autism?

It had been a real kick in the guts to learn of Angelo's autism diagnosis and I remember crying for six weeks afterwards. Sean and I knew nothing of the condition – in fact, my first instinct had been to wonder how long Angelo would live. I didn't know anyone else who had an autistic child.

So, what is autism? I didn't like the sound of it. It's such an ugly, harsh word. Basically, we felt that, after Angelo's diagnosis, we had just been left to get on with it, since there was very little offered to us in the form of advice or support. Some doctors assumed Angelo's condition was genetic, though, so far as we were aware, neither Sean nor I had autism in the family.

I realised I had to pull myself together and that feeling sorry for myself was of little use to Angelo, Patrick or Sean. I had a thirst for knowledge and I embarked on a voyage of discovery. The trouble was, the more I found out about autism, the worse the prospects seemed to be. The outlook, in my eyes, was so bleak and confusing. Nevertheless, I remained determined to find out all I could about the subject.

That, however, was not as easy as I might have initially hoped. First of all, I contacted the National Autistic Society, or should I say I tried several times without success. I should point out, however, that nowadays these problems have been overcome. Nevertheless, it was so frustrating trying to obtain knowledge at that time from an organisation that I just couldn't get through to.

At last I managed to speak to someone who told me she would forward some information to me and she recommended a useful VHS video that would be enlightening, which I paid for over the telephone.

Six weeks later, I had heard nothing from them. No video, no information. Coral rang the society a couple of times to hurry them along on my behalf. They apologised and, eventually, the leaflets and video arrived through our letterbox. Watching the video for the first time was a truly traumatic experience. In fact, after just three minutes, I ejected it from the player and felt as if I was going to be sick – not because of the children featured but because of the severity of their condition. Some were rocking, others swaying from side to side. No disrespect to the children, but I couldn't help thinking that, if this was all Angelo had to look forward to, well, that would be pretty hard to bear.

It got to the stage where I couldn't even keep the video in the house – I preferred to lock it away in the boot of my car. Meanwhile, Sean didn't want to read any of the information leaflets we had received. He simply buried his head in the sand and it seemed he was unable to accept that a child of his could have such a condition, which made me feel very alone in trying to come to terms with our situation.

Sometimes, even now when I'm at home with three other people, I can feel so lonely. Everyone seems to be doing their own thing. Patrick could be talking to himself upstairs in his room; Angelo, bless him, is in his own world, maybe playing on his trampoline in the garden; while Sean might be studying or using his computer. He has a Masters in IT, which means he spends a great deal of time fiddling around on the computer at home. For that reason I've always hated computers – to my mind, they are like 'the other woman' in Sean's life.

Because I wasn't computer-literate at the time, I didn't have access to the internet, although I had been able to find out a certain amount through my work with Health Call, a doctors' answering service. The deeper I dug, the more I found out, but sometimes that just added to the confusion. There were so many different therapies, most of which claimed to help but were very expensive, and we had no idea which way to turn for the best. At least, I thought, Angelo has a bigger brother to help look after him when he grows up a bit more. Even at this time I had convinced myself that Patrick would eventually grow out of his own problems.

I knew Angelo was still the same Angelo we knew and loved, but I found myself observing his strange behaviour more and more. In fact, I frequently spent ages just staring at him. He would often just spin himself around and around, and was, seemingly, a happy boy, although his moods were interspersed with tantrums. Patrick had tried to interact with him in his own way, blowing bubbles for him and playing on the seesaw, even reciting nursery rhymes coupled with clapping at the end of each rhyme.

The National Autistic Society's literature had highlighted the traits of people with autism such as ritualistic, repetitive behaviour and poor communication skills, and that, as very young children, sufferers don't tend to point to something they want but will lead you to it, and this was particularly apparent with Angelo.

Ros Blackburn is a prime example of how autism can be discovered by accident. Some years ago, Ros's parents thought she was deaf because she didn't speak and didn't seem to hear. Even their doctor confirmed she was deaf, then, as he went to write down his diagnosis, he made an error and crumpled up the paper, the noise of which Ros obviously heard.

Ros is now a very high-functioning young lady who goes around giving talks about her condition. She finds it difficult to read and is unable to make her own bed, but, if you speak to her, you would probably not realise she has a problem.

Ros is very articulate, although she still doesn't like people to come too close to her. In fact, a movie called Snow Cake (2006) stars Sigourney Weaver as a character based on Ros. Weaver spent some time with Ros as she prepared for her role in the film and I think she played the part really well. Ros was one of the first people with autism that I heard speaking at a meeting later on our voyage of discovery – and seeing and hearing her gave me real hope for the future.

Patrick had quite stilted speech, very literal. If you tried to hurry him along by telling him to pull his socks up, that, quite literally, is what he would do. I'd always told Patrick he should be careful of cars when crossing the road. One day, when he was standing on the side of the road with me, he looked right, then left, then just ran out into the middle of the road, causing a motorcyclist to take evasive action as he screeched to a halt before calling me a stupid *@!*!!

I grabbed hold of Patrick and shouted at him, 'What did Mummy say to you? I told you. I said you mustn't cross the road when cars are coming!'

'But, Mummy, you didn't say anything about motorbikes,' he replied.

Although they are both on the autistic spectrum, Patrick and Angelo are so different. I had one child who had limited speech and didn't want to be touched, while I had another who wanted to be touched and kissed, and didn't have such limited speech.

I discovered that some children with severe autism have no speech whatsoever, no eye contact; they may head-bang, maybe they never even say 'Mum' or 'Dad', and I can't think of anything more hurtful to a parent than never to hear those words. At the other end of the spectrum, sufferers may be boffins, really clever people who look down on people they consider not to be as clever as they are.

Although autism is four times more common than cerebral palsy, it remains a relatively unknown disability. It was first diagnosed in 1943 and is now known to affect more than half a million people in the United Kingdom.

It's a developmental condition that affects the way the sufferer's brain processes information. Sadly, there is no cure, although much can be done to ensure the person affected can be helped to develop the more basic skills they will require in everyday life, not least being able to communicate more appropriately with other people.

Because a child with autism usually appears like anyone else without a disability, it is often assumed by strangers that a related tantrum is either down to naughtiness or poor parental control when, in fact, it is neither. This was something I had almost become used to whenever I was shopping with Patrick or Angelo, particularly when they had been refused something they wanted. If only people really knew the true reasons why they sometimes behaved in such a fashion, then, perhaps, they would be more sympathetic.

People with autism often have many difficulties in life. Research at the time claimed autism was displayed by one in every 250 people to some degree. More recently, however, figures have suggested the ratio was one in a hundred until a report released by Cambridge Research Centre in 2008 revealed that one person in every 59 in the United Kingdom has some form of autism. It is more common amongst boys than girls and has now been recognised as the fastest growing serious development in the world.

More children were diagnosed with autism in 2008 than with diabetes, cancer and AIDS combined. Despite this, in the same year, the National Autistic Society released results of a survey that suggests that the majority of local authorities in England are still failing adults with autism, and criticised the 'astounding postcode lottery' in provision. Amazingly, it was found that just one local authority in England had undertaken a head count of the number of adults with autism in their area. In addition, 64 per cent of councils said they did not have a named team or individual responsible for autism, in contravention of Department of Health guidelines.

Difficulties with social interactions, social communication and imagination are apparent in people with autism. These three characteristics are collectively referred to as the triad of impairments. For a child to be diagnosed with autism, they have to present a certain number of difficulties in these three areas.

Broken down, social interaction refers to difficulties experienced with social relationships, maybe appearing aloof or indifferent to others; social communication problems would display themselves as difficulties in verbal and nonverbal communication such as not understanding gestures, tone of voice or facial expressions; and imaginative difficulties are apparent as an inability to develop play in an imaginative way or a limited range of imaginative activities.

A child with autism will, like a child with Asperger Syndrome, display resistance to changes in routine or exhibit challenging behaviour; they display indifference to others and will join in play only if an adult insists and assists them.

An autistic child may display little or no eye contact or speech; is often locked into inappropriate routines; some never become toilet-trained; they will guide an adult's hand to whatever it is they want; they will not play with other children; they will speak incessantly about a single topic such as a washing machine or vacuum cleaner; they will copy words parrot-fashion; will behave in a bizarre manner; will handle or spin objects, will laugh or giggle inappropriately; but will be able to do some things well and quickly, particularly if the task does not involve social understanding.

They will require specialised education and structured support if they are to maximise their skills and reach their full potential. They face myriad frustrations in life, particularly when they want to say something but someone else stops them from saying it, or when they want to say something but don't know how to express themselves, or when something doesn't happen when they expect it to.

That's why it's so important to have strong boundaries and structures in place so they can feel safe and begin to develop trust with others. They need to be taught to be more independent in order to develop their self-confidence and to be reassured that they do have something to offer, and that they can make a difference by reaching their academic, social and emotional potential.

People with autism have difficulty in displaying empathy and imagination; they often avoid direct eye contact or shaking hands; and may feel uncomfortable being in close proximity to others and are particularly averse to being in crowded places. They may answer rhetorical questions when in class groups with little understanding of colloquialisms.

When Angelo was diagnosed, my knowledge of other forms of autism such as Asperger Syndrome had been of limited importance to me because, as far as I was concerned, wrongly as it turned out, it didn't affect our family. My quest for information about Asperger Syndrome following Patrick's diagnosis uncovered the magnitude of the conditions in the autistic spectrum disorders. We hadn't realised the scale of autism, but it soon became apparent we were not alone in caring for a loved one whose life is blighted with the associated difficulties.

I learned that Asperger Syndrome was a form of autism that affected people in the higher-functioning end of the autistic spectrum. The more I found out, the more I began to understand the difficulties Patrick faces in life. Most people have a natural ability to look at someone else and be able to tell whether they are happy, sad or angry. They can guess their age or their status and read the signals given off by the other person. It's something most of us take for granted but, for someone with Asperger Syndrome, this is often too difficult to do. As a result, communicating and interacting with others is often beyond them.

People with Asperger Syndrome rarely have the severe learning difficulties associated with autism, and that's obvious when comparing Patrick to Angelo. Patrick's language skills – his vocabulary and more fluent speech – are far superior to Angelo's, although when people speak to Patrick, as is common with people with Asperger Syndrome, he doesn't always take much interest in what they say to him.

Many children with Asperger Syndrome are placed in mainstream schools but often they find themselves subject to teasing or bullying. That said, some cope well, achieving good progress, some even going on to further education and employment. Others, like Patrick, just cannot cope and require more specialist, individual attention. However, they are often of average or even above average intelligence but, sadly, even today, there are few educational facilities for children with the condition.

Despite his condition, it's clear Patrick is not stupid, although he has often convinced himself that he is. As with many who have the condition, Patrick's obsession with dinosaurs and trains has practically made him an expert in each field and it was heartening to read that, because of this side to the condition, many like him can go on to study or work in their favourite subjects.

The more I read about Asperger Syndrome, the more it

seemed I was reading about Patrick. There was his inability to understand a joke; his stilted, exaggerated language and the need to keep sentences clear and concise when speaking to him; the way he excels at learning facts and figures; his lack of social skills or consideration for the feelings of others; and his difficulty in understanding abstract concepts such as religion or literature and nonverbal signals.

People with Asperger Syndrome usually prefer their day to follow a set pattern – they do not react well to change or delays such as a traffic delay or a late train. They tend to be very punctual and, far from being a handicap in later life, these traits can actually prove to be assets when the child grows into adulthood and is seeking employment. Most employers would welcome an employee who is totally focused on their subject, hates being late, and is dedicated and reliable, wouldn't they? Of course, all this would need to be balanced by the understanding of employers and work colleagues.

As for the causes of Asperger Syndrome and autism, well, these are still under investigation. It seems some experts believe there is no single cause for Asperger Syndrome, that it arises from a variety of physical factors that affect the development of the brain. It is not assumed to be caused by either emotional deprivation or a person's upbringing.

Autism, it is believed, could be associated with a variety of conditions that affect the development of the brain before, during or soon after birth. Genetic factors are also considered to be relevant.

So now, at last, I was beginning to understand what Patrick, Angelo, Sean and I would have to spend the rest of our lives dealing with, but one thing common to both conditions was the importance placed on early diagnosis and intervention in order for sufferers to obtain a better chance of appropriate help and support.

Where on earth was that for Patrick?

Now, however, I can better understand why it's so difficult to diagnose autism as the spectrum is so wide. But at least, armed with more information, Sean and I were now in a position to make informed choices for our sons' wellbeing.

Of course, so far I have touched on only two aspects of the autistic spectrum's disorders. There are others, though. The term semantic-pragmatic disorder has been around for nearly 15 years. Originally it was used only to describe children who were not autistic. Features of the condition include delayed language development; learning to talk by memorising phrases instead of putting words together freely; repeating phrases out of context – especially snippets remembered from television programmes; muddling up 'I' and 'you'; problems with understanding questions – particularly those involving 'how' and 'why'; and difficulty in following conversations.

Children with this disorder have problems understanding the meaning of what other people say, and they do not understand how to use speech appropriately themselves. Soon after this condition was recognised, both research and practical experience yielded two important findings: first, that many people who definitely are autistic have this kind of language disorder – Dustin Hoffman's character Raymond in Rain Man being a typical example – and, second, most of the children diagnosed as having semantic-pragmatic disorder also have some mild autistic features. For example, they usually have difficulty understanding social situations and expectations; they like to stick fairly rigidly to routines; and they lack imaginative play.

Research has shown that there is probably a single underlying cognitive impairment that produces both the autistic features and the semantic-pragmatic disorder. The fact that children with semantic-pragmatic disorder have problems understanding the meaning and significance of events, as well as the meaning and significance of speech seems to bear this out.

The idea of an autistic continuum has been used to explain the situation. All the children on the continuum have semantic-pragmatic difficulties, but the degree of their other autistic impairments can be severe or moderate or mild. This parallels the autistic continuum relating to Asperger Syndrome, where all the children have a marked social impairment but those with Asperger Syndrome have only a relatively mild and subtle language impairment.

Pathological demand-avoidance syndrome (PDA) is a pervasive developmental disorder which, it is believed, is related to, but not the same as, autism or Asperger Syndrome. Individuals with PDA are typically socially manipulative with people, and, therefore, superficially socially skilled, and this sets them apart from those with autism and Asperger Syndrome.

The most central characteristic of people who have PDA is their obvious and obsessional avoidance of the ordinary demands of everyday life. This impacts in a very detrimental way in adult life when it comes to, say, meeting the demands of work. People with PDA lack a clear and defined sense of self, and, as a result, do not view themselves as being responsible for their actions. This latter characteristic is particularly significant in terms of social conformity.

For this reason, a person with PDA is highly motivated to avoid demands and is so able in this domain that they may even appear manipulative as a variety of strategies are used with such determination towards the desired outcome of escaping demands.

Characteristics are believed to include a continual resistance and avoidance of ordinary demands of life; sufferers may demonstrate surface sociability, but have an apparent lack of sense of social identity, pride or shame; there can be a tendency for rapid mood changes; they might be impulsive or led by a need to control; or they may be comfortable in role play and pretending.

A person with PDA may present a language delay or obsessive behaviour. They may develop 'illnesses' to avoid doing something or deliver an endless stream of excuses. Some 'normal' people may admit to doing this occasionally in order to get out of doing something they don't really want to do, but someone with PDA will do this almost all the time.

Chapter Three

Trials and Tribulations

The more I discovered about Asperger Syndrome, the more it dawned on me that Patrick was not my only concern in this field. As I read what I can only describe and recommend as a marvellously helpful and easy-to-understand book – Asperger Syndrome by Tony Attwood – a penny suddenly dropped: Patrick was not the only person in my family presenting the symptoms. So many of the traits Attwood describes in his book also seemed to apply to Sean.

Sean is certainly a little eccentric: he has very specific, pedantic speech; he's extremely intelligent; he likes structure to his life; he doesn't like holidays or changes in routine; he tends to relax only when he's studying; he has very black-and-white thinking patterns with no grey areas... I could go on and on.

I convinced myself I was reading too much into it – my emotions were already all over the place. However, my suspicions were further strengthened when I attended an autism workshop run by Christina Bertolucci.

Christina has a theory that everyone has a little bit of autism in them. As she says, we all like to have a certain amount of routine in their lives, to do things in a certain way – it's just that autistic people present more extreme examples. Christina actually took me to one side and quietly asked me – after Sean and I had attended three or four of her workshops – whether Sean had ever been diagnosed with Asperger Syndrome.

'What makes you ask me that?' I asked.

'Oh, nothing,' she replied.

Could Sean really have Asperger Syndrome as well? After all I'd read, it certainly seemed to me as if he might well have the condition; and later, when Sean and I were experiencing some difficulties, Christina, in a private chat, told me she believed that Sean did, indeed, have it.

To be honest, I was absolutely devastated, though it would certainly explain so many things that had happened in the past. For instance, our first meeting: 'Have you got a rod up your back?' he'd asked, which seemed a really strange thing to say, even though I'd been sitting bolt upright at the time.

Sometimes I find it difficult to tell what sort of mood Sean is in. He can look as if he is angry even if he's not at all. He's often telling me not to read so much into it. Sometimes he says it's just because he's really thinking carefully about something.

Sean has always been very independent – even moving down to London at the tender age of 18 on his own to study. In fact, ever since I've known him he's been studying. He's still studying even now. He has a thirst for knowledge and is always looking out for the next course to take up. He has a degree in economics and management; a Masters in computer science; he's a qualified barrister; he has a law diploma; he's completed loads of Microsoft engineering examinations; and he can read really quickly, just by flicking through books. And there are strong links with superior intelligence: Asperger Syndrome is thought to have affected both Sir Isaac Newton and Albert Einstein.

Then there was the fact that Sean just seemed to handle Patrick's and Angelo's conditions in a totally different manner from me: I'd been the emotional one, while Sean had either seemed to bury his head in the sand, or had handled things in a far more practical, matter-of-fact manner.

It would also explain why he never seemed as keen as I was to share a nice cuddle. Sean was never a touchy-feely person like me and, sometimes in the past, I have to admit I'd wondered if I had married the right person – I'd sometimes ask myself whether he loved me as much as I loved him.

Gradually, past experiences were now beginning to become clearer, to fall into place. Sean wasn't being awkward or inconsiderate at all, it's just the way he was. Nevertheless, there would be so many times ahead of us when this would prove problematic, particularly when certain emotional situations would arise and I would feel very alone in coping with them.

As for Angelo, as far as I'm concerned, he changed so much after he had his MMR (Measles, Mumps and Rubella) vaccination. Afterwards, he didn't want me to touch or kiss him; he'd spend a lot of time in the corner of the room and I really had to work hard to get him to accept any form of physical contact from me. We'd experienced nothing like this with Angelo prior to his having the vaccination. Now he was in a world of his own.

I'm not saying having the MMR jab causes autism, but I do believe that, if someone is predisposed to the condition, it may play a part in pushing them over the edge. I firmly believe that if Angelo had not had the MMR jab, he would have been as able as Patrick. He definitely changed for the worse after the vaccination. He had a high temperature, he suffered from measles and a severe ear infection, and so many other conditions.

All the walking, talking and everything he should have been doing – as he had been prior to the jab – had disappeared. When I look at photographs of Angelo taken before he had the jab he looked quite normal, and there was good eye contact. Afterwards, his eyes just had a glazed look about them and all eye contact disappeared. He would have major tantrums, scream and clap hands violently, fixate on the patterns on the wallpaper and play inappropriately with toys.

What's going on with this boy? I'd wonder. What's going on in his head? Sometimes when his behaviour got extreme I would become angry with him, then I would get angry with myself because it wasn't his fault. I just wanted to take away this horrible autism that had taken over my son's life.

There's an organisation known as Justice Awareness and Basic Support (JABS), through which parents have collected video evidence of their children prior to and after receiving the MMR vaccinations.

Members of JABS, a self-help group that neither recommends nor advises against vaccinations, has campaigned to sue the British Medical Council. JABS was set up to promote awareness and understanding about immunisations and to offer basic support to parents whose children have developed problems with their health after receiving vaccinations. The organisation has been battling for justice for vaccine-damaged children and for their rights to receive compensation. I have to say I have some sympathy with it, particularly as its views seem to back up my own doubts about the safety of the triple vaccination.

JABS' website claims the government accepts that childhood vaccinations could seriously damage a child and that a vaccine-damage payment unit has been set up to evaluate parents' claims on behalf of their injured children. But, according to JABS, the criteria are so strict that most claims are rejected, a child having to be 80 per cent disabled by vaccine with the onus on the parent to provide proof. After listening to some of the parents at JABS, I'm now convinced the MMR vaccination, at the very least, made Angelo's condition far worse than it might have been, had he been given the injections separately.

The British Medical Council tells us that autism manifests itself if it's not very severe when a child reaches 18 months, and that's when Angelo had his MMR jab – though they would probably insist that's when he would have shown clearer signs of autism in any case. But, to my mind, it's all to do with saving money. Why can't they give the measles, mumps and rubella injections separately as they still do in so many other countries?

The rise in confirmed cases of autism has soared in the UK since awareness and detection of the condition have improved. Is that anything to do with the introduction of the multiple inoculation? I'm convinced the MMR jab pushed Angelo over the edge and into a world of his own.

This argument received high-profile backing when seven medical experts – six of whom were from the Autism Research Centre – monitored 12,000 primary-school children and came to the conclusion that one in 58 of them may be showing signs of the condition. This is a staggering figure that almost doubled the previously believed number – and a figure that two of the experts involved in the study believed may be linked to the MMR jab. The study was conducted over a three-year period between 2001 and 2004. Two of the authors of the report, Dr Fiona Scott and Dr Carol Stott, suggested that the MMR jab could be a factor in this estimate.

Nationally, if the findings of the study are accurate, this could mean that 210,000 children under 16 may have an autistic spectrum disorder, compared with the one in a hundred that had been believed from previous studies.

We have to bear in mind, though, that this research was based on statistics, which is one of the reasons why the leader of the team, Professor Simon Baron-Cohen, rejected this view. Professor Baron-Cohen believed other factors could be behind the condition, such as children's exposure to hormones in the womb – especially testosterone – and he also believes the rise in figures might partly be attributed to a better diagnosis and a broader definition of the condition.

The medical world has been divided on this issue for years. Back in 1998, Dr Andrew Wakefield, from the Royal Free Hospital in London, voiced his concerns over the MMR vaccine, suggesting it could be the cause of inflammatory bowel syndrome and autism in children. For his trouble, Dr Wakefield's claims were derided as bad science and subsequently he found himself, with two former colleagues, hauled up before the General Medical Council to answer charges relating to their claims.

When he was about three years old, Angelo's tantrums often stemmed from frustration when he could not make anyone understand what he really wanted. It was very tiring being with him, particularly when he continually tried to pull me towards whatever he wanted.

He'd lead me to the fridge.

'What does Angelo want?'

Gradually I was able to get him to say, 'I want... ' and then I'd say, 'Yoghurt? Does Angelo want a yoghurt?'

Then I'd repeat it again and again until he gradually learned to say it himself.

The best thing the borough did for us was to introduce us to Jocelyn Phillips from Portage, who told me about pictures. She told me to take pictures of all the things Angelo liked, specific toys and clothes, places he liked to go such as a swing in the park. At the time Angelo had very little understanding when I spoke to him about where we were going and why. So, when I intended to take him there, I'd show him a picture of the swing with the word swing written underneath it.

'Mummy's going to take you to the park.'

I'd taken a picture of his favourite cup and I wrote the word cup underneath it.

'Angelo's going to have a drink now.'

This proved to be a most beneficial method of getting a message across, although at the time we were not sure how much information Angelo was taking in. Was he reading the words and understanding them, or was it more mechanical?

Whatever it was, it certainly helped him along. His vocabulary improved to such a point he would say 'drink' or 'apple' whenever he wanted one, or 'I want some', 'good night' or 'good boy'. Eventually I created a photograph album with a single photo on each page – a bed, a cup, food he likes and pictures of the doctor's surgery and the hospital, which were both used on an all too frequent basis.

Jocelyn's support helped to keep me sane and her method of putting pictures into words also helped Patrick, who was always looking for visual clues. Angelo's speech was still very limited, so a picture of Mum and the word Mum, or a picture of a car and the word car, predictable as they were, proved very helpful, particularly since, with Sean out at work, I was struggling to cope with two children with very specific needs.

Yet, although Angelo's speech was slow, his intelligence was never in doubt as far as I'm concerned. Using his letter cards he was able to spell difficult words such as dinosaur much earlier than many other children of his age.

Like Patrick, Angelo loves to fast-forward and rewind videos to his favourite sections of his favourite films. Even now, as we lie in bed, we often hear Angelo watching one of his videos with the phrase 'Disgusting, disgraceful, despicable!' being played over and over and over again. At three in the morning it's enough to drive you completely mad!

When he was a small child, his fear of water only made

matters worse. He'd scream blue murder at wash or bath times, and would not use a toilet because he could see the water in the bottom of the pan. Rainy days, needless to say, weren't easy. Angelo would also carry a blue brick around with him and, whenever he lost that bloody brick, well, woe betide us – he'd go absolutely mad. To save our sanity, I went out and bought a few more, just in case of emergencies. He often formed attachments to certain other toys. One favourite was a tea set and he would spend ages offering cups of tea to his teddy bear. Other particular attachments included a football and a toy hammer.

Like Patrick, Angelo would become most upset if I was out of his sight. The situation got so extreme that I had to reduce my working hours in order to spend more time with him.

Going shopping was a nightmare. When we got out of the car, if a motorbike or lorry went by he'd just scream, kick and throw himself on the ground, which would prompt Patrick to start shouting, 'Why's he doing that in the middle of the road?'

I decided we had to practise going to the shops. I would get Angelo out of the car and walk him to the traffic lights. Another day I might try to take him a little further down the road. Like this, I managed, within a two-month period, to get Angelo as far as the local shopping centre. However, when I did manage to achieve this, going around the stores was often problematic, particularly as Patrick had this thing in his mind about straightening boxes of cornflakes and other products on the shelves as we walked down the aisles.

Sometimes, if I was in a hurry, I'd help him straighten things up myself, then I'd realise people were looking at me and probably thinking what a bloody mad woman I was! After a while, though, I realised this was not good for Patrick. I was letting him control me. I'm the parent, I'm in charge and I have to give him boundaries. I discovered later on that the more autistic people find themselves in control, the more anxious they become. Responsibility provokes anxiety. Looking back, I realise that I was just trying to avoid any tantrums in the middle of a crowded supermarket.

So often Patrick was probably seen by others as a naughty child. If only the cards saying, 'This child is not naughty, he/she is autistic', currently supplied by the National Autistic Society, had been around at the time, maybe we wouldn't have had quite so many disparaging looks from other shoppers.

Angelo's mood swings were quite extreme. Sometimes he would be really high, other times really low. I noticed how different foods could trigger him off. He used to like eating angel cake but that would make him really hyper and he would eat only certain brands of certain foods. For instance, he loved custard cream biscuits but, if I bought any brand other than Crawford's, he wouldn't eat them. We tried to get him to eat vegetables but he just didn't want to know. He still won't drink milk – nor will Patrick – and I've since discovered that many children on the autistic spectrum have an intolerance to dairy products.

When Angelo was five, we travelled to Disneyland Paris for a short holiday. Sean didn't want to go at all really but he accompanied me, the boys and Coral. We went to Davy Crockett, a very nice self-catering area just outside the main theme park, where holidaymakers stayed in log cabins.

Our cabin had two outside doors, the first of which we locked; the other was blocked by suitcases to prevent the boys getting outside without being noticed. When we wanted to leave the cabin we had to distract the boys by moving the luggage to gain access to the door and made efforts to replace the luggage in exactly the same position afterwards.

However, one morning, our attention to detail must have slipped. As Angelo was sitting down on some stairs in the log cabin I got up to fetch him a chocolate bar but, in that instant, he disappeared. I wasn't too concerned: it had been only a short moment and he couldn't have got far away, could he? However, after realising Angelo had wandered off, Patrick became hyper and Sean went straight into panic mode. And, after a few moments, so did I, particularly when there was no response to our calls.

We knew that, if he got lost, Angelo wouldn't have the language skills to get himself out of trouble. He couldn't tell anyone his name or anything else about himself other than that he was hungry. Not only that, he had an obsession with caravans and the site was full of them. He could have wandered into any one of them.

The search began. We asked people in the other cabins if they'd seen Angelo, but most of them couldn't speak English, which made the situation even worse and more frightening. Despite our best efforts, four hours had passed, by which time I was beside myself with worry, dreading what might have happened to Angelo.

Patrick made things far worse, shouting out that someone had probably taken Angelo and chopped his head off. 'Oh, shut up Patrick!' I shouted. Coral was crying and Sean was in a desperate state as we climbed into a little golfing buggy to continue our search. I sat in the back, crying hysterically. 'What are you crying for?' demanded Sean angrily. 'That's not going to make it any better!'

On site, some building work was being undertaken about a 20-minute walk away from our cabin and it was there that a German fireman who didn't speak English spotted our little boy playing happily in the mud – minus his trousers and socks. Angelo was caked in mud, but I just didn't care, we were so relieved he was safe and well.

As for his trousers and socks, well, we never found them but they were the least of our worries.

When Patrick was five years old, he was very disturbed. He was soiling himself, sleepwalking and experiencing nightmares. He wouldn't even sleep in his own room because he feared 'the angry lady', who visited him in his room each night, so he had his mattress by the side of our bed while Angelo slept between Sean and me. I know a lot of children have imaginary friends, but Patrick would talk vividly about the angry-faced lady with long white hair, a red dress and no shoes. Now I realise she may even have had a happy face; however, a lot of autistic children find it difficult to interpret happy or sad expressions.

'She gives me a kiss on the cheek like you do, Mum,' he'd say. I remember thinking it was a really weird experience when Patrick informed me the angry lady had at last moved out of his room and was now residing in the wardrobe in our bedroom.

Meanwhile, if ever I left the house, Patrick would stand at the window screaming his head off. His behaviour prompted me to seek advice from our GP and I was reassured that boys generally develop more slowly than girls and that Patrick would probably 'grow out of it'.

But Patrick continued to scream on the way to school each morning. I felt so desperate, that I was a horrible mother. 'Stop it, Patrick, stop it!' I'd say each time he wrapped his legs around Angelo's buggy in an attempt to stop us getting to the school, and some mums would look at us, probably thinking I should get a grip on the situation, and I hated the looks of pity I got from the other mothers. Quite often it required a teacher to take hold of Patrick's legs while I took his arms in order to carry him into school as he kicked and screamed at us.

It was a draining experience. Patrick was not sleeping well, which meant neither were Sean and I. It was a nightmare and I always knew what to expect when I tried to take him back to school again in the morning.

Once in school, Patrick would not go into the classroom. Instead he spent most of the day in the corridor and refused to join his classmates in the playground. One way he would avoid mingling with the others outside was to make his lunch last the whole hour. Eventually, though, he did go outside, but we were told he would rather walk around the outskirts of the playground than play with the other children.

But, when he did join the others, it was clear he had no idea how to interact with them. A couple of times, because he didn't know how to ask for things, he would stroke the other children's faces to get their attention, until one of them thumped him.

Then he would tell us he didn't like school because 'the eyes' were looking at him.

'What eyes, Patrick?'

'There's eyes there, they're looking at me. I can see them in the classroom.'

Patrick was assigned a one-to-one support worker but she was able to spend only a very limited amount of time with him because she was needed for other children within the school as well.

Realising Patrick needed even more support, I also spent a lot of time at the school. Lunchtimes were particularly difficult for him because these were unstructured times. He continued to refer to 'the eyes', which obviously worried him. I eventually realised what he was talking about – his classroom door had the word classroom written on it and the two o's on the sign were, in Patrick's mind, a pair of eyes.

Furthermore, he was troubled by a 'mouth', which swallowed him at school. This was the pair of swing doors that led into the main hall. He didn't like the sounds in school – 'they hurt my ears'. It turned out he was referring to the sounds of metal chair legs scraping along the floor.

There were other instances that made Patrick stand out. For instance, when his teacher told the class, 'OK, then, everybody, stand up and get on with your work,' they would all do so, except Patrick, who would remain sitting on the carpet. 'Go on, then,' she'd say to Patrick, but he would just sit there. It was only later that she realised that, because she hadn't said his name aloud, he didn't think she was talking to him. 'Patrick, stand up,' she'd say, and he would do as he was told.

He would constantly draw angry pictures. Some would feature the school being blown up; others were pictures of himself in his school uniform with his eyes bulging and smoke coming out of his ears. He was even making furious tape recordings in which he expressed his hatred of the school. It was at this point that I realised some of the other children had been saying things to him and this was confirmed beyond doubt when, one day, he asked me, 'Mummy, what does "cuckoo brain" mean?' then, on another day, asking, 'What's a "bird brain"?'

The pressure on Sean and me was mounting up as we struggled to come to terms with Angelo's autism and Patrick's distress and consequent behaviour. I remember being at the hospital one day when Patrick decided to have one of his major blowouts. A woman standing nearby stared across at us and asked, 'Can't you control your child?' to which I angrily retaliated, 'Here you are, then, let's see if you can do any better!'

The woman's face paled and she looked down at the floor, uttering an apology and excusing herself by blaming her dislike of hospitals, which had been making her feel very tense and irritable.

Having both the boys at home and looking after them full-time meant I'd had to abandon my plans of being a working mum. My life now revolved around our sons. I felt trapped and, in many respects, my life was a nightmare – especially when shopping.

One day, while shopping in a supermarket, we passed a basket containing pink balls. Unfortunately, Patrick had become obsessed with the colour pink. I agreed to buy him a ball but he wanted them all. 'No, darling, one's enough,' I said, at which point he went ballistic. Patrick screamed and screamed and struggled against my efforts to calm him down. Other shoppers looked on in amazement and it was only with the help of one of the store's security officers that I was able to drag him back to our car.

Of course, undertaking any long-distance car journey with young children can be a nightmare, as most parents will readily testify. Again, I found this out to my cost when, in 1996, I decided to take the boys on the 266-mile journey from Hillingdon to Middlesbrough to spend part of the Christmas break with my family. This time Sean had decided to stay at home, so it was just Patrick and Angelo, who were six and three at the time, and I who made the long and boring trip along the M1 and A1 up north in our Ford Orion, accompanied by a bootload of Christmas presents.

As we travelled along the motorways in freezing-cold conditions, Patrick was endlessly asking me, 'Are we nearly there yet?' As we were 50 to 60 miles from Middlesbrough, a thick fog descended and I had to slow down to a crawl of 10 to 15 miles an hour. Things, though, were about to become a lot worse. Suddenly the car began to splutter and then came to a grinding halt in the middle lane of the motorway, a fault that was eventually diagnosed as a dodgy alternator.

We had found ourselves in an extremely frightening and dangerous situation. Frantically, I tried to restart the car, but without success. 'Come on, Mum, start the car,' Patrick called out. I could only watch helplessly as two lorries approached us from behind, then made our car sway as they passed us. I tried to call the Automobile Association from my, then analogue, mobile telephone but couldn't get a signal.

It was far too dangerous to stay where we were so there was nothing else for it: I would have to get out of the car and try to push it to the hard shoulder. I was utterly exhausted when I released the handbrake and tried to steer and push the car while Patrick, helpful as ever, was asking me, 'Why are you pushing the car, Mum? Just turn the key!' The car, though, rolled just a very short distance, only partially making it to the hard shoulder, therefore remaining a potential obstacle to cars approaching us on the nearside lane of the motorway.

I got back into the car, switched on the hazard lights, and tried to ring the AA again, but still there was no signal and no one stopped to help us. Staying where we were, though, was not an option. I retrieved Angelo's buggy from the boot of the car, wrapped the boys up and put Angelo in the buggy, then covered him with his favourite blanket that just had to go everywhere with us.

It was bitterly cold and there was a thick fog as I began to walk with Patrick and push Angelo in his buggy down the side of the motorway looking out for, maybe, a house or a petrol station where we might find someone who could help us. Not surprisingly though we hadn't got far before Patrick began to cry with the cold and I realised I should take the boys back to the shelter of the car.

Returning, I settled Angelo back in the car but, somehow, I managed to shut the door on Patrick's finger. He screamed and screamed, then Angelo joined in too. Desperate to calm the boys down, I began to sing, 'The wheels on the bus go round and round... ' This journey had become an absolute nightmare. I was stranded on a cold, foggy motorway with both my boys screaming their heads off. What on earth was I to do? Suddenly, there was a knock on the car window. I turned and screamed out when I saw a man's face pressed against the window.

'Are you a lady in distress?' he asked.

Seeing our predicament, he kindly offered to take us the rest of our journey in his car, so I took the decision to place my trust in him. He could have been anyone and I had to make an instant judgement as to whether his sudden arrival was either a blessing or just an extra aspect of the nightmare we were going through – but what choice did I have?

My anxiety was being sensed by the boys and my mobile telephone was still not receiving a signal. Thank God, though, that the driver turned out to be a very kind man who was making his way home after a business trip. I explained that we had been heading for my mother's home in Middlesbrough and that I'd had no success in contacting the emergency breakdown service. I decided to accept his kind offer and emptied our bootful of Christmas presents, Angelo's buggy and the boys into his car and off we went. Thankfully, the movement of the car helped to settle the boys quickly, and they both fell asleep.

Although this gentleman knew nothing of autism, he was very interested to hear more about this developmental disorder as we chatted along the way. When we eventually arrived at my parents' home, I offered him some money as a contribution towards his petrol costs but he wouldn't hear of it, and was happy just to wish our family luck in the future. In the end, all he would accept was a spare bottle of Italian wine and a panettone that I insisted he take in return for his kindness.

Chapter Four

Battling Bureaucracy

It was hardly surprising that there would be plenty of matters to raise when Sean and I attended Patrick's annual review at St Mary's School in June 1997, but the revelation that he had been diagnosed three years earlier with Asperger Syndrome without our knowledge really knocked us both for six – and that's putting it mildly.

Now we knew.

One of ours sons had autism, the other Asperger Syndrome. While recognising some parents of children with debilitating conditions face far worse situations than autism, at the time we couldn't help thinking how things could get any worse. Well, as far as Hillingdon Borough Council was concerned, it seemed some councillors were prepared to prove things could, indeed, get far, far worse if they were to have their way.

We first became aware of the barriers about to be put before us when it was time to try and get Angelo into mainstream education at St Mary's School. Angelo had already attended the nursery at the school, as I was keen to help him establish some form of interaction with other children.

His time at the nursery had not been without incident, though. One day, after managing to leave him there with a one-to-one support, I returned later in the day to pick him up, only to be informed by one of the support workers that he had gone missing for half an hour.

They had been so worried that he might even have left the premises but eventually they found him locked up in a galvanised shed full of bicycles, scooters and outdoor equipment – and it had been a boiling-hot day. Because Angelo had very little ability to speak, he had been unable to shout for help, as all the toys had been piled up in front of him.

I remember the looks on the faces of the staff at the nursery. They had been so shaken up by the incident and were, to say the least, very relieved to have found Angelo safe and well.

After I enquired about the possibility of Angelo joining Patrick at St Mary's School, we received a letter telling us that they didn't feel they would be able to meet Angelo's more specialised needs.

We were told he could be kept for a further term in the nursery because his needs were 'too complex' to handle in a reception class, but the afternoon sessions would not be a guarantee of full-time admission and would be subject to regular reviews. A taste of what was to come arose when I was informed by a statementing officer, 'You might as well take that extra term, Mrs Kennedy, because no one else wants your son.'

If I could have put my hand down the phone and strangled her, I would have done so. I was livid, frustrated and hurt all at the same time that someone could say something like that to me, particularly as this was in the wake of my reading all about the importance of early intervention. What a nasty thing to say! I was grateful to the nursery for offering Angelo the option of an extra term but speaking to this statementing officer made me feel as if she was just writing off any chance he might have for his future.

A number of meetings and assessments were held to establish the best way forward with Angelo's development. Because he would still not allow other children to come near to him and was showing only flickers of ability with words and numbers, it was considered that he was very much a baby, stuck emotionally at 18 months in development. This was particularly obvious whenever he resisted leaving his pushchair and also his attachment to a dolls' house at the playgroup. If ever Angelo could not find the dolls' house, he would refuse to stay there. He would make very little attempt to communicate with the other children and, despite being encouraged to work and play alongside a member of staff, this resulted in very little success.

In spite of our doubts, it was considered that the nursery at Grangewood School in Eastcote would be a more appropriate place for him, although significant concerns were raised as to how best to separate Angelo from me, particularly bearing in mind the significant stress that we, as a family, were undergoing at the time.

Meanwhile, Angelo's sleep patterns were showing no sign of improvement. In fact, they were worsening. It wore us down whenever he refused to settle. Most evenings he would become much noisier. He would laugh uncontrollably and begin running and jumping around the rooms. When, at last, he did sleep, it would be for only a short period of time before he was running around, jumping and laughing all over again.

The situation became practically unbearable and led me to ask a doctor for help. Two types of preparation syrup were prescribed on a short-term basis in an effort to calm things down, but they made them even worse, one causing Angelo to be completely hyperactive, the other turning him into a zombie-like state that made him very pale and lethargic with no sparkle in his eyes at all. He became very heavy-eyed and sleepy but, desperate for sleep as we were, there was no way we felt we could continue to administer the medication to him because of the adverse effects it was having on him.

At this time Angelo was also attending weekly sessions at the Child, Family and Adolescent Consultation Service, which he particularly seemed to enjoy but which, sadly, folded owing to a lack of resources.

At home, Angelo was constantly demanding my attention. However, I was encouraged by an improvement in his eye contact with me and by his allowing me more physical contact with him. One vignette from a psychotherapist's report emphasised this improvement: 'Angelo fell hard. I felt he must have hurt himself. He stood, seemed shocked. Mum went to comfort him. He went rigid. She could not hug him or comfort him. He was so resistant. He continued as if nothing had happened.'

Later she wrote, 'Angelo banged his knee. He stopped. He cried, ran to Mum who hugged him. They looked at his knee together.'

Problems aplenty remained, though. Angelo was fiercely resistant to being washed or bathed, and would become very easily distressed whenever his surroundings were unfamiliar.

At an interim review of Angelo's progress at St Mary's School I would have settled for two days' teaching with three days' home tuition, while Sean tried to convince the governors that home provision would, in fact, be cheaper for the borough than sending Angelo to a residential school. Nevertheless, we failed to persuade the governors to accept him at St Mary's because they felt the school would be 'unable to provide for his needs in the highly structured environment of full-time education and within the limited space available'.

Meanwhile, I was still struggling to get Patrick to go to school. One day, six months after his diagnosis with Asperger Syndrome, things came to a head. On arrival at the school, I really had to struggle to get Patrick out of the car. When I finally succeeded he put his hands and head against the brick wall outside the school and just sobbed and sobbed and sobbed.

'Please don't take me in that place any more! I don't like it! Please!'

Another mother taking her child to school was passing by. As I had Angelo in the buggy I asked her if she would ask Mrs Docherty, the head teacher, to come outside to see me. To be honest, I was at my wits' end.

Mrs Docherty came out and saw Patrick sobbing his heart out. 'This can't go on,' she said. 'What are we doing to this child? We're just damaging him.' She offered to write a letter to recommend Patrick no longer attend St Mary's and that he should be offered home tuition instead.

With this in mind, Sean and I decided to convert our garage into a classroom for Patrick, but getting home tuition didn't happen overnight. Eventually, however, a lovely lady called Vanessa arrived to give Patrick five hours of education a week – two and a half hours one day and two and a half hours another – but all that rather depended on whether Patrick wanted it.

Patrick would find it very difficult to distinguish what was real and what was not. He'd try to fit us into a world he'd seen portrayed in videos. While he had an obsession with *Thomas the Tank Engine* and anything to do with dinosaurs, he had at the same time an intense dislike of human beings. He thought people were rubbish and this was reflected in the angry pictures he would draw. He hated it if people came to our house. To him, they were intruders and he would shut himself away upstairs in his bedroom if anyone arrived. 'They're intruding. They're not showing respect,' he'd insist. As for me, I hadn't been showing him respect because I had taken him to school each day.

For some reason, Gordon the Engine in his *Thomas the Tank Engine* book had 'angry wheels'. Could it be the thought of steam coming from the wheels? If he saw models of the engines in the shops, he'd want them. If I told him I would buy him one it was never good enough, he wanted all of them and this, invariably, led to tantrums.

Patrick knew *The Gingerbread Man* and *The Three Little Pigs* videos word-perfect and would constantly ask the same questions over and over again to ensure he received the same answer each time. He would read dictionaries and ask the meanings of words he'd read so he could see that what he'd read was correct. He needed constant reassurance. He was a very anxious little boy.

His obsession with dinosaurs began after he watched the 1993 movie *Jurassic Park*. We've since been to visit the Natural History Museum in London dozens of times to satisfy his appetite for anything dinosaur-related. Nothing else there interests him. He can look at any bone on display and tell you what Cretaceous or Jurassic period it comes from.

I remember one particular incident when he was seven years old. It was the occasion of his Holy Communion at Our Lady of Lourdes church. Patrick was looking very smart and we tried to prepare him for what would happen. However, when he heard that the priest, Father Collin, would say 'Body of Christ' before giving him the host, Patrick became very anxious. At that time, we had no idea that many children with Asperger Syndrome can take anything said quite literally.

When it was time for Patrick to go to Father Collin, he pursed his lips and said that he didn't want the host because he would be swallowing Jesus Christ. After much explanation at the altar that it would be like eating a piece of bread, he finally agreed to take the host. 'Is there any butter on it?' he asked loudly. We were very fortunate that Father Collin is a patient man.

Mary Milne was head of client services on Hillingdon Borough Council. She was also in charge of the statementing process and I had already given her a pretty hard time over Patrick's and Angelo's statements – first, because there had been so many woolly comments in them and, second, because they were not applicable to children with autism.

A statement is a passport to get the right sort of support and education for a child and the financial package. If the statement is not right, you are not going to get the correct support, so it is crucial that the statement be absolutely relevant to that particular child. Children with autism require speech-and-language therapists, not because they can't speak properly, but because they have a communication impairment. They need to learn how to interact socially but, while looking at the statementing process, Sean soon realised that the council tended to write particularly woolly statements.

The statements would highlight the need for regular speech-and-language therapy, but what does regular mean? I have a regular Christmas dinner – i.e. once each year – but therapy should be held on a much more frequent basis. Parents who don't know this may think regular means frequent and often, but, if it doesn't, it's no use to anyone, especially if the child has a communication problem. With that in mind, Sean and I took a lot of time and effort to ensure the statements for Angelo and Patrick were exactly as they should be.

We already felt let down by the powers that be. Angelo was due to have been assessed for speech-and-language therapy in the nursery because it was felt the statement had not been meeting his needs, but this had not been undertaken because of a lack of funds from the London Borough of Hillingdon, the consequence of a £20,000 overspend. Two hours' autistic support for Angelo was, obviously, nowhere near enough and we were determined not to lie down and allow this situation to continue.

We were desperately looking for schools that would accept Patrick and Angelo. Our desire to find somewhere suitable saw me making dozens of telephone calls and, in all, I visited 26 schools within an hour's drive of our home after being told by the statementing officer of the London Borough of Hillingdon that the ball was in my court, that it was up to me to find a school because my son Angelo was 'unique', although we now know there are a vast number of children just like him in the area.

The officer's opinion seemed particularly harsh to me. Where would I begin? I couldn't understand how she could make such an assumption about a child she had never even met. It seemed so impersonal.

At first I looked for schools for children with autism, but the ones I visited were for children at the more severe end of the autistic spectrum, and some were like institutions. The scale of the challenge was brought home to me when I realised that one of the schools had just five places for the 55 applicants and several others were also full to bursting.

I was becoming increasingly worried. Having discovered the importance of an early start in education for autistic children, I was looking for a place that seemed more like a mainstream school that had been adapted in some way to meet the needs of my boys. To me it was obvious that there was no way Angelo would have been able to cope with around 30 or 40 other kids in a classroom.

I have since discovered that many teachers in mainstream schools have found it very difficult to cope with children with such specific needs when they also have 30 or more other children to teach at the same time, and that many parents of autistic children have been forced to send their offspring miles away from home to obtain a decent education, most notably to the specialist Boston Higashi School in America. This was even suggested to us by an educational psychologist but, after consideration, Sean and I decided against sending Angelo to a residential school and decided to press ahead with our search for a specialist school in the UK.

One establishment, however, did impress me: Springhallow School in Ealing. I really liked it there and thought it would be perfect for Angelo, since its classes were limited to eight children with one teacher and two assistants. Furthermore, the school had adopted the TEACCH (Treatment and Education of Autistic and related Communication-handicapped CHildren) methods and followed the National Curriculum at levels appropriate to each child's own development.

In a nutshell (although we'll come back to it in Chapter Six), TEACCH places an emphasis, among other things, on structured teaching, regular assessments leading to individual programmes and tuition, self-enhancement, cognitive and behaviour therapy and generalist training. There were individual programmes in speech and drama; an emphasis on social skills; integration with children from other schools; a variation in meals; and a warm, caring and happy environment.

The more I discovered about the school, the more it seemed just what we wanted for Angelo and Patrick. There were close links between home and school and a weekly home/school book was kept so parents had regular weekly contact. The school placed great emphasis on oral and written language developments. Each child was carefully observed and assessed on entry so that a suitable programme could be devised to cater for the needs of children, which would have been a huge benefit, particularly to a child like Angelo.

It seemed too good to be true and, unfortunately, it was. After further investigation, we discovered the school accepted only children from the London Borough of Ealing and they were already bursting at the seams and teaching in the corridors – such was the demand for specialised places.

Faced with the prospect of not being able to secure a school place for Angelo in the foreseeable future, we managed to obtain five hours of one-to-one tuition each week for him at home. His tutor was a very nice lady but she admitted to us that she didn't have a clue what autism was. Then, one day, she just sat on the floor and told me, 'I'm sorry, but I just don't know what to do with your son.' The poor woman just hadn't been given the appropriate training to work with autistic children.

Sean and I became like ships in the night. He was working in the IT department at Thames Water and was getting home from work at 6 p.m., which was just as I was going out to work myself at Health Call or to teach dance in a health club. Usually, when I got home at around 10.30 to 11 p.m., Angelo was awake. Eventually, he would go to sleep but for only a couple of hours, and then he would be awake for the rest of the night. The first thing I wanted to do when I got home from work was go to sleep, but that was impossible. Then Angelo would usually get up around 2 a.m. and that would be it. We had many nights like that and even a couple when he didn't sleep at all – they were real killers. This was no life for anyone.

All the books I had read on autism stressed the importance of early intervention. Well, I thought, where the hell is it? I certainly can't find it. I couldn't even find a suitable school for my own sons. For the next three years, the home tuition for Patrick and Angelo continued – ten hours a week for Patrick and, after a battle, we managed to get extra hours to bring Angelo up to five hours a week.

I remained disappointed not to have been able to get the boys into Springhallow School, but it just wasn't to be. Since there was obviously nothing else in the borough, another mother, Anne, and I set up a support group soon after Patrick had been diagnosed with Asperger Syndrome.

I'd first met Anne in May 1997, when Patrick was attending St Mary's School. I'd watched as her child had a tantrum in the playground. Hmm, I'd thought – I recognise that behaviour! Her boy looked around three years younger than Patrick, while Anne looked at the end of her tether. I went up to her to say hello.

'I don't mean to be rude,' I said, 'but have you got a few problems with your son? Does he have special needs?'

'How did you know?'

I told Anne I recognised the behaviour, since I'd seen similar from my own son. It turned out her son had been diagnosed with semantic-pragmatic disorder, which, as we saw in Chapter Two, is on the autistic spectrum.

Meeting Anne helped me to share the burden I was carrying and I like to think it helped her too. Between us we started a charitable support group which we called HACS – Hillingdon Autistic Care and Support. At first, HACS was formed with just a few local parents but, after a short while, it rapidly expanded – and all the parents involved were united in their disgust at the lack of knowledge of the so-called professionals on the subject of autism.

By now, I'd often taken Patrick along to Christina Bertolucci's Saturday club play scheme for children. It had taken him a while to settle there, as the sessions went on for four hours, but eventually he got used to it. After Angelo began to attend the sessions as well, I got to meet other parents, some of whom went on to become trustees of HACS.

Our charity started off on quite a small basis. Anne discovered we could use Our Lady of Lourdes Church Hall in Hillingdon free of charge. We met there one evening a month but, unfortunately, the main evening most suited to the majority of people coincided with my dance class, so it was always a bit of a rush to get to the meetings on time.

It was worth it, though. The meetings were usually quite productive and we all shared our experiences. Sean would come along, too, but he wasn't really into sharing experiences. He was more into the formal proceedings and he became the chair of the charity, while I took the role of vice chair.

Membership of HACS rapidly increased and we liaised closely with professionals involved with the provision of services for people with autism, and local and national organisations such as the National Autistic Society. We became a point of referral for families of those recently diagnosed as having an autistic-spectrum disorder and provided them with information, advice and counselling, and became involved in an intensive research programme relating to the different approaches available to working with people with autism.

Despite our activities in trying to run HACS and our continuing search for schools willing to accept our boys, the day-to-day problems and anxieties continued unabated. These were particularly apparent with Patrick in 1997 following the death of Princess Diana in a car crash in Paris. Patrick has an obsession with death. By the time this book is published he will be 18 years old and he's worried because he doesn't want to feel older because, as he says, he still feels young inside. I've tried time and again to reassure him that that's how most people feel, but he just doesn't understand, even now.

Back then, though, it was even worse. The issue of death played a major part in Patrick's thinking and he was so distressed when he saw Diana's coffin being carried at her funeral service on television. I know that several children in mainstream schools may have had similar issues but, in Patrick's case, this was far more extreme.

The questions were endless. 'How does it feel to die? How do I know there's a heaven? How do they know Diana's really dead? How do they know she hasn't opened her eyes in there?' Then his anxieties turned to anger against God. 'God is cruel. Why did he take the princes' mummy away from them? If God was good it wouldn't have happened.'

No matter how hard I tried to explain things to him, Patrick just became angrier and angrier. Then, when he saw so many people laying down floral tributes in London, he decided he wanted to do the same. He asked me to buy some flowers and drew a picture of one of his favourite characters at the time, Buzz Lightyear, from the 1995 *Toy Story* movie. Underneath, Patrick wrote, 'To Diana, to infinity and beyond.'

I tried to persuade him we didn't need to go into the city centre to lay down flowers. I was aware that, following Diana's death, the streets would be choked with traffic and I really didn't fancy struggling through it all. But Patrick was adamant and, after much screaming and shouting, we relented and agreed to take him. We got into the car and proceeded eastbound along the A40 towards the city centre. It was like a car park, with the traffic barely moving at all. We began to think we'd never get there. Meanwhile, in the back of the car, Angelo's fidgeting increased and he began screaming. The delays on the road had hardly made my mood any lighter and it was obvious that Sean was getting tenser and tenser by the minute. Then he cracked.

'That's it, we're turning back!' he said, to which Patrick went bananas and threatened to get out of the car.

'If you want to get out of the car and take your chances on the A40, Patrick, well, that's up to you!'

This journey was fast becoming a nightmare. Then I had an idea. I knew that, just a mile further along the A40, we'd pass the Polish War Memorial at RAF Northolt, where Diana's body had been flown in from Paris just a few days earlier. I decided to pretend that's where all her tributes needed to be taken and Patrick was taken in by my ruse.

On our arrival at the memorial, Patrick laid down his flowers and his picture of Buzz Lightyear among the poppies already there. Then he returned to the car, satisfied he'd done his bit for Diana's memory.

In February 1998, the London Borough of Hillingdon declined to finance an assessment for Patrick, which served only to further hinder his prospects of acquiring a school place. How many more barriers would we have to face? Sean and I felt we had exhausted every avenue in trying to get a decent education for our boys – and desperate times call for desperate measures. We decided to write to our local MP, John Randall, and he subsequently visited our home to discuss the situation.

We told John how we felt the local education authority (LEA) was in breach of its duty to arrange the special-education provision for Angelo. This had been set out in his statement of special educational needs with a recommendation that he attend a day school that catered for autistic children 'at the moderate/higher end of the spectrum; a small school with small class groups where staff are specially qualified and trained in meeting the needs of autistic children, thereby ensuring access to specific teaching strategies so Angelo can maximise his intellectual ability; a school that can foster feelings of security in an autistic child; a school that can offer speech therapy sessions and where speech therapists and class teachers liaise closely'.

John spent the best part of the day at our home, watching Patrick and Angelo, and he listened sympathetically to our plight. We were grateful when he offered his support and he agreed to write letters and make representations to appropriate government ministers on our behalf in an effort to speed things up. One of his letters was replied to by the acting group director of the London Borough of Hillingdon, who stated that, despite our assertions the borough was in breach of its duty, finding a day school to cater for children at the moderate/higher end of the spectrum had proved to be extremely difficult.

The letter went on to explain that the LEA (Local Education Authority) had made every effort to secure a place for Angelo at an appropriate school within daily travelling distance of Hillingdon. Six schools had been approached but none had places available. Because the specialist teacher at St Mary's School in Hillingdon had resigned, there would be no replacement in situ before Angelo was due to begin full-time education.

It mentioned that other schools were already oversubscribed and had their own waiting lists. The LEA had done its best but the London Borough of Hillingdon did not have adequate day provision at that moment in time, although the LEA had placed several children from the borough in out-of-borough schools, including the Boston Higashi School, at considerable cost to the council.

The letter recognised that Patrick's diagnosis of Asperger Syndrome had been drawn to our attention three years late and that the LEA had sought an explanation from the health authority for this delay. It had also requested a referral to a speech-and-language therapist to address Patrick's communication skills.

We were pleased to read this admission. It proved to us that the failure to notify us of Patrick's condition when it was first diagnosed had, indeed, meant that the education plans drawn up for him had failed to meet his individual needs.

On receipt of this letter we wrote again to our MP to inform him of this development and that the situation surrounding Patrick's latest assessment, which had been put off so often, was now bordering on the farcical.

We pointed out that the common themes running through Patrick's and Angelo's experiences were poor communication between the service providers; a lack of specialist provision for children with autistic-spectrum disorders in the borough; and that Angelo's therapist at St Mary's was experiencing very severe difficulty in receiving any remuneration from the borough.

At this point, the stress of battling the system had really getting to us both. The frustrations that saw us facing what seemed at times to be insurmountable odds had been coupled with our desire for legal action against the doctor who had not informed us of Patrick's Asperger Syndrome when it was first diagnosed. Had we known three years earlier that Patrick had this condition, we would have had a much better chance of receiving the appropriate support for him at the time, and the daily routine of dragging him to St Mary's might well have been avoided.

We felt somebody needed to make a stand in an effort to ensure as far as is possible that such a diabolical situation should not be possible again. We didn't want other parents to go through a similar experience, being told their child had Asperger Syndrome at a school review. It should never have happened like that. We decided to consult a solicitor to ask for legal aid to take the matter further. However, as the months dragged on, we had become so bogged down in a time-sapping

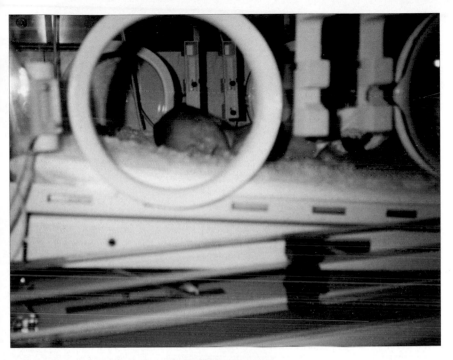

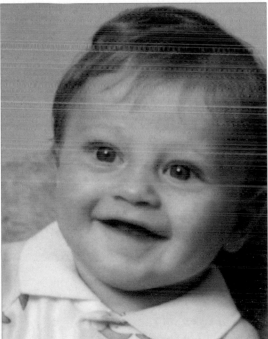

Above: 5 January 1990, Hillingdon Hospital, and my first born, Patrick, lies in an incubator unit. He was over two months premature, and was kept in the hospital until early March. Patrick weighed 3 lbs but went down to 2 lb 10.

Left: Angelo at 8 months.

Above: On holiday in Jersey. Patrick was fascinated by trains from a very young age, and we had just been looking at the ones in the background.

Below: More trains! This is the Great Western Railway at Southall. Patrick's 4, nearly 5, and my younger son Angelo's 1, nearly 2.

A hard day's night! Me, exhausted (as usual!), up at 3 or 4am with Angelo in his pre-school days.

Before the effects of MMR took hold of Angelo. Bright, alert, and fully engaged at 18 months.

Angelo was often very tactile and affectionate towards people, including his big brother Patrick. After the MMR, he wouldn't let anyone – including me – touch him.

Above: After MMR: Angelo in his own world, aged 5.

Below: Patrick at play with his dinosaurs in the back garden with a hose.

Above: At Disneyland Paris, where the boys really enjoyed themselves meeting some of the famous Disney characters. This is Patrick aged 7, in 1997.

Below: Patrick loves dinosaurs, and here he is alongside a much bigger one at LegoLand in Windsor.

Above: The boys on the computer, sharing (as brothers often don't!).

Below: Me and the boys at the back of the school, near the Terrapin buildings at Hillingdon Manor. At this time, Angelo wouldn't wear shoes on his feet, only socks!

legal process that we were unable to concentrate fully on matters more immediate and, very reluctantly, we decided not to pursue the litigation any further.

Meanwhile, a report from a psychologist regarding the extreme pressure our family life was under was sent to a chartered educational psychologist, Albert Reid. Mr Reid carried out a full psychological assessment of Angelo and made great strides forward with him, managing to get a few things out of him that, up to that point, no one else had achieved. Most pleasing was Mr Reid's accomplishment in getting full eye contact with Angelo and gaining his trust to such a degree that Angelo even sidled right up to him, something I never thought we'd ever see, bearing in mind that Angelo didn't know him at all.

For me, that was a really big thing. Mr Reid even managed to persuade Angelo to cooperate and focus on a couple of tests, which was marvellous. He'd found a pocket of hitherto undiscovered ability and, because of this, I was filled with renewed hope.

In summary, he concluded that Angelo would require placement in a school specialising in meeting the needs of children on the autistic continuum with specialised teachers on a teacher–pupil ratio of 1:6 with additional classroom support. A highly structured and consistent programme such as TEACCH would be beneficial, as would direct intervention from a speech-and-language therapist.

It seemed that all the experts were agreeing what was necessary for Angelo to develop but, unfortunately, neither the finances nor the facilities were in place in the borough to meet those needs.

Meanwhile, Angelo continued to be assessed. In May 1998, a contribution to a statutory assessment from the London Borough of Hillingdon recognised that provision should be made to address his narrowness of interest and rigidity of thinking, 'as these are interfering with his ability to learn'. He should be encouraged to cooperate in activities that are not of his choosing and efforts should be made to develop his listening and concentration skills, his language and communication skills, his play skills, social-interaction skills – particularly in relation to his peer group – and his self-awareness and independence skills.

Sean and I became aware of the possibility that Angelo might obtain a place at Meath School in Ottershaw, Surrey. We felt it would be ideal for both Patrick and Angelo, but the school held its own assessments and needed to receive paperwork and the agreement of our LEA to pay for the assessment. Because Patrick and Angelo were both still undergoing reassessment at the time, nothing came of it. We had been very hopeful of success but this too proved to be a non-starter.

When a similar request to place Angelo at Radlett Lodge in Hertfordshire was also turned down and we were informed that Hillingdon Borough Council was not in a position to increase the hours of home provision, we seemed to have come to the end of the road in our quest for a decent education for our boys.

Chapter Five

A Leap in the Dark

Despite all the heartaches and setbacks we just knew we had to do something. Apart from us, all the other parents at HACS had their children in a school. One of them, Alex Honeysett, also had a son, Sean, who had Asperger Syndrome.

Sean had been in a mainstream school from the age of eight to 14. His parents knew there was something wrong but when they took him to see doctors he was twice misdiagnosed – the first time a psychologist said it was just adolescence and, a few years later, Alex and his wife Sally were told their son had a personality disorder.

It was only through a care worker that Alex heard about Asperger Syndrome. When Alex and Sally finally got Sean an appointment with a specialist, she said, 'I don't know what's been going on here – your son's life has been wasted.' With an earlier diagnosis, Sean could have lived a more normal life because he has the intelligence to cope with work. As it was, he was placed in psychiatric hospitals after receiving inappropriate medication.

Alex heard that our children didn't have a school to go to and we quickly became friends. At one of our meetings, and in the light of our difficulties in acquiring suitable placements for Angelo and Patrick, desperation was beginning to set in. 'Let's set up our own school for autistic children!' I suggested. My idea prompted laughter from some of the other parents in the group. They insisted I was trying to run before I could walk but, fortunately, Sean and Alex supported me.

'We have to try something,' Sean said, readily admitting that he agreed that the foundation of our own school as a centre of excellence for people on the autistic spectrum would, indeed, be a great idea, and Alex quickly backed us up – in fact, over the coming months, he, as much as anyone, was very influential in generating the idea.

Someone else told us it was an impossible dream, adding that we wouldn't be able to do it without support. 'We'll find it somehow,' Sean insisted. Little did we realise that, from that point on, our lives would never be the same again.

Having our kids at home was not good for them or for us. We were determined our boys would go to a special school that, as far as possible, would emulate a mainstream school, but it would also be vitally important to limit the number of pupils in each class. Not only that, but, if we were to succeed, any school we may eventually establish would have to become a centre of excellence for the care and support of those with autism. Why settle for anything less?

Soon afterwards Alex, Sean and I heard about a residential

home for the elderly, Mountbatten House in Northwood Hills, which had stood empty for some time. One Sunday, Sean and Alex decided to take a look. The building was surrounded by a rickety old fence but Mountbatten House itself appeared very attractive from the outside.

Sean, all 23 stone of him, climbed over the fence and jumped down the other side to take a closer look, but in the process snagged his trousers on a nail to reveal far more of his rear end than was decent. It must have looked extremely suspect to have this big guy wandering around a deserted old council building while at the same time trying to cover up his backside. Sean took a look through the windows. There were lots of different rooms.

After he reported back, we approached Hillingdon Borough Council and asked if we could have a proper look inside, which, shortly afterwards, we did. The property was quite run down inside with a strong, lingering and disgusting smell emanating from the carpets, which had, presumably, been saturated with urine. That said, there were some nice grounds outside, which we felt could be transformed into a nice play area.

We decided to ask Hillingdon Borough Council if it would be possible for us to lease the building for use as a specialist school but were told we would need to make representations at a forthcoming council meeting, since we would face competition from a housing association who also had ideas for the property. Nevertheless, we went ahead with making our intentions clear at the council meeting in the hope of acquiring a base for our project.

However, after further discussions among ourselves, we soon

realised Mountbatten House didn't have a room large enough for use as a hall and would have required far too much work for our purposes. With so many small rooms and bathrooms, it would have cost far too much to refurbish the whole building. Looking back, I think it was probably desperation on our part at the time to find any property we could use, even if it had been only a stepping stone while we searched for more suitable premises.

Shortly afterwards, Alex heard about a disused special needs school situated very near to our home in Hillingdon. Moorcroft School, a former special school for children with physical disabilities run by the local authority, had stood empty for around 18 months and had fallen into a state of disrepair. When Alex told me about it I looked at it myself, and then we all went back to look at it together. We thought it would be ideal, and we couldn't believe our luck, even though it was quite run down. As Sean commented at the time, even the rats had emigrated.

Nothing much had been done to the premises for four to five years, as the previous occupants had known they would be moving on, so had done only the essential maintenance. The school had been cannibalised. When it was closed, all the neighbouring schools had been invited to come along and help themselves to anything they needed, such as desks and chairs.

By the time we looked around inside, the roof had holes in it and was leaking badly, trees were growing through the windows and vandals had smashed the sinks and toilets off the walls. The premises had catered for special-needs children but had since been deemed unsuitable for children with wheelchairs, so a new school had been built to house them nearby. We peered through the windows. The school was in a pitiful state. Blackboards and lockers had been removed and paint was peeling off the walls but, to us, it was perfect.

When we approached Hillingdon Borough Council we were told that a housing association had been buying up a number of buildings in the area and wanted the Moorcroft site too, but we countered that the building would make an ideal location for a specialist school for children with autism.

By now the housing association already had outline plans in place to build 38 homes on the council-owned site. It proposed to demolish the former special-needs school. The council was proposing to allow part of the adjacent 18th century mansion to be used for housing and to sell the remainder of the building for use as an institution, possibly a nursing home.

With time slipping away, we contacted the head of client services at Hillingdon Borough Council, Mary Milne, to express our interest in the site. Mary said she would see what could be done and suggested we put in a proposal. We took her advice and submitted a proposal for a suitable school for children with autism that was not like an institution and as near as possible to a mainstream environment – a safe environment where the children would be free from bullying.

The council and the education department were already familiar with Sean and me because of our ongoing battle to secure education for our boys. Sean had to give a presentation of our plans at a council meeting – as did the housing association for its own scheme – in a bid to persuade the council to our way of thinking.

Basically, the housing association had brought along a barrister to bolster their case. Nothing wrong with that, but they'd probably expected everything to go through in a smooth and uncomplicated manner as they put their case forward to the councillors and a representative from the Department of the Environment. After all, this was a public arena and they believed they had good public support for their plans.

The council, for their part, had also appeared sympathetic to the housing association, so we knew that Sean, myself, Alex and another of our supporters, the late Bob Hillier, would have quite a job on our hands to persuade them to look favourably on our intentions.

The representatives from the housing association and their barrister began their presentation and all seemed to be going well for them. Then questions were invited and Sean, although not on oath, was cross-examined by their barrister, who was obviously looking for weaknesses in our presentation.

If the barrister had reckoned that taking on Sean would be a walk in the park, he was soon made to realise he had a formidable opponent. Things started badly for the barrister, then got worse and the less said about the end for him the better.

'This plan isn't very feasible, is it, Mr Kennedy? You haven't applied for planning permission or change of use, have you?'

'It's already a school,' replied Sean. 'What do I need planning permission for? Do you really know what you're talking about?'

The barrister glowed red with embarrassment, and that, coupled with the fact that maybe there wasn't quite as much community support for their project as they may have anticipated, meant the housing association's case was scuppered.

Eventually, the housing association backed down and

councillors told us that, if we jumped through all the hoops they were going to put in front of us, there would be a possibility that we could use the premises as a school for autistic children, since there was obviously a need for such a facility in the borough.

Our plans were accepted unanimously. Sean was brilliant that night and, I have to admit, I was so proud to be his wife.

Now we had to really fight for the school. From that point on it seemed Sean, Alex and I would face endless bureaucracy as we tried to secure the premises. It was such a frustrating period. The negotiations and meetings seemed to go on for ever. We went to so many of them, some of which lasted for hours on end, yet not once were we ever offered so much as a cup of tea or a glass of water. In fact, I remember telling one councillor exactly how I felt. 'There's meetings about meetings – when on earth are we going to get some concrete information?' Sometimes after leaving a meeting we would be thinking, What on earth was all that about? We were working in the dark, not having done anything like this before.

We used every means at our disposal to get our message across. At one council meeting, Sean stood up to give a speech and used the opportunity to speak as melodramatically as he could. 'My kids are in the Last Chance Saloon,' he said. 'Can you really deny them what they really need?' If anyone had said no they would have felt awful. Sometimes we had hostile questions from members of the public but Sean refused to be swayed and didn't have any problem in dealing with them, such was his determination to get our message across.

I recall a time thinking that we'd been left hanging around for so long for a decision that, if one wasn't forthcoming in the near future, I'd break into the building and squat! Coral and Aunty Zita said they would bring me food and drink if I did. Furthermore, if we didn't get a decision, I'd ring every radio and television channel I could think of and tell them why.

Hillingdon Borough Council calculated that a figure of £450,000 would be required from us in order to get Moorcroft into a fit state, but our charity, HACS, had only £3,000, so where the hell would we get that much money from? It was obvious HACS couldn't raise anywhere near enough money and the banks wouldn't entertain lending so much. A series of further meetings over the next couple of months with Hillingdon Borough Council ensued but each time it seemed that the amount of money they demanded from us would change. The total went down to £250,000, then up to £825,000, then a million pounds, until finally they settled for £627,000.

When the figure of a million pounds or £825,000 was mentioned we were convinced it was the council's way of telling us they didn't really want our plans to go ahead, that they were deliberately trying to price us out of the market for the Moorcroft site. The figures bandied about by the council had been based on their surveyor's report on the property and the work that had been costed accordingly. What we couldn't understand was why all these extra works that were appearing and putting up the price hadn't been picked up in the initial survey. It just didn't seem to add up.

The building adjacent to the school had been used by social services and the council had originally hoped whoever would take over the former school would buy the entire site. The council knew we wouldn't be able to take over the whole site. However, in the end, they sold the social services building separately for £1.6 million.

Our proposal had to be put before all the local political parties and we were dismayed to learn we might have to spend around a million pounds on refurbishing the premises over the following five years to have any chance of acquiring the school. Basically, Hillingdon Borough Council wanted hard proof that we could raise the cash before giving us their approval.

Although we felt reasonably confident we still had the support of most of the council, one councillor made it clear how he felt about our plans when he informed Sean that the council was not there to do us any favours. As far as he was concerned, the council had wanted to sell the entire site and it was our fault that the sale had not yet gone through!

Undeterred, with Alex's assistance Sean and I put a business plan together over a couple of nights. We took our plan to a number of banks without success and rang several others but, although most of them agreed it was a good idea, they questioned what we really knew about running a school and, unsurprisingly, turned us down. It seemed HACS didn't have a cat's chance in hell of securing the money required to take over the site. Our hopes were further dented when, after approaching one charitable foundation for support, we were told, 'I'm sorry but we don't give to autism because it's not fashionable at the moment.'

We decided to contact the National Autistic Society to see if they would help fund our cause. Sean, Alex and I travelled up to London for a meeting with the chief executive at the society's City Road headquarters. The society had a serious amount of money, with lots of assets. The chief executive met us in a sumptuous meeting room and the meeting went on and on. We showed him our plans for the school and explained we needed to raise £627,000. We were rock solid on our business plan. Could the society help us?

The meeting went round and round and round with neither a firm commitment nor a refusal. In the end, a frustrated Sean just blurted out, 'Look, are you going to f***ing help us or not?' The chief executive was taken aback. 'We've got to look at things,' he said. 'We're constrained by our constitution... ' blah, blah, blah – and then he received a mysterious telephone call and had to leave immediately. The meeting, therefore, was over.

He did, though, send us a supportive letter and, afterwards, we became quite friendly with him. Apparently he still remembers our meeting. Thankfully, things have now changed considerably at the society. At the time, we felt they'd become rather dissociated from their core membership – maybe we didn't meet them at the best of times. They've improved vastly since those days. The information they give out nowadays is unrecognisably better than when we first approached them and they've worked very hard indeed to put that right. Hats off to all concerned.

However, by chance, a piece of luck went our way. One of the members of HACS, who had a son with autism, knew a bank manager from Barclays and offered to have a word in order to set up a meeting for Sean, Alex and me with him at Barclays'

Harrow branch. James Coombes had been a teacher before life in the world of banking and, I have to say, if it hadn't been for him I doubt very much we would ever have got a letter from a bank to show Barclays were prepared to lend us £627,000 for the refurbishment of Moorcroft in order to get it up and running again. James put an awful lot of thought and work into how we would be able to secure such a large loan and, needless to say, when it was finally agreed, we were over the moon!

Even then we were not home and dry. The next step was to persuade the council to give us permission to go ahead and for them to lease us the building. A meeting of the finance subcommittee was crucial to our proposal but, when Sean and I arrived at the Civic Centre, we were not allowed in. Instead, we waited outside for more than five hours. I was trying to get a microphone through the keyhole in an effort to get some idea of what was happening but it just wouldn't fit in. At the end of the day, though, it was a subcommittee meeting, not a meeting open to the public, so we had to grin and bear it.

Sean was struggling to hear what was being said behind closed doors and was encouraged when he thought he could hear some councillors expressing a degree of support for our project, even though they had reservations, since there were no models or templates for any similar projects that had gone before. As he said, the Education Act did allow for such a development but the Act itself was so convoluted. We arrived home at midnight with the matter still unresolved – apparently, we still didn't have enough cash, despite Barclays' offer.

The negotiations and discussions continued. We were determined not to give up, not after having come so far. It paid off. Our earlier doubts about whether the council was really on our side were eventually dispelled when we were generously offered a rent-free period for the first five years of a 25 year lease.

First of all, however, the council wanted proof that we could make this a viable proposition. We provided a plan and insisted we would have the school up and running within three years, even though some councillors reckoned we would need five years. We firmly believed in our cause and, in our plan, drew the council's attention to the three options available to them. They could do nothing, or utilise Moorcroft School by turning it into an educational facility for autistic-spectrum disorders, or create a new purpose-built school that could cost anything in the region of £2 million, plus interest. We were convinced our plan would be the most cost-efficient and effective of those three options.

The council had come up trumps after all and, we have to say, we have nothing but admiration for them, and particularly Mary Milne, because we could not have imagined another borough approving such a plan – even though we'd had to fight our corner so hard. I remember Mary telling me afterwards, 'I always knew you'd do something.' And it would be remiss of us not to acknowledge the support we received from Labour councillor Peter Ryerson and Conservative councillor Ray Puddifoot who, with MP John Randall, still help us to this day.

What came across to us at the time was that the local authorities were so paralysed. For months they couldn't seem to make any decision about anything, because nothing like this had been done anywhere, or else it was new territory to those who were doing it, too. It's just the way local authorities work.

The system doesn't seem to allow for decision making because there's such a lot of red tape. Everything's got to be double-, then triple-checked.

But we must now say a big, big thank-you to Hillingdon Borough Council, because, without any question, we couldn't have got where we are today without their support. Frustrating as it was at the time, the obstacles put in our way were by a couple of councillors who were very much in the minority.

While securing permission to use the site was a major hurdle to overcome, the small matter of raising enough money to cover all the expenses required was a significant task in itself. Prior to securing the loan from Barclays we had been looking at any way possible to raise funds. I arranged to top up our mortgage – without Sean's knowledge at the time – which added a huge amount to our monthly outgoings. I knew Sean would have said no, but I was so desperate. When I plucked up the courage to tell him I was surprised when he just said, 'Oh, all right, then,' before suggesting he should also ask for voluntary redundancy from Thames Water. It was a bit of a struggle but they gave it to him in the end and even let him have his company car at a cheap price when they heard the reasons for his decision.

Alex, Sean and I decided we needed to do everything in as businesslike a way as possible, and, with Dave Clark, we founded a new company, which became known as Moorcroft Manor Limited. Dave was an invaluable help to us. He had run his own company, which was based next door to where Alex had worked. After speaking with Alex, he had been persuaded to put some time and money into the school project, which proved particularly useful, bearing in mind his expertise with accounting.

Fundraising and publicity were now taking up a huge amount of our time but it proved very worthwhile, leading to donations large and small, both financial and practical. By taking on a number of sponsored keep-fit sessions, between other parents and myself, we were able to raise £20,000 – an amazing sum – and further cash followed after I spoke on LBC, the London radio station, about our hopes for the school. Within moments, £845 had been pledged and the phone lines were busy with other people sharing their experiences of living with autistic children, all of which convinced me of the lack of suitable facilities even further afield.

One listener who had an autistic child was on the phone line. She was crying and asked to speak to me afterwards. She told me she had felt so isolated with her problems and that it had helped her so much to have someone like me to talk to. The radio interview also prompted a chap called Nigel Seagrove to get in touch with me. Nigel's company produced signs. He suggested that, when our school opened, he would be happy to provide us with all the signs we may need free of charge, an offer that was gladly accepted.

By now our cause was receiving a lot of attention. The *Daily Mail* got in touch and they printed a two-page editorial on us and several other national newspapers and magazines followed suit. I did lots of talks and, from each newspaper article, a number of donations would arrive.

This generated a one-hour television documentary on our efforts to open the school. We were approached by a producer, Rachel Foster, who was responsible for *Video Diaries*, a series of programmes screened on BBC2. Rachel asked if I would be willing to provide ongoing recordings of our efforts to gain permission to acquire the school, right up to the point, should we be successful, of gaining the keys. Rachel asked me to leave a camera running and all I would have to do was to record the date and the time, and they would show me how to do cutaways.

The recordings, taken over a six-month period, were eventually edited down to two hours and then had to be cut even further down to an hour before I visited the studio to record the voiceover. The programme, entitled *Not Stupid*, aired in 1999 and took the form of a fly-on-the-wall documentary featuring all that was going on in our lives at the time. Patrick and Angelo were shown displaying signs of their challenging behaviour, Angelo having a tantrum when told he couldn't wear his dirty clothes and Patrick getting upset, first at being filmed and, later, protesting loudly about having to go to a summer play scheme.

The video then showed me walking around Moorcroft School and the extent of all the work it required. It showed Sean and me drawing up our business plan and proposals to Hillingdon Borough Council to set up what we hoped would become one of the largest specialist schools for autistic children in Europe.

The pressure Sean and I were under at this time was abundantly clear in the programme. With Angelo keeping us awake almost all night, every night, and the anxiety and stress we experienced in trying to secure use of the school, it's hardly surprising I looked absolutely worn out.

At least the video gave us the opportunity to put over the potential of some of the sufferers on the autistic spectrum. Earlier scenes had shown Patrick upset and declaring, 'I'm stupid, stupid, stupid!' Yet later ones showed him talking about his passion – dinosaurs – in great detail and with expertise. Furthermore, a fundraising concert by the brilliant autistic pianist Mark Bishop was included in the final cut, and that must have gone a long way in convincing the television viewers that some sufferers can lead very rewarding and fulfilling lives.

The boys and I were fortunate enough to be invited to the set of the BBC1 soap *EastEnders* in Barnet, north London. Rachel suggested we meet up with the actress Daniela Denby-Ashe, who, at the time, played Sarah in the soap and whose brother, Adam, has Asperger Syndrome. Rachel felt an interview to share our experiences with Daniela would slot nicely into the documentary.

While getting the boys ready for the trip I asked Patrick where he thought we were going.

'Out,' he replied.

'Yes,' I said, 'but who do you think we're going to see?'

He still didn't get it so I began humming the familiar *EastEnders* theme tune to give him a clue.

'We're going to *Coronation Street*!' he declared excitedly.

Well, that part of the documentary fell onto the cutting-room floor!

It was fascinating to see behind the scenes of such a famous soap. Apart from Daniela, we met Adam Woodyatt, who plays Ian Beale, Barbara Windsor, who plays Peggy Mitchell, and Michael Greco and Marc Bannerman, who played Beppe and

Gianni di Marco respectively. The set was absolutely huge. The frontage of all the houses in the fictional area known as Albert Square in Walford are all brick-built but are only a façade – there's nothing behind them. We passed a number of large trolleys, each of which carried flat-pack rooms with labels such as 'Ian's room' and 'Pat's room' affixed to them.

Daniela was full of praise for what we had been trying to achieve and it was really nice to meet her, even though it was freezing cold and windy. All was going well until Angelo delivered a truly messy sneeze all over Daniela's dress. I just wanted to die on the spot, I was so embarrassed, particularly when we realised no one had a tissue on them and I found myself frantically trying to clean her up by using a large leaf from a nearby tree! Fortunately, though, she was absolutely fine about it and just carried on telling me more about her family's experiences with her brother Adam.

But that was hardly the end of our eventful day. On the way home I spotted a Woolworth's store and decided to pop in. Patrick wandered off for a look around while I stayed with Angelo in his buggy. Suddenly Angelo spotted some Easter eggs wrapped up like footballs and demanded not one but all of them! When I said no, he went bananas, trying to wriggle out of his buggy and screaming loudly. I could feel the eyes of all the other shoppers looking in our direction. Angelo began to get even more hysterical and loud, so I lifted him from the buggy and tucked him under my arm with the intention of bundling him and Patrick back in the car as quickly as possible. Patrick, though, had other ideas when I called him to follow me.

'No, I'm looking at the DVDs!' he protested.

'Patrick, come here!'

'No, I want to see the DVDs!'

'Patrick, come here now!'

'I hate you!'

'I don't care, just get in the car!'

By the time I'd got the boys strapped into their seats, I was stressed out and sweating profusely. I remember spending the next five minutes driving around unfamiliar roads with the boys going completely mad in the back.

'I hate you!' screamed Patrick again as Angelo was frantically trying to undo his safety straps and yelling his head off.

God help me! I thought. I was almost at the end of my tether and my head felt as if it was about to explode.

I have to admit being glad when the filming of the *Video Diaries* episode was over. I'd built myself up for it and had been really worried about how it would come out. I was particularly concerned as to how the children would appear. They are not all like the guy featured in the movie *Rain Man*. They each have their own characters – funny, witty and bright.

For three days after the screening I received more than 50 telephone calls from parents of autistic children. Some rang to say they'd had no idea what we'd had to go through, and one mother, after having seen me getting up so often in the night to tend to Angelo, reckoned she wouldn't have been able to cope and said she'd have had to send him to a residential school and gone on Prozac!

A further £4,000 was donated to our cause by viewers after *Video Diaries* was screened and the producer also gave us

£1,000 for our efforts in making the programme. Then I wrote to McDonald's charity division, who gave us £5,000, and a group of Indian ladies whom I taught dance and keep-fit suggested we hold an Indian evening at a local community centre, which proved to be a huge success and further boosted our coffers – one lady even handed me a £50 note after I gave a speech outlining what we were trying to do. A £1,000 donation from Capital Radio's Help a London Child Appeal followed, as did several television interviews. I think I gave 18 of them altogether.

My first television appearance had been when I was just nine years old. I was dancing on a programme hosted by the late Jess Yates. Now, however, I had an important message to get across. I was desperate to promote our efforts regarding our school and, although I was appearing on television on a reasonably regular basis to do so, I have to say I found each experience rather nerve-racking, particularly if the interview was being transmitted live.

Many a time I felt the butterflies in my stomach as the cameras began to roll. I remember that, after completing my very first interview on the BBC, I telephoned my mum to see what she thought of it, but she'd missed it. At first I was even wondering if there would be anyone out there who would be interested in anything I had to say in any case, but those doubts were soon dispelled by the huge amount of feedback and support I received after each interview. Usually when I spoke on air the time seemed to fly past so quickly and I was often left thinking, If only I'd mentioned this, or Why didn't I mention that?

The publicity generated by our media campaign prompted a

Granada Television producer to get in touch. Would it be OK for him to visit us as part of a research project? The aim was to eventually produce a television drama starring the actor Robson Green about a couple who split up because of the pressures they were under while caring for their five-year-old autistic son. We were happy to agree to this request, thinking it would be a good way to highlight how autism and Asperger Syndrome affect not only sufferers but their families as well. Patrick was really happy when the producer arrived, and promptly began climbing all over him as he spent the best part of the day with us. He was particularly fascinated by the producer's Southern accent and got on really well with him.

We had been looking forward to seeing the finished drama and had expected to have been invited to its première but were disappointed not to have been. Nevertheless, it was a good drama, which showed very clearly some of the pressures that often divide the parents of autistic children, how they sometimes look to blame each other or someone else for the predicament they've found themselves in, and I know it rang a few bells with several of the members of HACS.

Meanwhile, I also appeared on Sky TV's programme *Why Me?*, a chat show that, this time, was about raising the awareness of Asperger Syndrome following a wave of press interest in autism-related stories. During the interview I chatted to Dr Rosemary Waring and, afterwards, several parents wrote to me to express their support.

Chapter Six

Hard Work, Policies and Procedures

It was an anxious wait but when I received the telephone call to say the keys to the school were available to us, I could hardly get down to Hillingdon Civic Centre quickly enough! I hurriedly got Patrick and Angelo into the car and went off straightaway to collect the keys. Needless to say, I was very excited, ecstatic, even though Patrick and Angelo had no idea what all the fuss was about. Anyway, any thoughts of school in Patrick's mind were full of negativity. To make it even more special, it was 5 January, 1999, Patrick's ninth birthday!

At last I had the keys in my hand. And then it hit me: I couldn't help thinking, What now? I drove straight to the school and let myself in. Bloody hell! I thought. Whatever have we let ourselves in for? Everything's in such a state. We're going to need a lot of help here.

Meanwhile, Angelo had seen fit to run off and explore. At first I wasn't too concerned, as everywhere had been locked up, but I was dismayed to find he'd discovered the climbing bars in the main hall and had instantly clambered right up to the top, and was balanced precariously on a tiny wooden platform many feet up from the floor with nothing to break his fall should he have slipped.

Seeing him standing there so carefree absolutely horrified me. One false move and that would have been it for him, yet there was no way I could leave to get help. I knew I had to climb up there after him – and I really hate heights. It was a nerve-racking climb but, fortunately, after some negotiation, my powers of persuasion saw Angelo safely back on terra firma. Not the best of starts, by any means!

Then I rang everyone I could think of to let them know the news – we were in business. Further exploration of the school brought home to me just how much work would be required to bring it into a serviceable condition and, I must admit, it was pretty daunting.

But there was no way I would accept failure. Firmly in my mind was the comment made by one councillor while we were trying to secure the school. He'd said he reckoned we'd be handing the property back to the council within six months. 'What do you know about running a school?' he'd asked. 'You won't be able to hack it.' He may not have known it at the time, but he'd just made me even more determined to make a success of the project.

Sean didn't arrive at the school until the evening. Alex was with him. After looking around the whole premises we all gathered around to discuss the best way forward, excitedly chatting while, at the same time, wondering what on earth we'd let ourselves in for!

Up until the point we received the keys for the school, Alex had been working for a warehouse company but, such was the scale of the task ahead of us, he decided to quit his job and work for us full-time as project manager. He would be the only one among us at the time to receive a wage, but this was to be a vital full-time role and we had already budgeted for such expenses with our bank loan.

Once appointed, Alex threw himself wholeheartedly into the project and, thanks to him, the organisation of the scheduled work over the forthcoming months went, largely, very smoothly. His enthusiasm for the task before him was matched only by his humour. I have to say he's a lovely man who likes nothing more than to have a jolly good natter!

It was clear that one of our priorities would have to be the school's flat roof, which was leaking like a sieve in places, but that was obviously going to cost a huge amount of money. Further inspections saw us quoted figures in excess of £100,000. We knew this would be a difficult sum to raise and considered having the work done in sections to spread the cost. One thing was for sure: the work couldn't be ignored, as we had rapidly-filling buckets all over the place every time it rained.

It was all hands on deck in the race against time to get the school up and running. Sean, Alex and I began the painting – with Sean ending up with more paint in his hair than on the ceiling! However, it soon became obvious we would need a lot more help if we were to have any chance of completing the project in time. We established a core workforce of seven or eight of us, but we also had a lot of occasional volunteers, including parents, brothers and sisters and grandparents of children who were hoping to get into the school.

One parent, whose daughter had autism, was an electrician and he took responsibility for the huge task of sorting out all the wiring at the school; and another grandparent, also an electrician, still helps us to this day. Another parent with an autistic son became the maintenance manager.

We've since become like one big family.

People would come in to help clean up, paint and so on. Prince's Trust volunteers cleared the area of old trees and paving slabs, while Middlesex Community Service would bring along people who had to work in the community on Saturdays. Alex and I would be on site to monitor what was going on.

Surprisingly, in spite of being made to come along to help out, many of the offenders, once their penance had been paid, still chose to come back to assist in any way they could, perhaps because of the camaraderie among our volunteer workforce. One lady, a drink-driver, had enjoyed working at the school so much that, a few months later, when she reoffended, she even asked if she could return to our school to serve her time. And she did!

I decided to ring around as many newspapers as I could think of to drum up support. I started with our local newspaper, the *Uxbridge Gazette*, and spoke to a reporter, Barbara Fisher, who has, over the past few years, been a huge supporter and also become a good friend. Barbara gave me several tips so far as dealing with the press was concerned. She advised me to keep all my correspondence short and sweet – they like conciseness – and suggested sending in letters on coloured paper so they would stand out among all the others received each day in the majority of newsrooms. It turned out to be very good advice.

We were very fortunate that our project captured the imagination of so many people and companies willing to help us along the way. When we acquired the school, the NatWest bank donated a whole load of toys, and David Kamsler, from the Link charity, which is based in Basingstoke, gave us lots of chairs and tables that had been donated to his charity at the end of the tax year when the companies renew their fittings and fixtures.

David also provided us with a huge number of large, heavy, blue carpet tiles, enough to cover most of the floor space at the school. Alex and Sean and I borrowed a couple of knackered old vans and drove down to Basingstoke to collect them from the company where they were situated. We had to lift them from the floors and load them into the vans. Although they were almost brand-new, there was a fault with them that meant the rubber backs were not quite as good as they might have been. That said, they were certainly good enough for our purposes. The vans really struggled on the way back to Hillingdon, such was the weight of the loads, and then we had to go back for more! We covered the classrooms and corridors, the staffroom as well.

The Pavilions Shopping Centre in Uxbridge chose the school as its charity for the Millennium, and four schools in South Harrow donated nearly-new furniture, including 90 desks. British Airways donated older-style PCs, office furniture, blankets for the relaxation room and a £5,000 cheque after they'd seen a number of newspaper articles. And we held jumble sales.

People would even leave things outside the school doors that they assumed would be useful to us – toys, computers, books, tables, etc. Some items had notes attached to them with messages such as, 'This is for the autistic children and the autistic lady!' Sometimes there were items we didn't really need but we took them to jumble sales and got money for them, so they weren't wasted.

Sixty British Airports Authority staff from Heathrow Airport helped to create a daily-skills living room and the company also donated £5,000 to help equip it. The room was converted into a classroom equipped with a kitchen, dining room and living area where the children could learn how to cope with everyday life. The American School, an independent private school nearby, which had had some autistic pupils in the past, gave us lots of books.

Although there was a lot of hard work to do, we also had times when we had a laugh. Outside there was grass everywhere, growing out of control. Alex, wandering around, found an enormous petrol motor mower that had been left in the grounds but we had no idea whether it would still work. We decided to give it a try. To our surprise it started and I decided to make a start on cutting the grass. Unfortunately, as I let out the clutch it roared off, much to Alex and Sean's amusement. It was so powerful it just lifted up and dragged me along behind it! Alex said he just wished he'd had a camera with him at the time.

Obviously, all this work at the school took time and, without Patrick and Angelo being in appropriate places of education, Sean and I would sometimes need to bring them along with us. For that reason it was important we could leave them securely while we worked and we had to ensure all the doors were locked so they didn't wander off while we were otherwise occupied. We made arrangements for the boys to receive their home tuition at the school and set up a classroom specifically for them to give them the opportunity to get used to their new surroundings.

Unfortunately, the burglar alarm used to go off an awful lot. Alex, Sean and I were the callouts, since we didn't have the money to employ security staff at the time. We also used to get false alarms and later we discovered that the alarm was faulty, which wasn't much fun when you consider it would often sound off at about 2 a.m.

Soon after we'd had a washing machine and fridge delivered, the alarm went off again, so Sean, Alex and I arrived at the school late at night to find a window had been smashed at the back of the premises. Then Sean saw two guys running off with the washing machine, so he jumped over the fence and gave chase. Seeing this big guy screaming and charging towards them, they sensibly dropped the washing machine and ran for it. Later, in a lane at the back of the school, a large amount of property was found awaiting collection, stuff that had been stolen from the school and other properties nearby. We got the washing machine back but it had been badly dented. Fortunately, though, the people who donated it to us in the first place replaced it.

It was nerve-racking to come out at the dead of night to a deserted school, not knowing who or what we might find. Sometimes, as we patrolled the premises, Sean would walk around holding a truncheon, though I'd warn him not to hit anyone with it because such is the law of the land that it probably would have been Sean who would have got into trouble rather than an intruder. Other times, Sean would go around on his own, which really worried me.

The break-ins highlighted the need for better security and, again, volunteers in the form of Waterside Parkland's manager Richard Wassell and his team came to the rescue to supply us with extra fencing and lighting. The most vulnerable part of the premises was the fence at the back of the grounds, which backed onto a field. This had to be heightened but we couldn't risk putting any spikes on the top because autistic children are renowned for climbing and we could not afford to risk their safety.

Another unexpected problem arose when we began receiving mail addressed to Moorcroft School that was intended for the previous occupants of the site. We hadn't changed the name because the former occupants had moved on but, although they were no longer based on our Moorcroft site, they had retained their school's name elsewhere. Obviously, this was a situation that needed to be urgently addressed to avoid any confusion. We decided to rename our school and held a meeting to decide upon it. After putting our heads together we came up with Hillingdon Manor School, which didn't take too much imagination owing to the fact that it is situated in Hillingdon and is adjacent to a manor house!

Of course, having the premises at last was only the beginning of a very long road we had to travel down. After all, what use is a school without any teachers? Bearing in mind this was hardly our field of expertise, we knew we had to bring in a head teacher first of all, who would be responsible for advising us on the number and calibre of staff required to enable the school to function effectively.

Policies and procedures would need to be put in place before any other appointments could be made, so the appointment of a head teacher became paramount – but how do you go about getting a headteacher for a school that is falling apart, with no pupils or staff?

It was hardly an attractive proposal, but I'd made a few contacts at Christina Bertolucci's workshops and I was aware of *The Times Educational Supplement*, which regularly carries advertisements for teaching professionals. I popped into our local branch of W H Smith, bought a copy and studied the way the advertisements were laid out in the situations-vacant columns. Then I noticed the paper carried a special-needs section, which also featured a good number of advertisements.

Looking at the existing advertisements, I got an idea of how our own advertisement should appear and what kind of requirements we should highlight. I was shocked, however, when I looked at the price we'd be required to pay for our advertisement: £600. Just think what we could have repaired with that sort of money!

We had set aside a certain amount of money from our bank loan to pay staff upon opening but, obviously, we needed to be able to sustain ourselves financially afterwards. We reckoned statementing fees would go some way towards helping out on that front.

And so it was that we put together the following advertisement:

HEAD TEACHER

Challenging placement in a new school set up by parents. Applicants need to be enthusiastic, determined and have knowledge of autism.

We soon received some replies, but there were some very strange or wacky applicants. One even wrote to us on some writing paper with the logo from the kids' TV programme *Rainbow* on the top of it!

Sean, Alex, myself and Dave, who was the only person out of the shareholders without a child with autism, conducted the interviews. Of course, knowing what to ask potential head teachers had to be researched prior to the interviewing process, and already I had a number of questions drafted. Previously I'd contacted Rosemary Siddles from the National Autistic Society, who dealt with education matters. Rosemary was very helpful in assisting me with a draft questionnaire and advised how much parents paid for their children to attend similar types of school.

One applicant, probably in her eighties, arrived for an interview. She was wearing a kilt, white training socks and trainers. She was one of several who turned up, none of whom we felt were suitable for our project. Fortunately, on the last day scheduled for applications, we received an application from Angela Austin. I'd read only the first paragraph of her letter when I thought, This is the one. Angela had expertise in speech-and-language therapy, she was a special-educational-needs teacher, and she had ten years' experience of working with people with autism. At the time she was working in a unit in Surrey for children with mixed disabilities. I called her over for an interview.

When she arrived at the school for her interview, Patrick was sitting in an office just off the main corridor near the entrance, reading one of his dinosaur books. Angela was very well-spoken, and well-dressed, with blonde hair, and she looked quite out of place in such a dilapidated building. As she walked past the office where Patrick was sitting, she noticed him and went in to say hello. At this time Patrick had the attitude that, if he didn't know someone, he didn't want to know them. He didn't want them in his space. He kept his book in front of his face and ignored her.

'Hello,' she repeated, 'isn't that *The Oxford Reading Tree Book on Dinosaurs*?'

Patrick glared over the top of his book as Angela started telling him what was in it.

'How do you know about this book?'

'I've already read it,' replied Angela and, within moments, she'd got around him.

I couldn't help thinking, This is the one! This is the one! She knows exactly how to speak to Patrick as nobody else could. As for the interview, it went really well. We explained our intentions to Angela of including pupils with a diagnosis of Asperger Syndrome, high-functioning autism and/or semantic-pragmatic disorder or pathological demand-avoidance, then she left to await our response.

Afterwards, it took little persuasion from me to convince the others that Angela was just the person we needed. It was agreed

I would telephone her the next day to offer her the job. Meanwhile, Angela had returned to Surrey, where, after telling her colleagues about our school, she was advised that she must be mad even to consider joining a school run by people like us.

When I called her the next day, she was surprised to hear from us so quickly and asked if she could have a little time to consider our offer. Fortunately, despite being advised to the contrary by her colleagues, she decided she would be happy to join us – but there was one condition. She wanted a teacher she worked with called Karen Croucher to come with her. Angela told me she had already asked Karen if she would be willing to relocate and Karen had indicated that she, like Angela, was interested in the challenge awaiting them.

We had no problem with that. If Angela thought Karen was up to the task, who were we to say otherwise? We knew we would have to put a lot of faith in Angela's ability and expertise if our school was to run effectively and efficiently.

When Angela and Karen arrived to take up their posts, we still had no idea how many pupils would be on the school roll when we opened. We knew, of course, that we needed more teachers and, after a series of meetings between us and Angela and Karen, it was agreed that the main responsibility for such appointments would be left to them.

Angela and Karen worked well in putting together a series of policies and procedures that proved their worth at a residential school they had previously worked at dealing specifically with autistic pupils at the more severe end of the spectrum. Their appointments were just the start of a dream team that would grow as the weeks progressed.

A broad, balanced, well-structured and stimulating curriculum would stretch the abilities of the pupils and it was decided to adopt the same TEACCH approach to lessons as those implemented so successfully at Springhallow School in Ealing. This approach plays a major role in the education of people with autism. Basically, TEACCH is a flexible method of teaching that was first established in North Carolina as far back as 1966. Its primary aim is to prepare people with autism to live or work more effectively at home, at school and in the community.

Hopefully, the following principles of the programme, complete with references for further reading, will clarify. As we saw in Chapter Four, TEACCH is an acronym for Treatment and Education of Autistic and related Communication-handicapped CHildren. It is a 'whole life' approach aimed at supporting children, adolescents and adults with autism through the provision of visual information, structure and predictability. Essentially, this means that the approach can be used in all areas of life for the whole of one's life. Having an autistic-spectrum disorder means that a person may have difficulty in organising their environment and sequencing tasks. Simply put, TEACCH teaches skills that will allow a person with autism to overcome these difficulties.

The TEACCH programme focuses on structuring the environment to facilitate skill development and independence. Clear physical and visual boundaries are established to help children understand what they are expected to do in each area. Visual supports are used to support children's comprehension.

TEACCH aims to provide the least restrictive teaching

possible. One-to-one support is available to children as they learn new skills. However, they are encouraged to develop independence and opportunities for integration and reverse integration are provided.

Every aspect of structured teaching is predetermined and organised to benefit the success of a person with autism. The programme emphasises certain skills and behaviours, but the effects of this work move into the child's personal life and everyday activities. The programme consists of precise methods to set up the learning and work environment, make schedules, create activities and teach the learner.

The physical layout of the classroom plays an important role in the implementation of the TEACCH programme because children with autism have trouble differentiating between events and activities. To address this, TEACCH creates several distinct areas for specific activities. Each activity is consistently done in its own designated spot, allowing the child to relate the activity to the work area and, therefore, allowing for more concentration and focus.

Students with autism are also very easily distracted, so minimal decoration of the room and dividers for each work area are necessary for the success of the programme. When working, it is beneficial for the students to be facing a blank wall to avoid added distractions. This can help students focus on the activity instead of what is occurring in the rest of the room.

Schedules are utilised when teaching an autistic child about a sequence of events that will happen during the day, as the child will be more capable of distinguishing between the distinct events and determining what he or she is to do next. The children receive their own daily schedule, designating times for activities such as play, structured play, work, independent work, snack and circle time.

The students learn what to expect next and this can sometimes motivate them to complete a task because they see that a more enjoyable one will follow. Each schedule is geared towards the individual student, allowing for a higher comprehension level. For advanced students, the schedule could be composed simply of written text, while other students might need pictures of their work stations or actual objects from these stations. The comprehension of these schedules helps the children to learn to follow directions and develop an independence they did not possess before.

The different work stations contain activities that the child becomes accustomed to and, therefore, he or she obtains more proficiency in the activity. In the work area, the child works with a teacher on activities dealing with topics such as shapes, colour and organisation. With the teacher's help, the child completes an activity and then moves on to another. Each activity is done many times until the child is capable of doing it on their own, in which case the activity is moved to the independent learning station. There, the child gains more independence, working alone to complete the activities he or she is accustomed to.

Structured play sees the child working with a teacher, using toys and games to help gain attention skills and learn to work with different objects such as blocks and balloons. The play station is where children can relax, use their own imagination and participate in whatever game or toy chosen. The children have their own times for each activity allowing for personal interaction with the teachers and stations.

There are two times during the day in which the group combines as a whole – snack and circle time. During snack, the teacher distributes a portion of food to each child only when he or she is asked for that specific food. The child must say the word for the food or hand over a card indicating a preference. This increases the communication skills of the children.

Circle time is a time when the children sit and sing songs to end the day. Each day the same songs are sung, allowing the children to become familiar with the songs and to anticipate what is next.

Underpinning the above is the need for assessment and measurement. It should also be stressed that the programme is highly individualised for each child. Finally, while the above describes how the method may be implemented among smaller children, the approach can be modified and thus made appropriate for older children and adults. In the workplace this approach could organise a person's day, what clothes they should wear, what they need to do before attending a meeting and so on. This 'structure' would allow a person with autism to work effectively.

TEACCH and connective education run alongside each other. It takes a very simplified view of autism, in that to understand the world the person involved has to take in lots of pieces of information and build interconnections between them.

An example of this may be learning a set of manners or ways of behaving, which is a good thing. But while correct etiquette is essential in the right situation, it can be a disaster in others. For instance, if Sean attended a dinner party for the Lord Chief Justice wearing a dark lounge suit and called everyone sir or ma'am, that would be fine. But, if he didn't realise that this approach is inappropriate at the works Christmas party or a shindig at the rugby club, he might be seen as not fitting in.

Thus, connective education teaches in a way that reinforces the interconnections between information. It can be applied to factual information and the learning of socially appropriate ways of behaving. To this end, what would be taught at Hillingdon Manor would be measured. An individual education plan would be rigorously monitored to enable the teachers to build on what is achieved in a very systematic and constructive way.

With the decision to adopt TEACCH at Hillingdon Manor, a mission statement and prospectus were devised. Within these were a number of pledges designed to cover every aspect of pupils' wellbeing. The school would provide a safe, excellent and effective learning environment for pupils within the autistic spectrum where they could minimise their disability and maximise their ability. This would be achieved through a curriculum of connective education, which would offer pupils the opportunity to make connections and gather meaning that would allow them to progress throughout the curriculum and in the world outside the school.

The staff would, through practice, promote the use of a consistent language-focused environment, which would address the so-called triad of impairment in autism – difficulties in social interactions, social communication and imagination – and they would work to provide an environment where the emotional, social and physical needs of the pupils would be met in such a way that the pupils would learn to be responsible for and manage their own thoughts, feelings and actions and their learning.

The ethos of TEAM, which stands for Trust, Empathy, Assistance and to discriminate what Matters (and what does not matter) in life, would be promoted. The school would be committed to providing a therapeutic environment that would ensure all pupils would be treated with dignity and respect, and their needs as human beings would be met.

Families would be trained, supported and encouraged to take on the specific philosophy and structures the school would employ to support their children with consistency.

A huge consideration would be how to encourage appropriate and acceptable behaviour. This would require an extensive good-behaviour policy, which would need to provide very clear definitions, aims and guidance about how pupils' emotional wellbeing and pastoral care would be supported by all staff. There would be a pastoral-support manager and each pupil would have a pastoral-support plan, which would be agreed by all staff involved and by the pupil's parents. It was hoped this plan would form overall targets for decreasing behaviours that inhibit learning, independence and acceptable behaviour.

The school would maintain a calm, low-anxiety environment that would support the pupils in keeping the school rules and boundaries, and staff would be trained to understand what happens in the brain in times of high anxiety and emotional charge. All behavioural incidents would be recorded, sent to parents and kept by the school, and would be open to scrutiny by any appropriate individuals or agencies.

Our policy would ensure that all staff would be committed to supporting pupils to comply with the rules and boundaries expected in mainstream education and in the world outside. This would require the introduction of a 'no blame' culture in which 'what works' is what is promoted, rather than making self or others 'wrong'. This would be adopted because pupils with autism do not learn or understand the rules and boundaries incidentally, as non-autistic people do. If they are burdened with being made 'wrong' by those of us who do understand, their anxiety levels will rise and their information processing breaks down.

The pupils' needs would be met in accordance with the human needs and resources identified by Joe Griffin and Ivan Tyrell in their book *Human Givens*. This requires pupils to make choices about their responses to their own behaviour. Staff would aim to encourage self-cognitive self-reflection and personal responsibility in behaviour management to support the development of the observing self.

Staff would also be encouraged to support the pupils to identify clearly the cause of anything upsetting them, then to discuss the cause with the child to guide them into making an effective choice about how to deal with the situation and how to clear up any negative results of behaviour that does not work, clearing up with whoever has been affected, and moving forward.

The school would also offer a parent-training session on a

termly basis to provide theoretical and practical information, and advice and strategies that would support the families of children with autism in the home. The sessions would cover such areas as promoting good behaviour, behaviour management, transactional analysis, relaxation, holding for wellbeing, and the Human Givens Approach which, in itself, requires further explanation.

The human needs as defined by the Human Givens Approach are as follows:

- Security: A safe territory and an environment, which allows us to develop fully.
- Attention: To give and receive. This involves a sense of autonomy and control; being emotionally connected to others; being part of a wider community; friendship, fun, love and intimacy; a sense of status within social groupings; a sense of competence and achievement.
- Meaning of purpose: This comes from being stretched in what we do and think.

With this in mind, a trained Human Givens therapist would be appointed to assist the pupils in solving their problems and helping them to move forward with emotional issues. This confidential service would also be made available to parents.

Because an autistic child may not fully understand when being told no, the good-behaviour policy adopted the stance that the word no should not be used when referring to a pupil's behaviour. Instead, the pupil's name should always be preceded by the word stop. No, however, could be used in answer to curriculum questions or in relation to unacceptable actions – for instance, the rule is 'no hitting'.

When dealing with misbehaviour, a pupil should be supported by the offer of a choice, linking the expectation with the action and the consequence. For example, the school expectation is 'to listen to the adult in charge'. The pupil may choose to listen to the adult in charge and do what works, or they can decide not to listen to the adult in charge, not do what works and not have free time at break time. One choice, therefore, is educationally, socially and physically advantageous to the pupil with an individually positive outcome; the other is unacceptable educationally, socially and physically with an outcome less desirable for the pupil.

If a pupil is experiencing upset or their information processing is reduced, further clarity would be required. In this instance, staff would hold out two hands, palms upwards. Pointing to one palm, a staff member would say, '[Pupil's name], you can choose that a and b will happen.' Then the staff member would say '[Pupil's name], or you can choose that c and d will happen.' Working in this way would require staff to know what each pupil's powerful positive and negative reinforcers are and this approach would also require close liaison with parents. If the pupil then refuses to choose, the staff member would say, 'Not choosing means you are choosing that c and d will happen.'

Of course, there would always be the possibility that a pupil's emotional charge would be so high they might become a danger to themselves and to others' health and safety. A physical-intervention policy was drafted that would be implemented if ever staff felt it appropriate to step in to deal physically with a situation. Staff would be trained in the use of ethical and legal physical intervention as approved by the British Institute of Learning Disability.

We also had to consider the probability that not all pupils would have English as their first language. We would need to reflect the cultural diversity that exists within our wider community. Of course, every aspect of education at Hillingdon Manor would be conducted in English but we needed to recognise that, for children who have English as an additional language, the complexity of their needs must be considered in addition to their communication impairment.

Our speech-and-language therapist would be required to assess the communication needs of these children and to work with curriculum staff and parents to develop an appropriate communication system that would include strategies and resources to support both understanding and use of communication.

The criteria for consideration for admission to Hillingdon Manor would include that the child's needs should arise out of their autistic-spectrum disorder, and some other related pervasive developmental disorders; the child would have their needs recognised through appropriate funding by the sponsoring local education authority; the child would have the commitment and support of their parents/carers to the educational approach used at the school through parents agreeing to a home–school contract; the principal would be satisfied that the needs of the child would be met; the principal would decide, using admission procedures, which children would be admitted to the school and would seek to ensure a balance of age, compatibility and gender; and admissions would be made on the basis of availability of placements, taking into account the above factors, plus a child's level of functioning, learning and difficulties and age.

The school would be 'human-being-centred', meaning it would place strong emphasis on equal opportunities with respect to gender, race, sexual orientation, religious belief and disability. The school would be committed to using the latest research into human brain functioning to refine and improve its practice. It would also be committed to keeping abreast of new research into autistic-spectrum disorders and to assess its implications for improved practice.

The policies adopted by Angela and Karen proved sufficient for approval from the Department for Education to open the school. Now, at last, we could advertise and release news stories to the media that we were hoping to open to pupils in the near future.

Thanks to the *Video Diaries* programme, teachers had become aware of our project and, learning that opening was near, some contacted me to express their interest in positions at the school.

This led to a further three to four days of interviewing, the panel consisting of myself, Angela and Karen. I thought I might feel a little out of my depth during this period but, surprisingly, that was not the case. I guess I'm a pretty instinctive person and I seem to know if someone feels right; but I've also learned that, just because someone presents you with a fantastic reference, it doesn't necessarily follow that they're all they're cracked up to be.

It was so important to get a good staff team – one that would work together – which ultimately proved difficult over the first 18 months to two years after we opened when some members of staff expressed a desire to do their own thing rather than work in the same manner as the rest of the team. Frankly, that just doesn't work with children with autism. Again, consistency is the key and that is what we had to strive for throughout.

Specialist speech-and-language therapists who could effectively address the communication disorder symptomatic of autism were particularly difficult to find. Individual education plans needed to be implemented for each child depending upon their specific difficulty. We were fortunate to discover a really good agency, which found positions for therapists from as far afield as Australia, New Zealand and South Africa. Many of the therapists who joined us from this source remained with us for two or three years, then, on returning to their native countries, told colleagues about us. They then applied to come and work with us, too.

Some of the staff who had joined us had children of their own with autism. One lady with an autistic son began working with us as a support assistant and went on to become our administrative assistant; our maintenance man had a son with autism; the grandfather of a deaf and autistic boy also joined us to cover the electrical work, as did Alex's brother-in-law, who also works on the maintenance side of things.

The borough referred children to us and we would look at the paperwork made available to see if we could provide a suitable learning environment for that particular child, basically, to see if they met our admission criteria. If so, they would then be assessed.

This sometimes proved very difficult. Because of their autism, some children find it problematic to be assessed, which meant we occasionally had to carry out this process in their own homes or go to the school or nursery where they were at that moment in time. This task fell mainly to Angela and Karen.

We were delighted when our MP, John Randall, invited Sean and me to bring the boys to the Houses of Parliament in London. After all the hard work at the school, a day out was a welcome treat. I didn't know how the boys would react but it was a new experience for them and a very interesting one for us. Angelo was mesmerised by the House of Lords, and all had been going well until he dived under a security ribbon and made a beeline for the Queen's chair and sat on it.

An agitated security man was quick to react and stepped in to shoo him off: 'Stop, you can't sit there!' Angelo instantly became cross – he'd liked the chair and wanted to remain seated on it – so Sean had to pick him up quickly and carry him off as he kicked and screamed in protest. 'Keep calm,' said Sean to the security man, 'my son's autistic.' Then he added cheekily, 'You'd better check the chair, mate, because he tends to wee on chairs!'

After Angelo had calmed down we went for lunch on the terrace of the Houses of Parliament, which we all enjoyed. On a table nearby was the then Chancellor (now Prime Minister), Gordon Brown, accompanied by some of his colleagues.

At the end of our visit John gave us a bottle of House of Commons wine that had been signed by the then Prime Minister, Tony Blair, for us to auction to raise money for repairs to the school.

Chapter Seven

A Dream is Realised

After much hard work by all concerned, the big day finally arrived. The school opened on 4 September 1999 and you could not imagine the lump in my throat as the doors opened and the children walked in for the first time. Sean could hardly believe it either. We'd done it!

We weren't the only happy ones. Other parents, many of whom had presumably faced similar obstacles to our own, were thrilled to have found somewhere their children could come, where they could learn in a calm and relaxed environment and be totally free from any bullying, which, unfortunately, many children with autism face when there is no option other than to attend mainstream schools.

Suddenly, we received flowers, donations, letters and cards of appreciation from parents, many of them pointing out that, if it hadn't been for our determination, their children would have been seriously disadvantaged educationally.

We started off with 18 members of staff and 19 pupils,

though Angelo and Patrick were the last two to be funded by the borough. We didn't find out we'd secured funding for them until a week before we opened, which was ironic, to say the least. I'd been thinking how crazy it was that, having got so far, I still didn't know whether my own children – the inspiration behind this project – would be able to attend themselves.

The classes had been named after colours and birds and other attractive things, which, we felt, added to the calming atmosphere. Although it was Patrick and Angelo's first day of schooling for some time they, at least, were familiar with the surroundings, having accompanied Sean and me to the school so often during the refurbishment project. Nevertheless, I was still wondering how they would cope. At this stage, neither Patrick nor Angelo comprehended that all this work we had undertaken had been because of them; that's become apparent to them only in more recent times.

Angelo had always loved being at his mainstream nursery – and that's what had made it so galling when we were told there was no place for him at St Mary's School. At Hillingdon Manor, he started his first term in Rainbow Class. Although he didn't mix well with other children, he seemed happy enough at the end of his first day and it was encouraging when eventually he allowed another child called Richard into his 'space'.

At the end of the first day, the staff, like Sean and me, were absolutely ecstatic. We were on a real high. Everyone was in a really good mood and no one could believe how well everything had gone – even though we were all absolutely shattered! There was such a nice buzz about the place and parents picking up their children were anxiously asking us how their child had got on. Seeing their faces when we told them their children had been absolutely fine was a very rewarding experience and Angela, when asked how she felt, told our local newspaper, 'I keep crying. I am always telling Anna this is a bad place for my mascara because I am always being moved by kindness and inspired by her dedication.'

Thirteen-year-old Matthew also enjoyed his first day at Hillingdon Manor. There had been suspicions he might be autistic when he was attending a nursery school but he had not been diagnosed with Asperger Syndrome until he was 12, and it was not until a year later that he received a statement of special needs.

This lack of accurate diagnosis had caused Matthew to endure a torturous time in mainstream education. He had become a source of derision and had been bullied ever since his days in the reception class. Not only that, but other children who made the effort to befriend him had found themselves the subject of bullying too.

Life, thankfully, was transformed for Matthew after he joined his peers at Hillingdon Manor and, at the end of his first day, he happily told me, 'When I sat down for lunch, nobody got up and walked away' – which, apparently, had been a novel experience for him.

On his second day at school Patrick became upset when a newspaper photographer wanted to get a picture of him and Angelo walking through the doors. Patrick is not a morning person, so he didn't feel at all comfortable with the attention of the photographer and made his feelings plain. Nevertheless, he was glad to be with other children. All his classmates in Blue Class had Asperger Syndrome, which is probably why he announced he now had friends – and he'd never really had friends before.

Each child was given a home–school book in which their teacher wrote down how the child's day had gone. The idea was that the parent could read the book at home and then tell us what sort of night their child had had and what to expect from them the next day. It's all about consistency in their home and school lives, which is of such importance with autistic children that it cannot ever be emphasised strongly enough.

Consistency is key. It's no use having a structured routine at school if it is not maintained at home. That is one of the most difficult things for a person with autism to come to terms with. Take Angelo, for instance. We talk to him in short sentences. Give him a long sentence to contend with and you'll lose him. At school and at home, everything is put over to him in a concise manner. That's the only way he can cope.

With the exception of one boy, all the children seemed more than happy to return the next day. In fact, this particular boy cried every morning when he was dropped off for school over the first two or three months but, as soon as his mother left him, he was absolutely fine straightaway.

The majority of pupils had already been statemented favourably, which enabled their parents to send them to us. Otherwise, there were just two children whose parents had to dip into their own pockets to finance their children's places with us at Hillingdon Manor, and that was a considerable expense: £22,000 a year per child. Local authorities were able to place children in the school for £27,000 a year but that compared favourably with the alternative of residential places, which would have cost in the region of £100,000.

Our aim was to keep class sizes limited to seven children per class. This was achieved with one teacher and one support worker to each class, while some children, like Angelo, required one-to-one support, depending upon their individual needs.

The first day at school for any child can be a traumatic experience. With autistic children entering a strange environment, with its new smells, new teachers and so on, we knew this would be a particularly difficult experience, so the decision was taken to admit some children on the first day and the remainder the next.

Surprisingly, the children all seemed to settle very quickly at Hillingdon Manor. I'd expected it to be mayhem but, within a couple of days, they seemed happy enough to be there. This has often been attributed to the calming environment generated at the school. Even when it's busy, it's usually a pretty quiet place to be, although, obviously, due to the nature of their condition, there were occasions when some children exhibited challenging behaviour and had to be held for their own wellbeing.

We even established a daily relaxation session for each class during which pupils lie on mats and listen to calming, soothing music. If they want a hand-to-foot massage, that's what they get, subject to parental approval of course, and, if they wish, the children are allowed to sleep. Breathing exercises were also introduced as an effective antidote to stress.

A relaxation room is utilised whenever a child's behaviour is such that they are not engaging in the lesson and need to calm down. They can go there with a support assistant until they feel better. Sometimes they just need a short while to relax, maybe wrap themselves up in a blanket or listen to some calming music through headphones or read a book. They know themselves when they are ready to rejoin their classmates.

Behaviour has to be managed quickly and effectively. Sometimes it's just not possible to manage behaviour in the classroom, so the relaxation rooms are very beneficial. All the staff are trained in 'holding for wellbeing', which means they know how to lead an autistic person, either by the hand or arm to an area where they are not going to harm themselves or anyone else around them physically.

Whatever their behavioural state, the children are always supported and safe. They may be encouraged to take up a particular relaxation position, maybe in the foetal position or any other familiar comfortable position that has been identified as beneficial to that particular child.

These sessions are most prevalent prior to lunch breaks or the end of the school day. Just think how useful they would be to people with autism in the workplace, to offer them a place where they could let off steam. But it just wouldn't happen, would it?

Karen, in her role as home/school manager, devised an award chart as a tool to help the children better understand the behaviour and attitudes of others. The chart would feature photographs of parents and teachers either smiling or looking annoyed. If there had been a behaviour problem during the day, an 'angry' picture of the teacher would be circled so both child and parent would recognise that things had not been so good that day. In the same way, parents could communicate with the school and their child, using pictures with various facial expressions.

Karen arranged for daily records to be kept that showed the targets set for each child in literacy and numeracy, and she carefully monitored the children's communication skills. Physical and verbal responses were monitored, as these were seen as a crucial indicator of an autistic child's progress. We also adopted a policy that every area of a pupil's achievement would be celebrated with the presentation of a certificate. Once a pupil gained five certificates, a present was given to them, which helped the children who might otherwise never have done so to experience their personal successes.

Children were encouraged to bring in their own packed lunches, which enables their parents to control their intake. This is particularly important for children on gluten- and/or caffeine-free diets, and for children who react negatively to additives. It is also important that the children learn appropriate social skills at mealtimes, which are overseen by a team of trained lunchtime/play supervisors.

It didn't take long for more and more people to hear about us. We had many visits from educational psychologists and psychotherapists, all eager to find out exactly what we were about. Then there were people from different boroughs with autistic children coming around to check us out and to compare notes. It got to a point where my main duty seemed to be that of tour guide because of the number of visitors who needed to be shown around every day, and I began to feel a little like a parrot, having memorised my talk for almost every person I accompanied.

An inspector from the Department for Education, David Gardiner, paid a visit to the school just five weeks after our opening. Since it was a new school, it was important that the powers that be realised how well, or not, things were going. It was pretty stressful for us, as David spent the day just wandering around the school and observing lessons. We nervously awaited his verdict. As it was, we were pleasantly surprised. 'I know it's raw, and I know the whole building isn't open yet,' he said, 'but, if I had a child with autism, I wouldn't hesitate to send him or her to this school.' Yes! What an amazing compliment! David commented on the calm atmosphere at the school and thought what had already been achieved with the children was remarkable. He liked the fact that we were operating as closely as we could to mainstream education.

Very few schools would have been inspected so soon after opening. David had been sent at the request of the department because there were so many outstanding approvals from local education authorities at our school. Because Hillingdon Manor at this time had yet to be registered with the Department of Education, this meant parents of children deemed to have special educational needs would be required to seek the approval of the Secretary of State for Education and Employment before their funding was to be put in place. At the time we had received 21 registrations for children and would need a further inspection for a registration of 42. Not only that, but quite a few London boroughs were becoming concerned at the number of parents requesting placements at Hillingdon Manor. They came to see for themselves and liked what they saw. At least we now knew we were on the right track.

There were other occasions that made all our hard work seem worthwhile, not least when one mother told me that her son Robert had actually told her that he loved her. He had been at our school for only one day and, when he arrived home, he said, 'I love you, Mum.' She rang me in tears the next morning: 'Robert's never, ever said that to me. He obviously feels happy in the environment at your school.'

Two months after opening, we held our first Christmas performance, which was entitled *New Beginnings* because we felt it was most appropriate for a new school and the fact that we were about to enter a new millennium. Lots of parents, carers and volunteers assisted with the setup of the production, which ended with a rendition of '*Walking in the Air*' from *The Snowman*.

Afterwards, there was hardly a dry eye in the school and a memorable evening was completed with coffee and mince pies as autistic pianist Mark Bishop played Christmas carols and classical music in the background. What a lovely way to end what had been a very busy, hectic and, at times, a very stressful year.

Six months after opening, Hillingdon Manor was officially opened on 4 February 2000 by the TV presenter Esther Rantzen. I'd first met Esther when we made a follow-up video diary, this time for Meridian Television. Snippets of the video were screened each week on the *That's Esther* show on ITV over a period of six months. I was interviewed a couple of times by the former wife of the ex-Beatle Paul McCartney, Heather Mills, who was one of the presenters of the programme, and she was very supportive of our project.

Three months later this was followed up by an appearance on the daytime TV chat show *Open House*, hosted by Gloria Hunniford. Gloria was very interested in hearing about autism and my boys. Norman Pace from the comedy duo Hale and Pace was on the show as well. He was there supporting the Meningitis Research Foundation. Afterwards, he shook my hand and told me that what we had achieved was marvellous. He was very nice to me.

I met Gloria again when Esther held a Childline event – a charity helpline which she founded for children with problems. This event was held at the Dorchester Hotel in London and I remember being amazed at being charged £5 for a glass of cola!

I went on another daytime chat show, this one hosted by Nick Knowles on Five. I'd been sitting in the audience with my friend Anne, with whom I had set up the HACS charity. It had been arranged that Nick would come up to me to say who I was and what I'd been up to, but it didn't exactly work out that way. When the time came, Nick came over and said, 'This is a surprise. You thought you were here just to sit in the audience to say blah-de-blah, but we'd like to bring you down to the front to acknowledge what you've done.'

And so it was that I was led down to the studio floor and presented with a huge bouquet of flowers and a foot spa because, they said, they'd heard I never relaxed and was always on the go.

As time went by, we regularly reviewed the way we taught the pupils. As good as the TEACCH method is – at first we had been convinced it was the only way to go – we realised that what works for one child doesn't necessarily benefit another. As a result we decided to adopt a more wide-ranging approach to run alongside the TEACCH method, because, obviously, all children are different. TEACCH remains the base on which we build, together with a therapeutic approach. There is a particular emphasis on speech-and-language therapy. The reason for this is twofold. First, autism is a communication disorder and, second, and very importantly, the effective use of communication within the school makes learning more effective.

The Pictorial Exchange Communication System (PECS) is the development of communication skills using an extensive communication system. You take a child who cannot communicate and, through the use of pictures, they get to understand the importance of other people and of communicating with them.

They then move on to another stage, where they can differentiate between objects and learn how to recognise them, and then they can make requests for those objects and, maybe, construct sentences.

The final stage of PECS is when the child can make comments about the outside world. PECS is generally used with autistic children. A child with Asperger Syndrome generally wouldn't use it. It's based on Applied Behaviour Analysis

(ABA). This technique is proven in enhancing the development of communication skills in autistic children, as it seems to teach the child to 'learn how to learn'.

The structured approach incorporated in ABA intervention involves breaking down skills into small discrete tasks, the teaching of which occurs in a highly structured environment.

There's also an emphasis on the different types of therapy at Hillingdon Manor – speech-and-language therapy on a regular basis. We have three full-time therapists at the school, which is incredible because normally they are so difficult to get hold of. Often in this borough, when a child needs speech-and-language therapy they get a block of six one-hour sessions and this is supposed to enable the child to deal with their problem. It's nowhere near enough, though. An autistic child's biggest hurdle is their communication problem so, at Hillingdon Manor, we're very well equipped to give them this vital support on a much more regular basis.

We have drama-and-music therapy, the use of which within the school broadens the range of learning experiences to each student, and there is an emphasis on the importance of exercise and physical activity. We also have psychotherapy for the older children.

While some people claim that semantic-pragmatic disorder is not an autistic-spectrum disorder, others say it is. We've currently got provision for a couple of pupils at Hillingdon Manor with this disorder. For them, it's almost like having autism but without all the impairments – a communication difficulty where the understanding and use of language is affected. It can be particularly difficult for families to cope with a child with this disorder, as the child can often struggle to understand what is being said to them and they find great difficulty in expressing their needs.

Basically, a child with this disorder may have poor language-processing skills; they may talk in parrot fashion or copy phrases they have heard. Some chat incessantly or repetitively and have difficulties when responding to questions. They may use wrong or inadequate words or even make up words of their own. Sufferers invariably have difficulty in maintaining a topic of conversation and may display some of the milder behaviours of autism.

We also utilise what are known as social stories. These were developed by Carol Gray, a senior lecturer in education and modern foreign languages at the University of Birmingham. Basically, social stories are a tool for teaching social skills to children with autism and related disabilities.

Social stories provide people with accurate information about situations they may find difficult or confusing. The situation is described in detail and focus is given to a few key points; the important social cues; the events and reactions the individual might expect to occur in the situation; the actions and reactions that might be expected of them, and why.

The goal of the story is to increase the individual's understanding of, make them more comfortable in, and possibly suggest some appropriate responses for the situation in question.

This, for instance, is an example of a social story:

Lining Up

At school, we sometimes line up.

We line up to go to the gym, to go to the library, and to go out to recess.

Sometimes my friends and I get excited when we line up, because we're going some place fun, like out to recess.

It is OK to get excited, but it is important to try to walk to the line. Running can cause accidents, and my friends or I could get hurt.

I will try to walk to the line.

As may be evident, social stories are relatively short, straightforward descriptions of social situations, specifically detailing what an individual might expect from the situation and what may be expected of them.

Having determined those areas on which one wishes to focus, the writing of the social story can begin. Again, a social story is usually a first-person, present-tense story used to provide students with as much information about a social situation as possible, so they are better prepared to face it and act appropriately.

There are four types of sentence used to present this information in a social story:

- descriptive sentences objectively address the 'wh—' questions: where the situation takes place, who is involved, what they are doing, and why they may be doing it;
- perspective sentences give a peek into the minds of

those involved in the story; they provide details about the emotions and thoughts of others;

- directive sentences suggest desired responses tailored to the individual;
- control sentences are authored by the students themselves as something of a mnemonic device – a sentence to help them remember the story or deal with the situation; these are not used in every story and are typically used only with fairly high-functioning children.

Below is another sample social story. Each of the sentences in this story has been labelled with terms in brackets to illustrate each of the above types of sentence (except for the control sentence – I've not yet had a child who has opted to use them, so I'm not even going to pretend to be able to dream up a good one yet).

Sitting in the car

In the summer our family goes to Spain for a holiday [descriptive].

The journey takes a long time because we drive [descriptive].

My dad is very quiet because he needs to concentrate on the road when he is driving [perspective].

It is difficult to drive in a noisy car [descriptive].

I will try to keep quiet and sit still in the car [descriptive].

We believe the extensive range of approaches adopted at Hillingdon Manor offer our pupils the best possible chance of finding a teaching method that best suits their needs and we remain open to trial other approaches as and when they arise as we strive to ensure the most appropriate individualistic requirements of our pupils, whatever their level of capability.

Chapter Eight
Branching Out

In 2000 Sean, Alex, Dave and I set up a company separate from Moorcroft Manor, which we called Autism Consultants Limited, through which we could offer provision to adults suffering from Asperger Syndrome and high-functioning autism. The aim of Autism Consultants Limited is to create employment opportunities, to organise play schemes and structured-activity groups, to offer informational events, training and conferences, and to raise the awareness of autism through education and community involvement.

Bearing in mind that the world of business was still relatively new to Sean and me, we decided we would be more secure to split our activities between two companies, just in case one of them went belly-up.

That's not to say we lacked confidence in our ability to steer the good ship Hillingdon Manor and its associated businesses on a fair course, particularly after hearing Hillingdon Borough Council's surveyor Gerry Edwards' comments. Gerry had been the surveyor responsible for the initial survey of Hillingdon Manor when we first approached the council with our proposal for the site and it was his responsibility to come around after fourteen months to check that the required work had been done satisfactorily. 'Hats off to everyone,' he said. 'You've proved all the doubters wrong.'

Alex was the only member of HACS with nothing to gain personally from the opening of Hillingdon Manor, since his son was an adult in his thirties at the time. Nevertheless, he had gone the extra mile following a number of late-night chats at our home prior to the acquisition of Hillingdon Manor. Now we found ourselves in a position to pay him back for his unstinting support. Sean and I had planned to get Hillingdon Manor up and running within a three-year time frame before, hopefully, being in a position to take things a stage further by creating an autistic centre for adults – and that could benefit Alex's son Sean, who was living inappropriately in a psychiatric ward at the time.

Eighteen months ahead of schedule, we found ourselves in a situation to progress with our plans and the search began for suitable premises. Of course, we knew we didn't have ready money to purchase other premises, so we decided to look for premises that were available on a leasehold basis.

I'd already read about the St Vincent's Hospital site in nearby Eastcote in our local newspaper but it was not until I was driving in the vicinity with Alex that I passed the sign for the premises. We decided to turn around and take a look for ourselves. At first glance it looked like the ideal place to form an adult centre. Some of the buildings were on one side of the road, some on the other. The premises included a building known as Fraser House and another known as St Mary's Centre. There was also a chapel in the grounds and the whole site was located in a lovely country setting.

After a cursory look, Alex and I decided Fraser House would make an ideal residential home, while St Mary's Centre could conceivably be transformed into a college for adults. We needed to take a closer look, so we knocked on the door of one of the associated houses, which, at the time, was occupied by a priest. We asked him whom we would need to speak to if we wanted to look around and were pleased when he informed us he had a set of keys and could show us around straightaway. No sooner had we set foot inside than we felt we could really do something there. I remember feeling a sense of excitement and could hardly wait to tell Sean and the others all about it.

After their approval, we decided to set up a meeting with John Davern and Jacqui Scott, who were associates of the group running the St Mary's Centre site. At the meeting we told them of our intention to open a centre for high-functioning autistic adults. John and Jacqui had already heard of our work at Hillingdon Manor.

Although it turned out Fraser House would not be available to us after all, as it was due for demolition, after considerable discussion and negotiation we decided still to go for St Mary's Centre, even though I couldn't help wondering how we would ever manage to accommodate a college and a residential home within its limited confines. Alex, however, is very good at visualisation and suggested a dividing wall through the middle of the premises. We measured up and went for it. An annual lease of £40,000 was agreed, which would need to be added to a significant rates bill.

Once the centre had been secured it was time for the work to begin to adapt it to suit our needs. Once again, there was a lot to organise and, once again, we were very fortunate to have many helping hands at our disposal. Even the Royal Navy became involved this time, sending men along to lend a hand with the mammoth task of painting and helping to put gym equipment together for us, which was installed to help the adults destress and to promote their feelings of wellbeing. A lot of adults with Asperger Syndrome suffer from feelings of anxiety, and this equipment would go a long way to relieving those feelings.

Volunteers from the Prince's Trust turned up to chop down all the brambles and clear the grounds, while offenders from the community services also came along to help out with a variety of tasks, and one client's brother, who had contacts, managed to organise the installation of fencing free of charge.

As the work progressed we were contacted by social services, who expressed interest in what we were doing. Would we be interested in a project they were developing – an independent house for people suffering from a variety of conditions? This, however, was not something we felt would be of interest to us – our project was solely for people with autism and Asperger Syndrome and we saw no reason to change our aspirations.

Over the following months we found our work and time split between preparing St Mary's Centre for opening and the running of Hillingdon Manor. It was an exhausting period but, because we had clear ideas of where we wanted to go and what we wanted to achieve, we knew all our efforts would be worthwhile.

After an article about Hillingdon Manor was printed in *The Times Educational Supplement*, we were contacted by Sally and Chris Eaton, who had opened up private mainstream independent schools of their own in Slough, having become disillusioned with the standards of education available locally at the time. They empathised with our struggle and they proved to be an invaluable help to us, particularly with their advice about dealing with the regulator Ofsted. Eventually a circle of friends would be formed between their schools and Hillingdon Manor, which enabled all the pupils to get together – a truly beneficial experience all round. Sally and Chris also helped us out financially, raising £3,000 towards the purchase of sports equipment.

The original *Video Diaries* documentary had ended when we collected the keys for Hillingdon Manor. For the follow-up, the producer of the ITV programme *That's Esther*, Richard Brock, wanted to show events leading up to the point when children came through the doors for the first time. Richard wanted to record our efforts in obtaining furniture and staff, and how Patrick and Angelo would cope with their new learning environment.

Material featured from the previous *Video Diaries* was added to footage taken by Esther's team. Filming continued even after our first birthday and compared the children's progress from the day they first joined the school with how they were a year later. The improvements were startling. You could really see significant differences in the children. This high-profile attention prompted a huge amount of support – both financial and otherwise – and we received many requests for information and advice about autism.

After filming had been completed I'd asked Esther how she would feel about being the patron of Hillingdon Manor, and she readily agreed. We've kept in touch ever since and she's remained a keen supporter of the school and of what we are trying to do. She is also patron of HACS and she played a large role in helping us to obtain an £18,500 Sunshine minibus, which she and former boxer Henry Cooper presented to us at a posh London hotel. HACS has since gone from strength to strength, and currently supports 275 families under the directorship of our close friend Toni Mullally.

Further large cash sums followed, not least a donation of £18,000, which had been raised after the Mayor of Hillingdon's decision to choose us as his charity of the year. A big party, attended by the mayor, was held to celebrate the first birthday of the school. We received a lot of congratulations cards and, up on the stage, I was presented with a beautiful gold watch. Yet again, Esther returned to help us celebrate and to offer kind words of support.

'I'm thrilled with the miracle that has been performed here,' she said, adding, 'I remember when all this was just a twinkle in Anna's eye. What Anna and the team are doing is a battle cry for parents all over the country. Parents of autistic children find it difficult to find the right education for their children. Integrated education, which means including children with different needs in the same classes, works for some, but can be an excuse for neglect.'

The fifth annual golfing event held by the Rotary Club of Elthorne, Hillingdon, raised a further much-needed donation of £10,600, which was set aside to help pay for improving the internet facilities and bringing in more computers. Our refurbishment project was still ongoing and we were still keen to get more children into the school to ensure its financial viability. I was still doing newspaper and magazine articles and countless TV and radio interviews to promote the school, but this had developed to such a stage that it was dominating my life and, to be honest, I was getting a bit exhausted by it.

So many people were inviting me to give talks and workshops here, there and everywhere. Often this meant getting up really early in the mornings to give interviews on BBC TV's breakfast news programmes and it got to a stage where I was beginning to feel burned out. I made the decision not to do any more promotional work or interviews. Since we'd got the keys to the school my life had been conducted at a hundred miles an hour without a break and I felt I just needed a bit more time to settle.

Don't get me wrong, all the publicity was very good for the school and we were grateful for it, but it had all got too much for me. I was starting to get recognised – even if I went into Safeway I'd hear people say things like, 'Oh, look, there's that autistic lady!'

A series of donations from parents, well-wishers, the Midland Bank, local companies, car boot sales and other fundraising events had been boosting the coffers of our so-called roofing fund for Hillingdon Manor and the decision was taken to have the work started. However, owing to a bit of a cock-up on our part, instead of having the work undertaken in stages, it was all booked to be done in one go, which, for a while, gave us a few cash-flow concerns, but, fortunately, these were overcome. The total cost of the work amounted to a staggering £165,000, but at least it was a job well done.

As the number of pupils increased, it became clear that our minibus was insufficient for our needs. However, we need not have worried because help was at hand in the form of the National Federation of Demolition Contractors, who very generously donated a second minibus worth £18,000. This came as a complete surprise. The minibus sported the school's name and had been fitted with seatbelts throughout and adapted to carry wheelchair passengers.

Two members of the Disney Corporation who were based in Hammersmith, London, heard about Hillingdon Manor and were keen to offer support. The husband-and-wife team decided to pay us a visit and really became involved in the project and offered to create a garden in the quadrangle.

The children were very excited when the resultant very special visitor came along to open the garden. Mickey Mouse arrived to cut the ribbon and the children individually had their pictures taken standing next to him. They were given lots of Disney goodies, including DVDs and books. We had a big party in the hall. Mickey Mouse was walking around and the kids just loved every moment of it. The husband and wife behind the visit returned now and again to help maintain the garden and, by putting in different plants and herbs, they transformed the area into a sensory garden, which is much enjoyed by the children to this day.

One young boy started at the school on the very day his

father died. His mum didn't want any money for flowers at the funeral. Instead, a bench with a plaque was purchased in his memory, which now stands in the sensory garden. Another man, Terry Crick, was a real character who enthusiastically maintained the garden area at the school. Whenever we had school fêtes or jumble sales, Terry was always instrumental in organising the events and ensuring all went well. He knew everything about all the kids in the school and had great respect for me, as I did for him. When he died we purchased a bench and installed it in the sensory garden in his memory.

After much hard work over a period of several months, in October 2000, St Mary's Centre was ready to receive its first residents. There were a lot of visitors from various boroughs – the social services, people from Connexions, others who had supported us when we founded Hillingdon Manor and who wanted to witness the next stage of our project, plus our trusty volunteers from British Airways, the British Airports Authority and the Royal Navy.

I gave a speech and cut the ribbon to open the premises, then everyone tucked into a specially laid-on buffet. Eight students arrived to look around the premises, plus several others who were in the process of waiting for funding approval from either social services or the health or mental-health authorities. We'd passed another milestone and I felt really great, but – as is typical of me, I suppose – I had already set my sights on the next stage of the project: the establishment of a domiciliary and outreach organisation. Looking back only holds you up when you're trying to move forward and there was still a lot more I wanted to achieve.

Sean and I had no idea when we started just how much attention our work would generate and, had someone told us we would find ourselves on stage with the Prime Minister, Tony Blair, and his wife, Cherie, one day, I don't think we would have believed them. However, it happened. Sean and I were among other people nominated for the Unsung Heroes Award by *Daily Express* readers, which resulted in our attending a presentation ceremony in Kent. This was the first time we had been out on our own since having the boys. Coral looked after them while we attended the function and stayed overnight in a smart hotel. There we met many other people who had all achieved something worthy of recognition and had, like us, been nominated for an award by the newspaper's readers.

Sean hates being the centre of attention but he accompanied me to the stage, where Tony Blair and his wife presented us with the Co-operative Bank's award of a beautiful crystal bowl engraved with the words Unsung Heroes 2000 Finalists. As we stood with Mr Blair somebody took photographs – which unfortunately didn't come out – and then a buffet was held. Afterwards Mr Blair and his wife circulated and, I have to admit, I was sorely tempted to say something to him about the lack of funding and the difficulties in obtaining it for children with autism, but I bowed to Sean's persuasion not to. It wasn't the time or the place, he said.

Mr Blair admitted that autism puzzled him and wondered if there would ever be a cure. I was surprised I was able to bite my tongue when he shook my hand and told me we should be very proud of what we had achieved. That may have been so, but we'd had little help from local government and, if Her

Majesty's Government had put in place the support so obviously needed by so many thousands of people with autism and Asperger Syndrome and their families, we wouldn't have been forced to do it all ourselves in the first place!

It was encouraging, though, to hear our school being described as a 'flagship for autism', and other educational psychologists from other boroughs told us that they had been preaching 'the gospel of Hillingdon Manor', which was quite an accolade.

Our work was bringing us to the attention of several politicians and, as a result, Sean and I were invited to attend the launch of the All-Parliamentary Group on Autism. This is one of the largest all-party groups in Parliament and is made up of backbench MPs and peers from the House of Lords who have an interest in autism and want to lobby the government to improve autism services.

The group launched its manifesto in May 2003. It is a ten-year programme to which MPs are asked to sign up – a series of measures by which successive governments can be held to account. It contains targets in a range of policy and service areas, and MPs who sign up to the manifesto are committed to working to achieve these objectives. More than 300 MPs and peers have since signed up to the manifesto.

It was an uncomfortable meeting for Sean, as he had been involved in a car accident while driving on the M3 motorway, and his spinal injuries meant he had to wear a body brace at the time. This had been a particularly difficult period for us, since Sean had been in hospital for a couple of days following the accident and then needed bed rest for the next few weeks. At first it had been suggested he may even have needed an operation to get him back on his feet, but two sessions of physiotherapy each week finally did the trick. I remember being completely exhausted at the time because Sean, being incapacitated, was in no fit state to be able to help me with the school runs, shopping or other jobs around the home.

At the meeting we met many politicians and household names, including Charles Clarke, Peter Mandelson and Dame Stephanie Shirley, with whom I have remained in contact. Dame Stephanie is a highly successful entrepreneur-turned-philanthropist who arrived in Britain as a five-year-old evacuee via the Kindertransport from Austria in 1939. Her son, who had autism, sadly died. She later visited Hillingdon Manor and told us we should be very proud of what we had achieved.

We had told Hillingdon Council we would be opening only half of the school at first but, in fact, with the work on the roof completed, the whole school was eventually up and running after just 18 months because of the demand from parents for such a facility.

In February 2001, a care agency known as Summacare Limited was set up by the directors and shareholders of Moorcroft Manor Limited. The aim was to become a respected and professional domiciliary and outreach organisation that would play its part in inspiring a level of confidence between service users and purchasers.

We wanted to support children and adults within a range of disabilities that would include autistic-spectrum disorders, behavioural issues and learning and physical disabilities, while promoting social inclusion and offering personal support as part of a dual-purpose support package. We also wanted a company that would be able to offer live-in respite support and that would play its part in safeguarding services for children. Since its early days, Summacare Limited has specialised in the employment of carers for children and adults with autistic-spectrum disorders and other special needs.

Given the doubts expressed in our ability to make a go of this project by some councillors and others a couple of years previously, extending the services we were able to provide gave us a huge glow of satisfaction. Even better was to follow with our very first Ofsted inspection at Hillingdon Manor in June 2001. Any teacher in any school will tell you how much pressure an Ofsted inspection heaps on them, and it was certainly no different at Hillingdon Manor. In fact, our being a fledgling establishment, coupled with the fact we were dealing with children with very specific needs, meant the pressure seemed intense for all concerned.

Prior to the inspectors' arrival, there had been a lot of hustle and bustle. The staff, quite naturally, were stressed out, working really hard and putting in extra hours, and checking out the building to make sure everything was up to scratch. On the day of the inspectors' arrival I remember sitting in my office while, every few minutes, a member of staff would pop their head around the door to ask, 'Are they here yet?'

I was heartened when I noticed that one of the inspectors was David Gardiner, who had visited the school and had been impressed by what he had seen when he checked us out for the Department of Education inspection shortly after we had opened the school. The inspectors sat in the classrooms to observe the lessons in much the same way as you would expect them to in a mainstream school. Then they went through all our paperwork, the policies and procedures, and checked to see if we were following them through.

During the two-day inspection Angela kept popping into the office to ask for further documentation that had been requested by the inspectors. This gave us the opportunity to ask her how things were going. Because the inspectors were within earshot we were whispering and Angela resorted to a series of thumbs-up or thumbs-down signals, depending upon what we'd asked her. The mood was lifted somewhat when one of the children gazed up at a female inspector, put her hand on one of her breasts and loudly declared, 'Wow, you've got big bosoms!'

When the inspection team had finished their work, Angela, the senior members of staff and I were called into a meeting to hear their verdict. With so much riding on what they had to say my stomach was in knots and I know my colleagues felt much the same. I was feeling sick and sweaty, aware that, because the school had received so much media attention, a substandard Ofsted report would be absolutely catastrophic.

But we needn't have worried. We received a glowing report and, as soon as the inspection team left the premises, we were all absolutely elated and found ourselves jumping up and down and kissing each other. Now we had a brilliant reason to crack open some bottles of wine and champagne! We could hardly wait to spread the news to the parents and, almost at once, we were flooded out with messages of congratulation and cards. After so much hard work and a fair bit of stress, the team headed off for a celebratory meal at a nearby restaurant and nightclub. The relief was palpable.

Reading the report gave us all a huge boost. Under the section headed 'Main Findings', it stated, 'Hillingdon Manor is a good school which very effectively meets the needs of pupils on the autistic spectrum and has the potential to develop even further. Teaching is good in 100 per cent of lessons and is very good or better in 42 per cent of lessons.'

The report went on to say,

The curriculum is broad and balanced and effectively meets the needs of the pupils. Pupils and adults are respected and treated with dignity, with pupils responding well to the very good role models provided by staff. They show care and concern for each other and, as they overcome their own difficulties, they support and help other pupils.

The section of the report headed 'The Management and Efficiency of the School' heaped praise on Angela and her staff:

The head teacher provides a very effective leadership and management of the school. She has a clear vision of the work and further development of the school, which is shared and owned by the directors, staff, and parents.

The aims and values of the school are positively reflected in the practice of the school. Effective policies and procedures have been established in the relatively short time that the school has been open to ensure that the school is well run and that statutory requirements are satisfactorily met. Good support is provided by the deputy head teacher who has established good relationships with staff and has their confidence and trust. Good curriculum support is also provided by the two curriculum leaders with special responsibilities for the lower and upper parts of the school.

Together, the head teacher, deputy head teacher, two curriculum leaders, pastoral and support managers form an effective management team. They provide effective monitoring and evaluation of planning, the quality of teaching and of the individual progress made by the pupils. They are supported by the whole staff.

Staff morale is very good and all staff are, justifiably, proud of what has been achieved in the time since the school opened. The school has successfully established a strong ethos where learning and personal success are effectively promoted, valued and celebrated.

No wonder we were all so happy!

The success of our Ofsted inspection saw the school registered by the Department for Education and Employment, which we knew would be necessary if we wanted to follow all the criteria of a mainstream school. Being registered was a huge step forward for the school. It meant we no longer had to write to request the approval of the Secretary of State every time we wanted to accept a child because they had to agree to the funding of the child's statementing. Jumping this hurdle was a huge relief. As we ourselves had been, parents were desperate to find placements in specialist schools for their autistic children, yet funding was always very difficult to secure. Now, that obstacle had been overcome. The added bonus was that the long and drawn-out process of waiting for approval from the Secretary of State was no longer necessary.

Our work at Hillingdon Manor was making news locally and much further afield, even internationally. I even received a telephone call from a lady from Singapore. She informed me that she and her husband were about to relocate in the United Kingdom and they hoped we would be able to accommodate the educational needs of their autistic son.

The frustrations and despair Sean and I went through while trying to find places for Angelo and Patrick were often brought back to mind when I met other parents desperately going through the same experience. We even had a lady from Dubai arrive at the school. Obviously fabulously wealthy, she turned up in a posh Mercedes car accompanied by two huge, sunglasses-wearing minders. It doesn't matter how much it would cost, she told me, she wanted to secure a place for her son at Hillingdon Manor. Unfortunately, though, the poor boy's needs were so very complex that we couldn't have catered for him, as he also suffered from other conditions as well as autism. Nevertheless, his mother persevered and, after an impassioned plea, Angela agreed to allow her son to spend a week with us and then to review the situation. By the end of the week, though, it became clear that his needs were even more extreme than we had at first thought and, because his aggressive behaviour was so intimidating to the other pupils, we could not allow him to stay.

I remember showing a parent around the school and then

having to tell her that, at that particular time, we didn't have any places available that would be suitable for her son because his needs were so acute. She explained how desperate she was and how she really liked the feel of our school, and it broke my heart to have to turn her away. Just as she was about to leave through the main entrance of the school she broke down in tears, sank to the floor and begged me to reconsider: 'Please, please, I want my son to come here.'

By this time I was getting pretty emotional myself as all those feelings came flooding back to my mind. 'Please don't do this,' I pleaded. I gave her a hug and told her that, although we didn't have a place for her son, I wished her luck in finding a place elsewhere. As she left I had a huge lump in my throat.

Yes, I knew exactly how she was feeling.

We hate to turn anyone away, but we must stick as rigidly as possible to our admission criteria if we are to get the best out of our pupils. Hillingdon Manor is a school for high-functioning autistic children and all the children in the school should be as similar in terms of needs as possible. Children with more complex needs are catered for more appropriately in other specialised schools, although it is often very difficult to secure places for them.

We soon began to attract visitors wishing to know more about our methods. Among them were students from Brunel University in Uxbridge, who had a particular interest in autism. A few of them have come to us as an extension of their studies and we have trained them as they have worked alongside the children. Among them have been a couple of psychology students taking part in a six-month placement as a part of their sandwich course. They enjoyed the experience so much they remained with us and secured teaching posts at the school. Another Brunel University student went on to become a manager at the school.

Students from the university played a pivotal role in an innovation to yield spontaneous responses by designing a multisensory interactive 'wall' – a piece of textile linked to a computer that will say a word or make a particular sound whenever it is touched. Different textiles produce different sounds and teachers also have the option of recording the sounds and words they want the children to hear. Hillingdon Manor was, in fact, the first school in the United Kingdom to use this device.

Our links with the university remain strong and have proved beneficial to both parties, and the famous scientist Professor Heinz Wolff, who is based at the university, has been a long-term advocate of our projects, frequently helping out with fundraising and helping to raise the awareness of the autistic spectrum.

A BBC television video about us was posted on the internet and was seen by a distinguished psychologist in America who, many years earlier, used to live near Hillingdon. He contacted us and asked if it would be possible to visit the school for a closer look. He duly arrived and claimed to be very impressed with what he had seen. He told us that, in America, they had been trying to include autistic children in mainstream schools while, at the same time, closing some of the specialist schools. That was the last thing they needed to do, he said.

He explained the difficulties teachers had been finding: they were unable to cope and a lot of autistic children in America were requiring psychotherapy because the educational provision in the mainstream schools was so inappropriate. I suggested we visit America to see, first-hand, how they dealt with education for children with autism in the specialist schools that were still up and running. 'I wouldn't bother,' he said, adding, 'It would be better if they were to come to this school to see how it should be done!'

Following our visit to the *EastEnders* set, Patrick had become keen on watching the soap on television, particularly the hard-man character of Grant Mitchell, played by his favourite actor, Ross Kemp.

Patrick would talk about Ross/Grant all the time – yet another obsession. A friend's brother often went out with Ross for a drink and told him about Patrick's obsession. Very kindly, Ross decided to visit the school to meet Patrick and the other children, which was a huge boost to all concerned. I hadn't realised Ross had a bit of a reputation as a sex symbol, but the rest of the staff did and, while he was chatting to Angela in her office, it was surprising just how many people found a reason to be passing by or to pop in for one reason or another! To be honest, I think the staff were as excited as the children over his visit – if not more so.

While Ross was with Angela I found myself chatting to his agent, who declared himself to be most impressed with what we had managed to achieve and, I believe, it was he who nominated me as Wondermum 2003 in the *Sun* newspaper, edited by Ross's partner Rebekah Wade. Although there was no ceremony or prize attached to this recognition – which the newspaper features each Mother's Day – after the publication of a two-page spread about me and other women considered worthy of the award, the phone hardly stopped ringing with offers of help and support, which were truly appreciated.

Hopefully, the other mothers recognised at the awards received similar support. Among them was a woman who campaigned to save a closure-threatened haematology research unit after her 18-year-old daughter had died of leukaemia, and a mother who developed a natural cure for eczema after witnessing the dreadful side effects of the conventional medications prescribed for her daughter.

Other awards followed. I received the Local Hero Award for Voluntary Endeavour, which was sponsored by the Nationwide Building Society, and, after being nominated as a Hero of London by listeners of the LBC radio station, I won their weekly wine award – an absolutely enormous bottle of Baron Philippe de Rothschild wine and a certificate for my 'contribution to improving the quality of life for people in London as voted for by the listeners of London News Radio' – but I don't drink alcohol! In fact, I hadn't even been aware I'd been nominated for the award until someone stopped me in the street to tell me. I opened the bottle at the school and shared it out with the staff and we all celebrated together – after all, I couldn't have done it without them. It was very heartening to think people had taken the trouble to vote for me and I later appeared on the station to thank them all.

Esther Rantzen returned in May 2003 with a camera crew to record a film to be included in her weekly television show, which would form the prelude to a discussion on the arguments for and against inclusion in mainstream schools of children with special needs. After it was transmitted, I was invited to speak on a BBC Radio 4 programme with a woman who was claiming all special-needs schools should be closed down. Not surprisingly, her argument really annoyed me and I ended up telling her she didn't know what she was talking about.

Chapter Nine
Moving Forward

As the reputation and standing of Hillingdon Manor increased, we realised that we had rapidly outgrown the premises owing to an intake of pupils that now totalled fifty-three. Quite simply, as Angela pointed out, the school was no longer large enough to accommodate the number of classrooms required if we were to keep class levels to a maximum of eight children. Not only that, we had a number of pupils aged between four and five mixing with 15- and 16-year-olds. We were determined to continue to provide quality rather than quantity and were aware that, if we were to try to cram too many pupils into Hillingdon Manor, we would be answerable to the Department of Education.

In January 2003 it was decided to look for another property to accommodate the older pupils, in effect an Upper School. This time, the work in founding a new school was shared out among the directors, HACS, and me plus Angela, who, in fact, took the lead, as she was the expert with reference to education and Ofsted. We asked a local estate agent to look out for a large building that may be suitable for conversion and he came up trumps, pointing us towards a large office building in Church Road in Hayes, not too far from Hillingdon Manor.

The building had stood empty for 15 months, but we liked it as soon as we saw it. It certainly had potential and it had a nice feel to it, although we wished it could have been slightly larger. There was a good-sized shingle-covered area outside, which we considered would be suitable for a play area, and a reasonably-sized hall downstairs. What we particularly liked about the property was that it had formerly been used as office space, so we felt it would be easier to emulate the feel of an office environment in the students' minds.

The office was on the market for £930,000 – a huge sum – and, on top of that, we knew we would have to put another considerable amount aside to adapt it for our purposes. We decided to canvas the local residents to establish whether or not any of them would have any objections to the opening of a school for children aged between 12 and 19 with special needs nearby. Thankfully, there were no objections and, after negotiating the price down to £850,000, we put our heads together to draw up a finance plan.

Unlike having to start from scratch, as we did with Hillingdon Manor, our plan this time was a little more straightforward: we would use Hillingdon Manor as a guarantee for the loan we required and, once again, Barclays Bank came up trumps. We had earlier created a development fund for special projects and this had helped to keep the loan down to a minimum. Although it was scary to spend such a large sum of money, this time the burden was shouldered among us all, but at the backs of our minds we knew we would all be liable financially as individuals, should things not go to plan.

Despite all our careful planning, it was an informed gamble on our parts that, once we had successfully acquired the property, we would still need to obtain funding to get the students in, as it would be a gradual process in getting them enrolled. Before any building work could begin we had to write to Ofsted for permission to get our capacity increased and we also had to ensure we had all the required structural plans approved by the council.

There was not an awful lot to do to the building to convert it for use as a school, as it had already been refurbished to a good standard. Over the following few months we spent £100,000 bringing the premises up to our specifications. One of the larger expenses was the erection of a long conservatory, which ran along the rear of the premises and would be used as a corridor, eliminating the need for students to walk through one classroom in order to reach another. The large shingled area was covered with tarmac for use as a playground and, while all this work was in progress, Sean got to work setting up all the computers and whiteboards. Again, David Kamsler from the Link charity was instrumental in providing a good number of desks for the new school.

Now we needed more staff. Angela decided we required a new head teacher for the Upper School, reasoning that she couldn't effectively run Hillingdon Manor and the new one herself. However, she had the perfect candidate in mind: Sean

Pavitt, who had already particularly impressed us all with his work as a teacher and then as the curriculum manager at Hillingdon Manor. As far as we were concerned, Sean would fit the bill perfectly. He is a great teacher and, prior to his appointment at Hillingdon Manor, although he had only recently qualified, he had already undertaken plenty of voluntary work with autistic children and had demonstrated a really nice way of working with them. Sean even met his wife at Hillingdon Manor. Cheryl was working there after attending a placement from Brunel University and then found herself in charge of children at the school who have more complex needs.

It was very pleasing when Sean agreed to accept the post of head teacher at the Upper School and it's been really lovely to watch him progress over the past few years. Following his appointment, he and Angela liaised to recruit the extra staff required. Sean's elevation to head teacher meant a shuffle-round was required. Pam Sickelmore, who had been Angela's deputy, stepped up to the role as head teacher at Hillingdon Manor, while Angela assumed the responsibility as the principal of both sites.

The following September, after much hard work by all concerned, the school was ready to accept its first students. I remember a huge feeling of pride and delight as we opened the doors that day, although Patrick, having moved up from Hillingdon Manor School, was a little apprehensive. He'd got used to life there but, after his first day at the Upper School, he declared he had really liked his new surroundings. I was very pleased because, even for a mainstream school pupil, moving from one school to another can be a very traumatic experience – and it's always going to be a far more difficult move for a child on the autistic spectrum.

I could hardly believe how far we'd come. Opening another school had proved beyond any doubt that there was a demand for what we had set out to do. Because of the huge amount of referrals, and the desperation of parents whose children were struggling to cope in mainstream schools, Hillingdon Manor had rapidly outgrown its capacity and this was the only logical step we could have taken. Several of the pupils walking into the Upper School that morning had graduated from Hillingdon Manor; the others were new referrals.

The first day went pretty smoothly. The decision to adopt the same ethos as at Hillingdon Manor was a straightforward one, and obviously helped the students through this transitional phase in their education – they knew from the start how things worked and what was expected of them.

Again, Esther Rantzen returned, this time to perform the official opening of the Upper School on 6 February, 2001, and she was thrilled to see the progress of some of the children she had first met at Hillingdon Manor. Esther was generous in her praise, as was our MP, John Randall, who wrote the following article in his weekly column in the *Uxbridge Gazette* after touring the premises.

The other day I visited the newly-opened Upper School of Hillingdon Manor Special School. There I saw what can be achieved through hard work and dedication.

It gave me real hope. If we could extend what has been achieved there into the world we live in and into each of our own lives we really would have a country to be proud of.

The school's code for its pupils should be on display in every home and certainly should be included in every political manifesto. It states: 'All humans need the following to have their needs met – security, attention – to give and to receive it; a sense of autonomy and control; being emotionally connected to others in part of a wide community; friendship, fun, love and intimacy; a sense of status for social groupings; a sense of confidence and achievement, meaning and purpose which come from being stretched from what we do and think.'

It might be up to politicians to help fulfil those needs, but perhaps each one of us should take responsibility ourselves to making our country one to be proud of.

I was thrilled to read John's ringing endorsement and made a point of telling the staff that he was right: we had all contributed to something to be proud of. I photocopied his article and sent it to all the parents, and I still have a copy of it on the wall of my office.

Our aim at the Upper School is to teach the students more about their autism or Asperger Syndrome and to prepare them for a life in the workplace. That, of course, is easier said than done, as, according to Carol Povey, from the National Autistic Society, 49 per cent of adults suffering from autism (how I hate that phrase – how does one know they are 'suffering' when they are not in pain?) are at home without employment and just 15 per cent have employment.

Nevertheless, at the Upper School, students are encouraged to study for GCSEs, while others may study for GNVQs or the accredited Award Scheme Development and Accreditation Network (ASDAN) courses, which offer approved programmes and qualifications to develop key skills and life skills.

One day a week is set aside for a healthy-eating day, when students, under supervision, are given the opportunity to prepare fresh fruit and vegetables, and then to present it appropriately to other pupils and staff.

Students are given many opportunities to practise what they learn in the school setting in the world outside school. This is achieved through involvement with the immediate community around the school, work experience locally, the use of local sports facilities, and involvement with mainstream peers in the local comprehensive school. Then, if the students reach a specific level of ability in dealing with mainstream situations, they have the opportunity to reintegrate and study at the local comprehensive school.

In 2004, four years after we'd opened the original West Middlesex College and residential home at the Eastcote site, we had to close them both down because the council ruled that the site where they stood was to be returned to green belt land. We had known all along that this would happen, but had successfully put off our eviction from the site on a number of occasions in a bid to buy time. The buildings would now be demolished so people could wander around there and walk their dogs. It was a significant setback and I was gutted.

We needed to find somewhere else as soon as possible. Through an estate agent, we found Colne Lodge, a big office building that had stood empty for some time on an industrial estate, and we made plans to transfer the West Middlesex College facilities into it. A £40,000 lease for ten years was secured with the right to buy after that period. The location, unfortunately, was not the most attractive, but it suited our needs. That said, I'd still love to be able to pick it up and put it somewhere else.

First of all we needed to secure approval for change of use and planning permission. Our efforts to secure the property saw us in competition with a group of people wanting the premises for use as a Buddhist centre, but we prevailed in the end.

The new college opened its doors for students for the first time in February 2006. Now it has a large room downstairs, which is used for large social events, and upstairs are the classrooms, which include an ICT suite; a wellbeing room, where students can go if they feel they need some quiet time to destress and listen to music; and a staffroom, which offers a lovely view over the river Colne.

To ensure the needs of each applicant are met, strict admission criteria have to be followed. Successful applicants will be funded by the Learning and Skills Council. They will have a diagnosis of autism or Asperger Syndrome and have abilities between moderate learning difficulties and university entrance. They must have the potential and ambition to study and work in a mainstream environment and have the desire and determination to function as an independent adult.

Our mission at the college is to ensure we enable adults with an autistic-spectrum disorder to develop the skills, knowledge and understanding that will enable them to achieve as fulfilled, meaningful and independent a life as possible through the provision of a high-quality, stimulating and personalised education programme that meets their needs and interests.

Basically, we are aiming to improve their quality of life and to promote a better understanding of autistic-spectrum disorders and we believe this can be achieved by the implementation of individual learning plans with a multidisciplinary approach.

Because there is always the highest regard for the safety of students and staff, those who exhibit physically challenging behaviour are not accepted at the college. However, we have the means to assess the behaviour of potential students through programmes that have been designed to empower the student to manage specific behaviours. The establishment of non-challenging alternatives is of great importance.

The principal, staff and, when required, the consultant psychologist work together to produce effective behaviour-management plans. Naturally, all plans are instigated with the full cooperation of the student. All staff receive ongoing training in the delivery of behaviour-management plans.

Parent and/or carer involvement is encouraged. The staff aim to establish a collaboration in order to share expertise and generalise a student's new skills. Educational workshops are run and college open days held. There is regular communication between the college and the parents/carers, who are also encouraged to participate in college events and celebrations.

As with Hillingdon Manor and the Upper School, parents/ carers and staff liaise to plan optimal educational programmes, to assess progress accurately, to formulate individual learning plans and to conduct home visits.

The staff team at the college are particularly empathetic to the needs of the students and their families. All are professionally qualified and experienced, and more than 45 per cent of them have experience of dealing with the challenges of autism in their personal lives which, obviously, is of great benefit to the students.

Here, students are able to develop their academic, life and vocational skills through a creative, stimulating and personalised educational programme that promotes enhanced wellbeing and social inclusion. The aim is to provide a calm, reassuring environment alongside a comprehensive, high-quality curriculum with an emphasis on intensive individual support and development.

The principal carries out a rigorous initial assessment and thorough baseline assessments are executed throughout the first term. This ensures that a clear understanding of the needs of each individual student are realised. Learning plans are designed to identify realistic and achievable targets for each student.

To offer the best opportunities for students' development, it is vital to maintain a good ratio of students to staff. We provide a minimum student-to-staff ratio of two to one with a minimum student-to-teaching-staff ratio of four to one. This allows each student to receive the individual and personal attention they require. Furthermore, one-to-one teaching is allocated for weekly tutorials and student guidance counselling. We also access the services of speech-and-language therapy, psychology and, if it is required, other specialist services such as occupational therapy and sexual counselling.

The students are given access to ongoing in-house training and external courses and qualifications in understanding autism and Asperger Syndrome, behavioural intervention, curriculum development, health and safety and first aid.

The goals for students are wide-ranging. Our staff try to enable them to participate independently and achieve to the best of their ability, and help them to develop positive self esteem, a sense of worth and respect for themselves and for others. They are guided to a stage where they can relate and communicate in an effective and constructive manner, and taught how to access and use technology.

It's important that the students are able to understand and influence the world in which they live and that they are able to develop their physical abilities and coordination skills; that they can participate in new activities and extend their range of experiences. The staff help the students develop their cognitive abilities, such as reasoning and problem solving, as well as helping them develop their moral, social and cultural understanding.

A strong emphasis is placed on values such as mutual respect, recognition and ethical behaviour; equal opportunities; open communication; a focus on achievement and improvement; a commitment to students, staff and the community; and continual and constructive self-evaluation.

To reinforce those values, strategically placed noticeboards feature reminders of some of the expectations required of the students:

> *Be responsible for your own learning! Plan, participate*
> *and review;*
> *This is YOUR college! Help improve it by sharing*
> *your ideas;*
> *Make the most! Take advantage of tutorial and*
> *counselling services;*
> *Think of your health! Inform staff of your medical needs*
> *or if you feel unwell;*
> *Think about security! Keep your possessions safe in*
> *your locker;*
> *Make positive choices;*
> *Obey the rules! Don't bring weapons, drugs or alcohol into*
> *the college;*
> *Care for yourself and others!;*
> *Be safe! Follow the Health & Safety and Fire procedures;*
> *Be fair! Treat staff and students with respect*
> *and consideration;*
> *Behave appropriately! It helps keep you and those with*
> *you safe;*
> *Be assertive! Ask for help and tell staff if you are unhappy;*
> *Celebrate diversity! Enjoy what makes us all unique;*
> *and finally:*
> *Respect the college environment! Keep it clean and tidy.*

There is an emphasis on intensive individual support and development. By formulating individual learning plans with a multidisciplinary approach, the students are encouraged to be independent and to reach their full potential.

The team have designed a curriculum that is broad enough to provide each student with a wide range of concepts, experience, knowledge and skills, all of which are necessary to increase their level of independence. The curriculum is relevant, by which I mean that all learning is connective, and it provides a strong foundation that prepares the students for the responsibilities and experiences they will face when they are able to lead a more independent adult life.

The curriculum comprises three main areas: the core curriculum, which is overarching and is embedded through all areas of learning; the vocational; and the life-skills and independence curriculum.

The overall curriculum is, in many respects, like a menu from which the appropriate learning for each individual is selected. All programmes contain elements from each area but the balance and nature of what is offered will be selected to meet the individual need.

The programme for a student with good practical and basic skills who has the potential to work will, for example, focus on the development of work-related skills. It is likely to include the opportunity to access a college of further education and to achieve nationally accredited vocational and literacy and numeracy qualifications, and will prioritise the independence skills required in order for the student to live and work as independently as possible – such as independent travel, managing benefits and bank accounts, and cooking and shopping.

For another student who, perhaps, has limited communication skills, poor literacy skills and difficulty participating in learning, the independent learning programme might prioritise learning from within the core and independence and life-skills area.

Students learn wellbeing skills, which show them how to take care of and be responsible for their physical, emotional, mental, spiritual and environmental wellbeing. Subjects include fitness; swimming; hobbies and pastimes; anger management; anxiety management; community participation; music, drama and arts and crafts.

Through vocational skills the students prepare for the world of employment. Subjects include seeking employment; preparing for employment; work experience and a college business project. We feel confident our broad curriculum can provide students with all the necessary strategies and skills they require if they are to move on towards independent living.

The college has developed strong community links, which enable the students to generalise and apply the knowledge, skills and attitudes they have learned to other situations, thereby broadening the range of learning experiences available to them. Community participation is encouraged by making full use of local and wider facilities. These may include shops, libraries, leisure centres, cinemas, theatres and art galleries. Trips are organised to parks, the coast, various towns and the countryside, as well as places of historic interest such as castles, stately homes and museums. Outings to airports, railway stations and factories also prove popular.

Not only is the college blessed with good quality staff, but it also has a highly respected patron. Professor Uta Frith, FBA, FmedSci, FRS, studied experimental psychology at the Universität des Saarlandes, Saarbrücken, and subsequently trained in clinical psychology at the University of London's Institute of Psychiatry.

Since completing her PhD on autism in 1968, Uta has worked as a scientist funded by the Medical Research Council and is now professor in cognitive development at the University of London and deputy director of the UCL Institute of Cognitive Neuroscience.

Her main focus of research is developmental disorders, in particular autism, and also dyslexia. Her book, *Autism: Explaining the Enigma*, has been translated into ten languages and she has successfully conveyed the results of basic research to a wide readership, including parents and clinicians. Uta was one of the initiators of the study of Asperger Syndrome in the United Kingdom, where her work on reading development, spelling and dyslexia has been highly influential and her outstanding record includes 31 highly cited papers in the field of psychiatry/psychology.

At the same time as we acquired the replacement site for West Middlesex College, we had plans to open a residential centre for eight adults aged 18 and over – a completely different kettle of fish from one for children. It would be a really difficult task to find a suitable building to replace our facilities at the former St Mary's Centre and to get it to comply with the regulations set down by the Commission for Social Care Inspection, which carries out a spot inspection every year and publishes a report on every aspect of the home. The rooms would need to be a certain size and we'd need eight bedrooms. Again, we would require permission for change of use and to be able to secure funding from social services or the National Health Service, or from the Learning and Skills Council for each student.

We eventually found a six-bedroom building in the Greenway, Uxbridge, advertised in the local newspaper for £650,000. There were also several other rooms that had the potential to be converted. We managed to get it for £635,000 – again with a mortgage through Barclays Bank.

The building, which we've named The Old Vicarage, would be separate from the college, which we felt would be more real-life – normally a person goes to college and goes home again afterwards. Not only that, the building needed refurbishing and extending to add a further two bedrooms and install showers and bathroom in each person's room. A conservatory added a further £30,000 to the bill, and the lounge was extended. It was a big project, which, at times, proved quite stressful.

In October 2005 we moved in. It's a lovely house. The adults had got used to living at the St Vincent's hospital site, so moving to The Old Vicarage was stressful for them, too, but it all turned out for the better in the end. A lot of forward planning by care manager Lorraine Harland had been undertaken to keep the stress levels to a minimum, including a project plan entitled Operation Move. Staff rolled up their sleeves and worked extra hours to help ensure everything went smoothly.

The home itself is set within large front and rear gardens, which gives it privacy from the road. There are facilities for laundry and cooking, together with many recreational facilities such as Sky TV, games consoles, a pool table, basketball hoop, a computer room with internet access, and four communal rooms on the ground floor.

Esther officially opened the home and said how nice it was to find a place like this that didn't smell of cabbage and disinfectant, and that she'd be happy to live in a place like it herself.

The Old Vicarage generates a safe, homely and attractive aura – a safe environment where the residents have twenty-four-hour support. Here, the aim is to prepare them for life in the outside world and to diversify their range of abilities as much as possible. The ethos of the West Middlesex College also applies here. Great efforts are made to enhance residents' self-esteem, self-worth, confidence and personal identity, as well as their cognitive abilities, coping strategies and communication skills.

The admission criteria are the same as at West Middlesex College, plus an ability or willingness to cooperate with the home's relevant policies and procedures in order to maintain a safe environment for all residents. New arrivals must also demonstrate an ability to co-exist without any major disruption to current users of the home and be willing to undertake meaningful day activities. They must also be willing to undertake an assessment to determine whether or not The Old Vicarage is able to meet their needs.

We aim to provide a care package, led by the needs of the resident yet supported by a quality staff team, who are understanding of and responsive to the needs of the individual.

The home is run by a well-established, friendly and professional team. Ongoing training is provided to ensure all staff are kept informed of current research related to autistic-spectrum disorders.

Although the home is registered to take residents from 18 years of age, we've had some aged up to 40. We try to support the residents in all aspects of their lives and have supported their access to many areas such as language night schools, physiotherapy, private maths tuition, personal fitness training, a dietician and chess tournaments.

Just as at the West Middlesex College, residents at The Old Vicarage have the opportunity to enjoy organised excursions into the wider community. The home has its own eight-seater minibus, which enables staff to take residents on a number of activities such as dry-slope skiing, golf, fishing, bowling, boating and ice skating. For the less energetic, trips to theatres and cinemas are regularly organised, as are annual holidays, which are truly beneficial experiences for the residents.

The final months of 2005 were most satisfying. Not only was The Old Vicarage finally up and running, but Hillingdon Manor won a nationwide competition run by British Telecom. The prize included a cheque for £1,000 and a variety of electronic equipment.

It was another proud moment for all the staff involved, as the school was chosen as one of the most effective communication-centred educational establishments in the country, which was deserved recognition for the high quality of work going on there.

We aim to ensure that the highest standard of good home-care practice at The Old Vicarage is maintained. This was confirmed following an unannounced Commission for Social Care Inspection in June 2007. The inspection resulted in a very favourable report, which, although very satisfying, came as no surprise to us. Nevertheless, reviews of the service at The Old Vicarage are regularly held in order to aspire to providing the best-quality service possible. There is never a reason to be complacent.

Residents will leave the college after three years, either to take up a place of employment or an apprenticeship elsewhere or, maybe, to secure a place in a mainstream college. Because the college at the time of writing is still in its infancy, very few students have yet to reach that stage.

Chapter Ten

Unity is Strength

My personal ambition in life is to remain fit and healthy so I can carry on with this work and to look after my family. I worry about what will happen to Patrick and Angelo, come the time Sean and I are no longer able to cater for their needs, but we hope to be able to cover every aspect of their future support care before we end our days.

Hopefully, we can also offer the benefit of our experiences and offer advice to others. If someone in your family has been diagnosed with autism, please remember there is help out there. It's so important to talk to someone – don't try to carry the burden on your own. Talk to other parents with autistic children. It's important not to feel alone. The National Autistic Society has come on in leaps and bounds since we first tried to contact it and is a very good source of useful information. Alternatively, you could, of course, contact us at Hillingdon Autistic Care Society or at Hillingdon Manor.

Try to remember, however dire the circumstances may appear

when you're faced with this situation, that you are not alone! In the London Borough of Hillingdon alone, it was estimated there were 2,129 people with autism in late 2007. I've found it helps to have an interest that allows me to have some time just for myself. Dancing is my way of coping with the stresses of day-to-day life. I can appreciate how some marriages can be put under immense pressure when trying to cope with an autistic child – whether it be the ending of the relationship or taking to alcohol, cigarettes or Prozac. Dancing gives me something to look forward to – something that's just for me.

I can also use dance to help the pupils. I teach dance at Hillingdon Manor School several times a week. The children love the mixture of dance and exercise. This is undoubtedly my favourite part of the week because I can enjoy watching the improvements they are making each week. Dance stretches the imagination and bodies of autistic children and there are other benefits such as stronger muscles and bones, better coordination, agility and flexibility. Dance also improves their spatial awareness and balance, which many autistic children often find difficult. I've found that dance increases their physical confidence and their mental functioning, which is particularly apparent after they have performed in front of their parents.

It's very rewarding but, on one occasion, while teaching dance at West Middlesex College, I stepped onto my left foot and went over on my ankle. I was in agony, having ripped my Achilles' tendon. I didn't want to shout out in pain in case I alarmed the students, so I asked them to sit on the mats to perform floor exercises.

After they had completed their exercises and relaxation session, the lesson ended and they left the room. I was crying in pain and hopped into the staffroom before being sent to hospital for treatment. My leg was set in a plaster cast for three months. I was still able to go to work at the school each day, though I had to hire an automatic car to do so. The injury took five months to heal and, although I was still exercising at home, I desperately missed the opportunity to dance.

The diagnosis of symptoms on the autistic spectrum still needs to be improved, but it is getting better, resulting in more adults now being identified with the condition. Unfortunately, some of them have already been misdiagnosed as having schizophrenia when, in fact, they've had autism all the time. As a result, many individuals have been given inappropriate medication, which may have damaged them, and now, instead of having autism as their primary disorder, mental-health issues are more dominant because of what the drugs they have been prescribed have done to them. If only the correct diagnosis had been given at the outset, earlier intervention for autism could have been made and it wouldn't have cost the boroughs so much when these people reach adulthood because some progress, however limited, could have been made.

When people ask me what I hope for in the future, one of my main desires would be to see the process offered to families after a diagnosis of autism improved to such a degree that it is easier for them to understand what it is and how they can cope. Parents need far more support to show them the direction they should go. Here, in Hillingdon, we have at least got HACS, which was set up with parents and families in mind, and Hillingdon Manor as a place of learning for children with autistic tendencies. That's a lot more than in most areas, so there's a lot more that should be done nationwide in that respect. People should not be just left alone to deal with it.

As Sean and I discovered, it's a real minefield, particularly when it comes to getting the right sort of education and statementing for an autistic child. I know things have moved on in a slightly more positive way since Patrick and Angelo were diagnosed, but there are still problems.

Speaking to various parents, I've learned that getting a statement of special educational needs for preschool parents is still difficult, even ten years on. Boroughs are saying let's wait! But wait for what? Getting a statement is the beginning of the journey for parents. They need resources allocated for their child. Lots of local authorities have been moving away from the statementing process. Sometimes the people who are making the decision whether the child needs a statement, or what support is in the statement, are people who have never met the child and know nothing about autism!

It would be great if there could be more specialist schools because not all kids can cope when sent to mainstream schools. There's a good argument for both specialist and mainstream schools. Put simply, every child deserves a decent and appropriate education to help them cope with life in their early years and to guide them on their way to adulthood.

Also, it's important that professionals such as doctors, teachers, social workers and others get the proper training to know what is best when dealing with autistic children. For

God's sake, what is the point in giving teachers a half-day's training session on how to teach autistic kids? I'll tell you now: there's no point at all. I should know – I've been living with it for years and I'm still learning!

I've met so many GPs who have very little idea about autism. I know there are many disabilities out there but autism affects at least one out of every hundred children! Well, that's a significant ratio, so surely our GPs should receive adequate training so they know how to recognise and deal with the symptoms.

I get frustrated at what I see as the disjointed networking between organisations that deal with autistic children. Some like to keep their information close to their chests, but why? We should all share in order to increase the awareness of all aspects of the autistic spectrum and then we can all fight the same battle together. Are we not all trying to get the best we can for people with autism? After all, it's not a competition!

Following the countless battles Sean and I had with Hillingdon Borough Council, it seems things have turned full circle and there is now a working relationship between us and council officers. The council has, in the past, helped with the funding for autistic children to attend the Higashi School in Boston. Some time ago, when we enquired about the possibility of sending Patrick and Angelo there, it would have cost £54,000, which we were expected to fund ourselves.

It's ironic how things can change. Once we were locking horns with the council as we struggled to obtain educational provision for our boys, yet nowadays we find ourselves cooperating with them as they refer children to us and, to be honest, I just feel glad we can help. We're here. Use us, because we're a vital resource for the borough, even though we're still considered to be an out-of-borough resource because we're an independent school.

A while back we received a visit from the director of education from Hillingdon Borough Council. To be honest, we got the impression he wasn't too keen to come at first, particularly when he told us he could spare only about twenty minutes of his time. It was pleasing, therefore, when he stayed with us for nearly three hours. I like to think that means he liked what he saw. We often get requests from people in the teaching profession who wish to visit Hillingdon Manor and sometimes we receive enquiries from other boroughs wanting advice.

The school continues to receive recognition, one of the most recent being the Business Achievement Award for Excellence in Education, an independent award programme that acknowledges business excellence across a wide range of disciplines and is recognised both locally and nationally. This award was a very welcome seal of approval and, although Sean and I are often recognised for our roles in founding the school, this award deservedly reflects the fantastic efforts of everyone else involved in the project, and our last Ofsted inspection went very well indeed, which ensured we crossed the final hurdle on the way to obtaining full Department of Education approval. The school is now widely recognised as a centre of excellence for the care and support of those with autism – our original aims have been fulfilled.

Since Hillingdon Manor opened, we have modified our procedure for admission by including assessments, which now means that potential pupils spend up to half a day on the premises. After this assessment, if it is felt we can meet the child's needs, a home visit is made by a member of the home–school team. When a pupil is accepted, the parents and local education authority will be informed of the placement. Once the LEA agrees to fund the placement, a starting date is given, subject to availability.

Sometimes it is deemed appropriate for a pupil to be given an assessment placement for a specific period to determine the effectiveness of the placement for that particular pupil. New pupils have a three-month observation period, during which time they are assessed to provide a baseline from which individual educational plans are constructed. However, pupils are not admitted on a first-come-first-served basis. They are admitted when a suitable vacancy occurs within a compatible group. This also applies to children whose referral is subject to Special Educational Needs Tribunal procedures and decision.

A baseline assessment is carried out in the initial six weeks. During this period, staff will observe all aspects of the child's level of functioning. Baseline assessments include the setting of targets for individual educational plans and the setting up of pastoral support plans.

All placements are subject to a probationary period of up to six months. During this time, a review is held to consider the needs of the child and the ability of the school to meet those needs and the level of resources necessary.

Our curriculum, which is tailored to suit individual needs, is designed to assist pupils to integrate as well as possible into society and offers a truly eclectic approach, which includes the use of physical education; connective education, which features connections for generalising learning; TEACCH; speech-and-language therapy; a social-skills and communication group; Makaton signs and symbols; transactional-analysis therapeutic structures; relaxation, massage and yoga; music therapy; drama therapy; behaviour management; a circle of friends and buddy system; the Duke of Edinburgh Award; daily-living skills; Picture Exchange Communication System; counselling and healthy eating. When teaching children with Asperger's Syndrome and autism we try to adhere to the following guidelines. As far as possible, we try to ensure that we provide an area in the classroom where they can have their own personal space and avoid distractions; we aim to ensure that the classroom has an element of continuity – not too many changes at one time; we prepare the children well in advance for any changes in school routine, if possible, as this can be very distressing for them; we use a daily visual timetable for younger children and keep instructions clear and simple, checking that they understand by repeating the instructions to them individually as they may not understand that general instructions are for them unless their name is used; we use ICT to support their learning in a variety of ways and use visual and concrete materials to support understanding of conceptual vocabulary.

Great efforts are made to teach the pupil how to interpret social signals and we use social stories to support a learner in specific social situations (e.g. turn-taking) and we give them the opportunity to explain their anxieties. We give logical explanations when asking them to do something new and ensure that they understand that school and classroom rules apply to them. We always speak to them in a calm and emotionless manner, with little variation in tone/modulation of voice and we explain jokes, idioms and figures of speech – what they are, what they mean and how they work, as far as can be understood, and that people often say things that may not seem logical or literal.

Sometimes I feel as if I have an invisible radar on the top of my head because I always seem to be bumping into people who have a connection with autism. A couple of ladies who work in the new Moorcroft School, which was relocated from the site now occupied by Hillingdon Manor, recognised me and asked if I had any advice or information that would assist them in teaching two children with autism in their classes. They had obviously had great difficulties in coping with their condition and were particularly interested in any information I could give them that referred to anger-management issues.

I agreed that I would speak to our speech-and-language therapist on my return to school and I would ask her to provide the ladies with a social story that could be used to help an autistic child relate to and understand what's happening to them. This small link between our two schools has since blossomed and, today, a circle of friends exists that helps our children with more complex needs to integrate with children from other schools.

The bestselling novelist Nick Hornby and his now ex-wife Virginia Bovell's son Danny was born in 1993. Danny is autistic. Nick and Virginia found themselves faced with a similar dilemma to ourselves and eventually joined a group of other parents of autistic children in north London because they felt their children deserved better educational provision than was being offered to them at the time. As a result they founded a nationwide charity of their own – the TreeHouse Trust – and opened a school in London, which specialises in autism education.

I was invited to attend the opening when Virginia paid a visit to Hillingdon Manor after watching a documentary about us on television. She generously donated some money to the school and has since kept in contact with us. At the opening of the TreeHouse Trust School I once again met Cherie Blair. I was surprised she remembered me from the awards ceremony in Kent but she was interested to hear how things had been going for us.

The TreeHouse Trust School had been set up on a temporary site, and, at the time of going to print, a replacement school is being built at a cost, I believe, of around £10,000,000, which will be partly funded by the government and the rest by the TreeHouse Trust. I can't help thinking we could have opened five or six more schools like Hillingdon Manor for that sort of money.

We often see headlines in newspapers saying things like 'This is the cure for autism!' or 'This is the best thing for autism'. If only it were that easy! I have to say, I feel many of the stories offered to newspapers are from people whose real intention is to make as much money as possible from parents who are at the end of their tether as they struggle to cope with their autistic children. Let's face it, there's no magic wand. The most appropriate and effective approach is for parents and teachers to work together in a consistent manner. We've seen at first-hand how effective this approach can be.

I'm happy to say our Upper School has gone from strength to strength. One thing we've noticed is that, when all the students get together, it's clear how well they have matured into young men or young ladies. It now has 28 students, the majority of whom have graduated from Hillingdon Manor. The students study at the Upper School until they reach the age of 19, and then, if they are capable, they can graduate to West Middlesex College or a mainstream college. Although it's still early days, to date three students have already done so, while others have moved on to mainstream colleges. It's so rewarding to observe their progress and it really thrills me and fills me with pride as much as anything else – if not more so.

At present we have students from 15 different local education authorities, including Hertfordshire, Buckinghamshire and Berkshire, attending our centres. Taking care of their needs, we now have a hundred staff working at the residential home, the college and the schools.

Chapter Eleven

Trouble and Strife

After identifying the need for students who require more intensive support in communication skills, we established an intensive-communication life-skills residence – a converted Portakabin – in the grounds of Hillingdon Manor. This facility has a bathroom, a bedroom, a kitchen and a lounge, where the students can live semi-independently – which fits into my plan of plugging the holes many sufferers of autism face as they go through life.

The classes here have a high adult-to-pupil ratio, providing both one-to-one and group teaching that promotes individualised teaching and learning styles to meet the specific special educational needs of every student. All teaching and learning practices optimise the student's ability to increase their knowledge and skills. In addition, opportunities are given to practise and generalise these skills in a variety of meaningful contexts and environments within and outside the school.

Teaching is multisensory and communication-centred, which

creates opportunities to ensure learning, progress and independence in settings meaningful to the students, who also have the opportunity to gain ASDAN (Award Scheme Development and Accreditation Network)-accredited qualifications.

In October 2006, as our reputation for excellence spread, we felt the need to expand the Upper School, as it was already approaching full capacity. For that reason it was decided to purchase another property known as The Lawns, which is set in the grounds of Hillingdon Manor. The plan was to use The Lawns as a facility for students aged between 16 and 19, and the intention had been to convert the building to cater for 28 students.

You could be forgiven for thinking that, after we'd got Hillingdon Manor up and running, everything that has been achieved since then has been plain sailing and that our businesses have blossomed and almost run themselves. But, unfortunately, trouble was on the horizon as we began to look into ways of financing The Lawns and the following months were as stressful for Sean and me as any we had experienced before.

The problems began when we realised we couldn't afford to buy The Lawns without outside financial backing. Originally the property had been on offer for £920,000. We could have just about scraped the money together but it would have left us short the following January with reference to VAT and corporation tax. For this reason the directors and shareholders agreed we couldn't do it on our own and decided we should contact other service providers to assist us.

After initial investigations, we were contacted by two other specialist providers who expressed an interest in buying Hillingdon Manor. This led to a prolonged period during which the directors were trying to decide which would be the best group to align with. If we were to go with the first group, they would have wanted to buy us out. That would have meant I would no longer be a director or a shareholder, I'd just be working for them – but I didn't want to give away all we'd worked so hard for.

My preference was to go with the second group, who said we could buy up to 20 per cent of the shares and I would remain a director of the company. That, sadly, is where the conflict between Sean and I and the board of directors began. Three of the directors/shareholders, who wanted to retire, were keen to go with the first group but I had no intention of going down that route at all. They could have offered me a job worth £2 million and I still wouldn't have been interested! I felt we had an awful lot going for us at Hillingdon Manor and that we were something really special – I didn't want to see us becoming part of a huge anonymous group. We're a specialist provision, and that's how we should stay.

Nevertheless, I found myself being strongly urged to go with this group and to take the job offered to me and to work my way up in the new company. Maybe I could even work my way up to a directorship in the future, they suggested. The directors were telling me they wanted to do what's best for the children – and that of course would be paramount – but did they really think I didn't want the same thing?

Of course, whichever choice would eventually be made, I knew I would still want to be involved, but, then again, I knew it just wouldn't be the same. I wanted to remain a director, and to extend the board of directors. Sean, on the other hand, didn't want to be a director but preferred to help out in the areas of education law and legislation.

I felt that by going with the second group we would have more chance of staying special because this particular group didn't have any schools at all for children with autism, although they have expertise with children with emotional behavioural disorders. This group wanted to set up a separate company and to use our school as a template, and that appealed to me far more because what we are doing at Hillingdon Manor could then be replicated up and down the country.

The two choices caused considerable conflict between the directors, with me out on a limb battling against the first offer. This resulted in some directors accusing me of being selfish, which, naturally, caused me a lot of hurt, upset and extra stress. I was at an incredibly low ebb and my spirits were hardly lifted when we received some anonymous letters – some of which contained some very unpleasant comments about Sean.

I was livid and felt Sean had been really badly let down by some people in the way they treated him. Some of the horrible things said against him caused unbelievable stress to us all as a family and it's something I would never, ever want to live through again. Matters became so unbearable I truly began to feel I was beginning to lose my faith in people and, although I'd never had a panic attack before, within two months I had two: awful tight feelings across my chest and a frightening inability to breathe.

The pressure was immense and I even began to doubt myself.

I lost an awful lot of faith in some people as our family life became almost intolerable. Coral, however, was a mountain of moral support and backed Sean and me to the hilt. How I wished I had the money to buy the other shareholders out to put an end to all this hostility.

Then, in June 2007, the waters were further muddied when a third provider also expressed an interest in buying us out – it was as if we had a for sale sign at the front of the school. This further added to my stress. I was finding the whole situation particularly hard to cope with and was frequently feeling sick to my stomach.

The staff were also becoming unsettled by rumours and counter rumours floating around the school. Something needed to be done quickly to put minds at rest. After a meeting among the board of directors to try to thrash out our differences, a meeting with the staff was arranged at which I explained to them the need for our company to acquire more capital if we were to purchase The Lawns and be able to refurbish and staff it to an adequate level. Quite simply, we had outgrown our existing facilities.

I told the staff why we needed to attract outside investment towards this goal. We had looked at our businesses carefully and asked ourselves, Where are we now? Where do we want to go? How are we going to get there? We had looked at employing the skills of a consultant or possibly employing an experienced non-executive director who could provide regular impartial assessments of what we had been doing. Another option had been to use a management consultant to help us identify how best we could strengthen or change our management structure.

I then informed the staff of the two educational and care-service providers actively expressing an interest in amalgamating with our businesses. Putting aside my own misgivings, I told the staff that these options would not only allow for future development but would also help create cross training between the schools, improve resources, increase and improve our reputation, improve on morale, improve on staff development and opportunities for advancement and, finally, extend the board of directors.

We had already spoken to key staff working for the service providers who had expressed an interest in amalgamating with us and found them to be most helpful and with a good understanding of the autistic-spectrum disorder.

After my speech I was heartened by the support of the staff. Several of them came up to me and gave me a hug, and told me they realised how difficult all that had been happening must have been for us as a family. I became quite emotional and told them of my concerns for children like Angelo, who were in the intensive life-skills and communication classes. After the age of 19, there was nothing in the borough for them and that's why I felt we needed to press on and set up a life-skills centre that would complement the work done at West Middlesex College.

I know that, on reaching 19, Angelo will not be able to live at home because his needs are so complex. He, and others like him, will need to become more independent, but suitable specialist residential homes are non-existent in the borough. In fact, they are miles away. We needed to choose the most suitable service provider that would allow us to make this happen more quickly.

Of course, rumours of unrest were bound to filter down to the parents, who became most concerned at how things might develop. Some were very upset and didn't want us to sell out to anybody. Basically, they just wanted things to carry on as they were. In their eyes, if something isn't broken, why fix it? One mother even approached me in the playground and told me that I should not believe any rumours that she had started up a parent action group. I told her it was all news to me, yet, in the light of this, I realised we needed to call a further meeting to reassure the parents that Hillingdon Manor did indeed have a future.

And so it was that the parents gathered to hear about the recent developments. I explained how the meeting was intended to allay their fears and to assure them of everyone's desire to expand the services on offer – not as some had feared, to break up all that had been accomplished.

We had every intention of attracting and retaining quality staff to ensure quality and good practice; we intended to purchase The Lawns, and Portakabins would be leased and placed on the school's site to enhance the provision of intensive-communication life skills.

That said, I outlined the difficulties facing small specialist schools such as Hillingdon Manor. We had little opportunity to make extra money outside of that generated by fees. Maintenance and expansion plans would be limited without the extra finances an amalgamation would generate. I tried to reassure the parents that, whichever the choice of service provider partnership, Hillingdon Manor did have a good future.

Like me, parents liked the homely atmosphere, the good staff–pupil ratio and the feeling that the children are known individually to staff and are valued; that our staff were loyal and dedicated, always willing to go the extra mile, and that they enjoyed teaching our children and that this individualism was our unique selling point. The staff are passionate about the special education our pupils need and feel them to be part of an extended family. Whatever happened, this would not change. Then I promised all present that we would advise them of any developments just as soon as practicable.

Afterwards, some parents came to see me and told me how pleased they were that I was digging my heels in and encouraged me to continue to do so. I was so reassured when they told me things would never be the same if I were to leave. They wanted to continue to be able to see me every day, and for me to carry on giving their children dancing classes. I was so touched by their support.

Later I spoke to Esther Rantzen about the situation and, fortunately, she too was right behind us, telling us we shouldn't throw away all we'd achieved. Then Patrick, realising something was going on, asked me to explain what had been upsetting us so much, so, in simple terms I did, and asked him what he thought I should do. 'You should carry on doing what you've been doing, Mum,' he said. 'Don't let anybody else tell you differently.'

We knew we faced a big, big decision within a few weeks if we were going to succeed in buying The Lawns because the LEA had been asking whether or not we had the provision in place and we needed to acquire the necessary planning permission from Hillingdon Borough Council. We'd already assessed 33 more children, so we knew we must expand – and quickly – and we were constantly being asked by parents of prospective pupils whether or not we'd got planning permission for The Lawns in place.

Planning permission was eventually secured, despite one objection, and I have to say that Dave and Alex played instrumental parts in gaining approval. That's their bag, planning and maintenance; they're particularly good at that sort of thing. However, our joy was almost immediately tempered by the news that we'd been gazumped: if we still wanted to buy The Lawns the asking price was now a cool £1 million! This would mean that a further £20,000 would need to be added to the already steep deposit and this was money we had earmarked for the refit of the science laboratory, domestic science kitchen, new toilets, IT facilities and fencing, among other things. I was absolutely fuming!

Further meetings between the directors and shareholders, although lively and stressful, eventually saw an agreement reached between us all. We would probably amalgamate with the second service provider after all. This, we concluded, would be the best way forward for the school and its associated facilities. I was left to comfort myself with the thought that at least I would still be in a position of some influence over the running of the school, albeit to a lesser degree than before.

At the same time were very aware that the children and young adults at our establishments are special and vulnerable individuals and I and the other directors owed it to them to ensure that their future would be safe and secure with us. Of course the successful conclusion of the sale would be subject to us obtaining a number of reassurances from the consortium. In fact, as we write, that is where we stand.

All this aside, our problems were far from over. Suddenly, we discovered the asking price for The Lawns had spiralled by yet a further £100,000; then our human-resources manager, Kevin Mullally, noticed some men in suits wandering around The Lawns. 'Are you looking to buy it, too?' he asked and was gobsmacked when he was informed they already had – and that they had exchanged contracts for the property a month before!

And so it was that our interest in The Lawns ended with all our directors and consortium partners unhappy. Meanwhile, the problem of overcrowding at the Upper School remained unresolved and time was running out before the new term was due to begin.

Desperate times called for desperate measures. The decision was made to obtain a further three Portakabins to house the extra Upper School students and to make use of the Mencap building adjacent to Hillingdon Manor until a more satisfactory solution could be found.

It seemed to me the whole issue of purchasing The Lawns had opened up a very unpleasant atmosphere between some of the directors and Sean and me, and, in the end, it had all been for nothing.

Above: Hillingdon Manor, when we first arrived in January 1999 – look at the state of it! We had to have great powers of imagination to see beyond the drab exterior.

Below: Work in progress. Carpet tiles (donated by The Link), roll cages and stud boards litter the inside of a standard classroom at Hillingdon Manor. It was a real mess. This one was transformed into our art room.

Above: The exterior starts to take shape after a few weeks. We had a lot of help, including from a group of people on probation in the local community.

Below: It took us a lot of sweat and tears – and about nine months – to get to a stage where we could even start to move our stuff in. We opened in September 1999, providing educational facilities for 19 kids, catering for ages three and a half to 19 years old.

Above: Our first Christmas in the school, and here I am at the bazaar on a stall selling cake and jam which some of the parents donated. We had a great turnout and the kids loved it.

Below: Summer 2000, and our inaugural sports day in the school grounds. I ran in the parents' race and the boys did relay and obstacle races; all the kids received certificates of participation, and we gave out medals and cups. On the front right is my Aunty Zita, a great help and staunch supporter.

Above: Angelo on our roof. He climbed up next door's scaffolding and got into the chimney pot where he sat, swinging his legs. He was 12, agile and I couldn't persuade him to get down!

Below: Firemen and Sean try to get him down. Angelo refused the offer of help from the fireman with a polite 'No thank you!', but eventually he decided to come down from the chimney. He tried it again the next day!

Above: West Middlesex College, which we officially opened in February 2005. The college is a day centre catering for up to 15 students aged 18 plus on the autistic spectrum.

Below: The Old Vicarage residential home, complete with eight bedrooms for eight residents from 18 years upwards. We have had residents in their 40s, and theoretically there's no age limit.

Esther Rantzen has been a great friend to our endeavours. Esther and
I pose at the official opening of the Old Vicarage; she said she'd like
to move in herself! Local press and MPs attended – it even caught the
eye of the BBC's *Newsnight* programme.

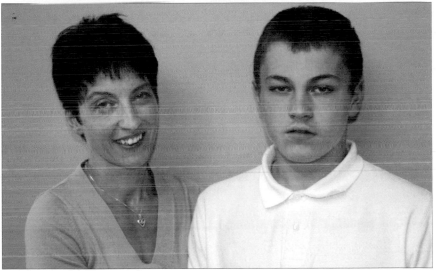

Above: Patrick with Chris, his drama therapist, with whom Patrick has a 1-hour session every week. Patrick loves his drama and it helps him to develop his imagination, to relate to other people through role play, and with problem solving. Patrick is on his way, I hope, to leading a fully independent life.

Below: Angelo, aged 14, and me. He will always need support, but he's making great strides towards becoming independent.

Above: Patrick is 18 and growing into a lovely young man. He's now attending mainstream college one day a week and work experience once a week.

Below: Now I can see the light at the end of the tunnel. I hope it's been worth it for my two sons and all the other people we've helped towards proving they're simply Not Stupid!

Chapter Twelve
Patrick

So where are we now as a family? Well, as individuals, we have all changed significantly since we embarked on this journey. When Patrick was out of school, his behaviour, even though I loved him, had turned him into a child I really didn't like that much. Nowadays, he's a completely different young man.

At the moment Patrick is very much into Eminem's music. He seems to enjoy the 'bad boy' image portrayed by the rapper and frequently asks if he can go out and wear a hood. I always refuse, but he just cannot see why. He cannot appreciate the danger he could find himself in if he tries to mix with the wrong sort of people, or how he could be so easily led astray.

Patrick is very good at mimicry. He does an excellent impression of the comic actor Jim Carrey and grew up with my Northern accent even though he's not local to the area, which is common between autistic children and their mothers. Now, however, his Northern accent seems to have subsided to some degree and he is beginning to sound more like a Londoner.

My brother Tullio now lives in London, too. He's a jokey sort of character and gets on well with the boys, particularly Patrick, who has taken a shine to him. Patrick insists that Uncle Tullio 'puts me out of my misery because he makes me laugh'.

Patrick has become a handsome and sensitive young man. He keeps himself clean and presentable and he's kind and thoughtful, although when he gets a bee in his bonnet about something he can be quite selfish. That said, once he's got it off his chest, he'll usually say, 'Sorry, Mum.'

He's made incredible progress and I'm sure he wouldn't have done so without our school. In fact, even if I had to go through the heartaches and ups and downs of the last few years all over again, it would be well worth it just to see how well he's come on.

Patrick will definitely continue to need support in a work environment but I am convinced he now has the ability to get a job. However, while I don't think he'll have a problem getting work, I wonder if he will be able to keep it. That could be another matter owing to certain anxieties that sometimes overtake him, and he's still a bit vulnerable and naïve.

At the time of writing, Patrick has a girlfriend! We are so pleased for him, particularly as it's done his ego the power of good and because he had been convinced no girl would ever be interested in him. She has been very understanding and, when she discovered that Patrick had a fear of the police, she even arranged for him to be shown around a local police station in the hope he could overcome his anxieties.

His fear of the police almost cost him his life in June 2007. Patrick had popped down to our local corner shop to buy some shampoo. While on the way he heard the siren of a passing police car and instantly panicked, so much so he ran straight into the road in front of two other cars and was extremely lucky not to have been run over.

His anxiety was heightened even more when a police car stopped. A couple of policemen got out and stopped him running any further. 'Why were you running?' one of them asked. 'You were almost killed.'

Patrick began to panic even more. He told the policemen he had Asperger Syndrome. The policemen apologetically admitted they had no idea what this was. Then one of them searched Patrick's pockets for drugs. He asked that, since Patrick had this syndrome, did he need to go to hospital? Patrick declined and asked the policeman to telephone me on our home number.

My heart sank when the telephone rang and I realised I was talking to a police officer. Whatever had happened? However, I was told not to worry, but that Patrick was panicking and had become very anxious. At the time I was wearing only my pyjamas, so Sean popped down to the corner shop to collect Patrick and to speak to the policemen.

To be fair, the police officer and his colleague had been very kind to Patrick. They told Sean they felt he was a good lad, and that Patrick should have some assistance to help him cope with his fear of the police – maybe visit a police station – and that he was a very lucky lad still to be alive.

Patrick was still very shaken when he arrived home but, in a weird way, I think this experience may have done him a favour in that his perception of the police had been that they were to be feared at all times. Now he had seen them in another light.

They had been helpful and kind, yet he was most disappointed that they'd had no idea what autism was.

Of course, having his first girlfriend has led to his bombarding me with a myriad questions, which, at times, has driven me crazy! Patrick analyses everything I tell him and everything his girlfriend tells him to ensure there are no hidden double meanings. It's bloody hard work to give advice, give it again, and then again when, all the time, a little voice in the back of my head is screaming, 'Shut up!'

Patrick tells me of his difficulties when he was trying to explain the intricacies of Asperger Syndrome to his girlfriend. 'Why can't I be normal?' he asked me. I tried to reassure him by telling him it didn't mean anything, that he'd always been the same person since the day he was born, that it's not as if he'd just found out he was different.

All I ever really crave for in my life is some peace. Is that too much to ask? I always know if Patrick is about to give me a hard time with all his questioning because he usually starts the conversation off with, 'Sorry, Mum, but... ' That said, he is far more aware of the pressures he puts on Sean and me nowadays. He's definitely more empathetic, but still insists on getting his own point across first!

Patrick didn't even like human beings at one time – now he's got friends, and people really seem to like him. Although he had convinced himself that no girl would ever like him, I have to say the opposite is the case. He has plenty of female admirers, several of whom have expressed an interest in going out with him or even being his girlfriend.

So far, I've been most impressed in the way he's handled such situations. He has made a point of trying to let them down gently by telling them he already has a girlfriend and that, in no small way, is down to the strategies he was taught at Hillingdon Manor, the Upper School and at East Berkshire College in Maidenhead, through role play, to deal with these situations in a sensitive way. He even told me he felt bad afterwards in case he had hurt anyone's feelings. There's no doubt he's learned to be loyal, understanding and considerate and, I have to say, as a result, I am immensely proud of him.

Patrick began attending East Berkshire College whilst still at Hillingdon Manor in September 2006. This was a big step for him. His progression to this mainstream college came about after Sean Pavitt assessed him as being capable enough to cope. Patrick had been doing well at the Upper School and Sean felt moving on to East Berkshire College would help prepare him for a degree of independent living.

When he first attended East Berkshire College he did so for one day a week, this was a particularly stressful time for Patrick. Prior to being picked up by the minibus on his first day, he had been very anxious, though I wasn't because I felt Patrick was in the good hands of members of staff from the Upper School who would be shadowing him.

Of course, Patrick's anxieties were not unexpected. After all, he was used to attending a school with another 79 students, but, with 1,600 students in East Berkshire College, it was obviously a daunting prospect for him. However, with the support of staff at the Upper School and the staff at his new college, his fears and anxieties were allayed within a couple of weeks and he now travels to Maidenhead twice a week, spending the rest of the week at the Upper School, where he has already completed his Duke of Edinburgh bronze award and, at the time of writing, he's working his way to gaining his silver award.

In 2008 Patrick was due to leave the Upper School so a special goodbye assembly was held for him and two other students. All three were presented with a Hillingdon Manor school diary that showed pictures throughout the years of them with their classmates. It was a very emotional occasion and I was glad when a member of staff passed me a box of tissues!

It was decided that training would be required to prepare Patrick for the journey he would need to undertake to get from our home to the college, as this would consist of a combination of bus and train journeys. This was practiced throughout the summer holiday period until we were satisfied Patrick would be able to cope with the daily commute.

Patrick is now undertaking a Higher Options course, which covers maths, English, IT, vocational and art. He is hoping to commence a media studies course next year.

Looking to the future, I can envisage a time when Patrick will be able to look after himself, although with some support, which is why I'm trying to plug every hole, support-wise, for him now before I'm dead and gone.

Sometimes he watches the original *Video Diaries*, which we recorded in 1999, and, more often than not, it makes him cross. 'I was a real brat when I was little, wasn't I, Mum?' I tell him he wasn't, that he was just a little boy with a lot of difficulties in his life. I remind him of the problems he experienced in mainstream school and try to reassure him that, now he's spent time developing his education at Hillingdon Manor and East Berkshire College, he has developed into a really nice, handsome young man, which he truly is.

In 2006 a charity called HCPT – The Pilgrimage Trust – took Patrick and four other children from Hillingdon Manor to spend a week at Lourdes in France where Christian pilgrims regularly gather. Once there, Patrick telephoned me two to three times each day and, even after only the second day, wanted to come home because Lourdes was 'too holy' and there weren't enough shops selling Eminem CDs! 'The shops here only sell holy stuff.' He asked if I would be putting up a Welcome home, son poster on his return, which made me laugh, but I did it anyway. Once home, Patrick gave me a bottle of holy water and a party cake, which Angelo particularly enjoyed.

At the time of writing Patrick mentioned something to me that happened in the past that still upsets and angers him – a particularly sad incident that had a huge effect on us all as a family. 2004 was not a good year for us. Not only did we have to shut down and relocate the original college, but I lost the baby I was carrying at the time.

When I first became pregnant I had experienced a range of emotions. I remember being at home on my own after the pregnancy test and walking around in circles in the lounge. At first, Sean was none too happy about the prospect of the arrival of another child, but he soon got used to the idea. As for me, I was rather selfishly hoping for a little girl because we would then have a greater chance of having a child without autism. Not only that, when she grew up, she would be around to look out for her brothers after Sean and I are dead and gone.

But, just 12 weeks into the pregnancy, after attending the hospital with Aunty Zita for a scan, I was told our baby had died and that I had a cyst on my ovary. I was devastated. Was I being punished for wanting a child without autism and thinking a girl could, in later life, look after Patrick and Angelo? I couldn't help thinking so – after all, these were not good reasons for wanting to bring another child into the world. Coping with those emotions was made even harder because Patrick had become very angry with me. Didn't I want the baby? It was my fault, and God was bad.

After taking just two days off work, I threw myself back into my routine. I needed to keep busy, but I remember hating all the looks of pity from the staff when I returned to work, as I'd told them only a couple of weeks previously about the pregnancy.

I have to say I was surprised and had a huge lump in my throat when Patrick raised the subject three years later. He told me how upset he had been when I lost the baby and how much he would have liked to have had another brother or sister, particularly as Angelo is so autistic they cannot even have a conversation or go places together on their own.

These days I am noticing Patrick can be embarrassed about Angelo's behaviour even though he knows it's not his fault and that Angelo's difficulties are more apparent. Patrick can become cross with Angelo for his autistic behaviour and sometimes I need to remind him that Angelo's frustrations can manifest themselves in a different way from his own.

I would love to be able to get into Angelo's mind – if only for a while – so I could get an insight into his world, realise what he understands, feel what he feels, and know what he likes and dislikes. So much of Angelo's world is a mystery to us.

At least Patrick is able to express his emotions, his hopes and his fears, which is why it would be far more enlightening for him to tell you, the reader, of how he sees his life, rather than have me try to do it for him.

What follows, in Patrick's own words, is how a 17-year-old youth with Asperger Syndrome sees his life as it is today, how he reflects on his childhood, and how he sees his future.

Among my earliest memories are my school days at St Mary's School. It wasn't very nice for me because they didn't know what Asperger Syndrome was so they couldn't meet my special needs. Also, some of the other children would take the mickey out of me sometimes.

I found this very confusing. They called me names like 'bird brain' and 'cuckoo brain' but I didn't know what they meant. I didn't understand what was going on so I asked Mum why they were calling me names. She was surprised the other kids had been calling me names. I remember feeling quite scared at the school. I would feel intimidated by people's faces because I didn't understand their expressions. I used to run away because I was a bit of a wimp.

I felt different from the other kids and I remember kicking off because I didn't want to go to school. I was having tantrums every day, but I didn't know I had Asperger Syndrome or what it was. I remember kicking and screaming on the way to school each morning and some woman trying to make me feel better by showing me her earrings, but that didn't work. I made up excuses not to go to school, sometimes telling my mum that there were weird things she didn't know about in the school, such as the ground would open up there and I could fall through it.

I couldn't understand what my teacher was telling the class. When she told us all to do something like stand up, all the others would stand but I never realised she wanted me to stand as well because she hadn't said my name.

I remember drawing pictures of me blowing up the school. I drew myself holding a detonator with my eyes sticking out and smoke coming out of my ears because I was so angry. I would grab my hair and tug at it. I was trying to pull it out because of my frustration. I didn't feel as though I fitted in. I was kicking against my frustration and I used to think I was really stupid. I would make furious audio tapes saying how much I hated the school.

I really like Eminem's songs. Sometimes, when I listen to the lyrics and I hear him expressing his anger as he refers to his past, it reminds me of my own past and my audio tapes. It reminds me of the times when this or that was happening to me and I was getting so upset that I was trying to tear my hair out. Eminem's lyrics remind me of that feeling.

Not everything at school was bad, though. Most of it was, but sometimes it was quite exciting. I enjoyed taking things in to show my class – anything to do with Thomas the Tank Engine or the Jurassic Park movie. I'd take in toy engines or dinosaurs. I was obsessed by them both. I still like dinosaurs, but I'm not obsessed by them any more. I *still like any programmes to do with dinosaurs because they remind me of when I was a kid. But there'll never be another film with dinosaurs that can ever be as good as Jurassic Park.*

I used to get fact mixed up with fiction. I used to think what I saw in movies was real, that it was actually true. In Jurassic Park the rampaging dinosaurs and special effects fascinated me. I was really influenced by all that. Were they really real? The movie really influenced my interest in films and special effects and I'm currently reading the Jurassic Park book by Michael Crichton.

Jurassic Park and The Lost World – Jurassic Park are probably the first movies I remember watching. I bought all the toys that went with them so I could act out the scenes. Sometimes, after watching the dinosaurs in the films I would get a bit over-excited and try to bite the wheels off my toy cars while pretending to be a rampaging dinosaur.

I used to enjoy going to the Natural History Museum in London to see the dinosaur skeletons. That was because of Jurassic Park. I still go there, but not just to see the dinosaurs but because I'm familiar with it. That's not such a bad thing, is it? I find prehistoric animals really interesting. Life back then was nothing like it is today. I'm not so interested in cavemen but it's interesting to learn about our planet before we were on it. It would be fascinating to know if there was life on Mars, wouldn't it?

I can't remember lining all the things up on supermarket shelves but I do remember collecting all the Thomas the Tank

Engine toys. In fact, if I didn't get the toy engines I wanted I'd scream and scream. I remember lining them all up in straight lines. Why? Because I'd been watching the videos and I was trying to recreate the exact episode with my trains.

When I was a kid I used to have so many problems, but I enjoyed being a kid. It's just a shame I couldn't do some of the things like the other kids my age that I might have really enjoyed. Most of my childhood was happy, it's just that I had problems.

When Mum took me out of St Mary's School I was really happy. Wow, I thought, this is freedom, I don't have to go back and I can do whatever I want to at home. I can watch cartoons or Jurassic Park or play on the computer, maybe watch Disney films like The Lion King and so on. But then I had a home tutor. That was a nightmare. I just didn't like being told what I needed to do. I didn't enjoy that at all.

I was a bit worried on my first day at Hillingdon Manor School because I thought it might be a bit like being at St Mary's School, but it wasn't – it was good. Once I got used to it I had more fun and made more friends. It was easier to make friends because the other kids were in the same position as me and we could understand each other better than we could at St Mary's. I liked talking to the other kids and messing around with them. I felt I fitted in much better there and I felt a lot calmer than I did at St Mary's.

All in all, it was excellent at Hillingdon Manor School. Sometimes I wish I was still 10 or 11 or 12 and back at the school because I miss some of the good things I did there.

I liked to draw and play with my friends, and the teachers were very good.

One day actor Ross Kemp came to the school. He played Grant Mitchell in EastEnders and I was very excited because I watched it on TV. I was interested in the programme and I was a fan. I'd look up the internet for clips of the programme and I really liked Ross's hard man image. It was very impressive. I have a thing about looking like a bad boy. I like that image. I've been influenced by Eminem's lyrics. Eminem's image is great, the way he poses. I like that. I've got a poster of him in my bedroom. I'm much more confident now, though I don't like people to think of me as a big softie. I like to think I can be a bit hard at times, maybe a bit stern.

I was very nervous when I first met Ross but he was a very nice guy. I met him again last year and that's when I realised he's not such a big man after all, though that could be because I'd grown quite a bit since I'd last seen him. He's not big, just bald.

Moving on to the Upper School was a bit nerve-wracking but I got used to it in the end. I particularly remember, when I was 14, moving into Elm class. That was good. The Upper School teachers are very good. They've been preparing me for life ahead but I still feel a bit immature – Mum often tells me I'm immature when I start acting out scenes from films or videoing myself just for a bit of fun. When I play the same Eminem song over and over again she finds it very irritating. It gets on her wick! But I just like the rhythm. Anyway, she said it was OK at first.

In my last term at Hillingdon Manor I did quite a lot of work experience. I worked in McDonalds, Woolworths and Iceland. Part of me was sad to leave Hillingdon Manor but part of me was happy to be moving on, even though I was anxious.

When I left Hillingdon Manor I attended East Berkshire College one day a week, which was later extended to two days a week. It was a bit daunting going there for my first day because it's a lot bigger than the Upper School or anywhere else I've ever been, but I've got friends there, one called Colleen and another called Jo. It's kind of frustrating because there's a girl there with a crush on me and she asked me out but I'm already in a relationship. I've got a girlfriend.

Sometimes though I think girls are nothing but trouble. Sometimes I think why bother with them, but I guess I can't resist them! I like girls a lot. Normally I find it quite easy to get on with them – depending on what sort of questions they ask me. One girl asked me if I thought she was pretty. I did, but I didn't know what to say to her. I was scared to admit it because I've got a girlfriend.

At East Berkshire College I've been getting used to communication. I've studied tourism which is quite interesting. Finding out where Wales is was very interesting. I like it at the college. I've rediscovered art and I find that very relaxing. I've made some new friends but I still have some difficult moments. Although it's a mainstream college there are students in wheelchairs and there are students with Down's Syndrome and other problems. I think several of the students know what

Asperger Syndrome is now and I think I fit in OK. I can ask them questions to see if they understand my problems and that's something I could never have done when I was at St Mary's. That often comes back to haunt me.

School can get boring sometimes and I'm often very relieved when it's time to go home. Sometimes I lose concentration during the lessons – that's been happening for a long time. I'm quite good at relationships and I still like reading dictionaries, which is good. I'm very good with computers, though I can't fix them. I just use them for the internet and playing computer and video games.

I find computer games very entertaining. Loads of kids do but most adults find them quite boring. I like Lara Croft Tomb Raider, Half Life, Jurassic Park: Operation Genesis, Doom 3 and Resident Evil.

I like playing video games and watching action movies. I'm interested in movie making and I'm interested in animals, though I don't like rats or mice. I love sharks and tigers. I really like to see wild animals. I'd love to get close to a tiger or a lion because I've been influenced by the Crocodile Hunter, Steve Irwin, on television. I was a very big fan of his and was very upset when he was killed by a stingray.

I love animals and, sometimes, I have more respect for them than I do for people. I feel more comfortable around animals than I do with people. At one time I didn't really like people at all. I'm still a bit wary of some people but I like talking to people even though I'm not always sure what they're going to be like. I like people who are nice, especially if they've got a good sense of humour. If it's an evil sense of humour that's even better! I like my Uncle Tony. He makes me feel at ease. He lightens me up when I'm in a bad mood and he tells me I can ring him up at night if I'm not happy. Now I have a new interest – painting Warhammer models. I often go to Games Workshop in Uxbridge and take my models along to paint. The staff there are really helpful and give me a lot of their time.

Nowadays I like to hang out with my friends. I like to socialise with people, maybe find new things on my computer, or watch good films. I think Bruce Willis is an excellent actor. I love the Die Hard series of films. My friends and I play in the arcades and go out for drinks, but we're not allowed in pubs. I like bowling and chatting to girls – that's my obsession at the moment. When I was younger I always thought girls were YUCK! But now I'm older that's so different. I can't resist looking at a pretty blonde girl and thinking to myself, 'She's fit!' But when I'm with my girlfriend I wouldn't do anything like that in case it was to hurt her feelings.

She's a really nice person. I was very happy to have a girlfriend and she often sends me text messages. I was tearing my hair out at first because it was a new experience for me. She didn't want me to keep dressing up like Eminem, though. When I had an annual review at school my tutor Chris even told me: 'Patrick, put it this way, she's met YOU not Eminem. It's YOU she wants to be with!'

My girlfriend tells me she likes the way I look, my personality and the way I treat her. That makes me feel very good, even though we sometimes have misunderstandings. Because I've been scared of policemen I wasn't amused when my girlfriend told me she wanted to join the police force but, recently, a meeting was arranged so I could talk to a policeman and that made me feel a lot better. I explained to him how I felt but he explained you don't always have to go to prison for certain things – it had to be for something really bad.

I went on and on at my girlfriend, trying to explain what Asperger Syndrome was, but she just told me it didn't matter – it didn't bother her, which is good. I think I did her head in a bit when I kept going on about a bad boy image. She thought I was just being silly.

She seems to understand my problems. I was not impressed when she told me she wanted to be a policewoman – what would she do if I did something bad? Maybe I was getting a little paranoid. Of course, if I killed someone she'd have to report me. But I wouldn't do that.

I get quite embarrassed about some things in my childhood. I remember Princess Diana dying and how curious I got about that. Then there was the picture I drew for her of Buzz Lightyear. That's definitely embarrassing, especially as I wrote 'To Infinity and Beyond' on it!

I remember going to Disneyland Paris and being scared of going into The Haunted House. I thought everything in it was real, but when I returned a couple of years later, I thought how pathetic I'd been for being so scared of going in there. It felt so different although nothing much had changed there... but I had.

I cringe when I see the Video Diary. Watching myself having a tantrum is a nightmare, it's just awful. I find that particularly embarrassing, especially if I'm watching the video with other people. Some of it was very good though, like the bit where I'm showing off my hand puppet of a T-Rex dinosaur and visiting the Natural History Museum.

Mum looked very tired in the Video Diary but I don't really think it was really my fault, although it must have been very challenging for her to look after me and Angelo. Sometimes I feel that, if I hadn't been born, she wouldn't have had to go through all that. If I watch the Video Diary now, I fast-forward it past the tantrums. I was very confused when it was filmed.

Nowadays I feel that I'm quite old. I'm nearly 18. Sometimes, when I get up in the morning I'm slow and feeling knackered, maybe I'll be in a bad mood or feeling achey. I'm getting to be like an old man! I'm starting to feel my age.

Mum and Dad are amazing. When they were first setting up the school I was thinking it was just for me. Now I think 'Wow!' – how can parents do something like that? When I look around the schools, well, I guess me and my brother are the start of all this – does that mean I'm going to be famous because I've caused Mum and Dad to achieve something? (joking).

I'm very proud of Mum and Dad, though sometimes I forget that it's because of me and Angelo that they've had to do so much. Now I'm older I can appreciate better how hard Mum and Dad have worked though I've got used to them both looking after me since I was so young which means I still ask them for support even though I'm more independent now. I can cook my own food, make my own breakfast in the mornings and go to the shops. I can get a bus on my own but, one day, the bus broke down and that made me start to panic. I was asking the driver what was going on and getting very worried. Then I realised that I had no credit left on my phone which made me even worse.

Mum's really nice. She understands me. She's a good person, though sometimes she can get on my nerves. No offence Mum, that's what all parents do. Usually, she gets stressed out when I keep playing the same Eminem song. But I do love her.

Dad's very intelligent and can be very funny, though sometimes he can get a bit irritating. All dads are like that, aren't they? Dad can be very informative and he teaches me a lot. I love him too.

I love my brother but he's got into a habit of throwing things he doesn't want over the fence into our neighbour's garden which gets really annoying. I don't play with him as much as I used to, but I do still tickle him and all that stuff.

I enjoy his company. We have a good relationship but we often just do our own things. He's started to take an interest in some of the things I like such as computers. He's getting quite good at using them now and he likes to look at some of my old dinosaur toys.

I feel very protective of Angelo. Once, when a kid hit him, I hit him back. I can't go out with Angelo. I wish I could. I wish he was a bit more like me. Although I have difficulties, his are much, much worse than mine. I can get a bit upset at times because it would be really great to have a brother I could hang out with, maybe even go out for a drink. If only he was like that. I can do that with my cousin Nico, but he lives a long way away in Middlesbrough.

Angelo realises more than some people think. I reckon he can understand quite a bit of what people are saying, even though he can't express his feelings or what he understands. I've got used to the fact that he has so many difficulties in his life, but I do feel very sorry for him.

Angelo does love me too, I'm sure of that. Sometimes he'll look for me around the house – even when I'm away for a few days in Middlesbrough visiting family. When I spent a week there Angelo was convinced I was stuck in my room and kept looking in there for me.

As for the future, well, we'll have to see. I think my future could be good. I've often wanted to be like Steve Irwin. Now he's gone perhaps I could take his place. I'd like to take big risks by getting close to wild animals or swimming with sharks. At one time I wanted to join the army but Mum said I wouldn't like it because I wouldn't like being shouted at by a sergeant. Sometimes I've wanted to be an actor because I love films, or maybe I could be someone who makes films with special effects – someone like Steven Spielberg who made Jurassic Park.

I'd like to take my driving test when I'm 18 so I can take my friends out for a spin – but I wouldn't want to be a taxi service for them, and I'd like to settle down with someone one day, though I'm not sure I'd ever want to get married.

There's been times when I've been ashamed that I have Asperger Syndrome because I've thought it could cause me to do strange things, like getting angry and a bit aggressive. More recently I've become more curious to find out what it's all about. Having said that, the most important things in my life have probably been the experiences I've had that have made me the person I am now.

Would I change anything in my life? Well, I wish I didn't get so obsessed with things, but that's just part of having Asperger Syndrome.

But, yes, I would like to change that.

Chapter Thirteen

Angelo

While Patrick will be able to fend for himself to some degree in the future, the same cannot be said of Angelo. He is, and will remain, a very vulnerable individual. Several past incidents involving Angelo still give me nightmares because, even today, the possibility remains that they could recur, as his sense of danger remains as limited as it ever was. We cannot take our eyes off him for a second, and we found out the hard way what can happen if we do.

In the summer of 2003, when he was 10 years old, Angelo performed another disappearing act when we took a caravan holiday near Great Yarmouth in Norfolk – undoubtedly the worst holiday we've ever had. As always, Sean didn't want to come along in the first place and his mood didn't improve when the school's Sunshine Variety coach, which we had borrowed, broke down on the way. 'That's it,' he said. 'We're going back home!' But, desperate for a much-needed break, I wouldn't hear of it.

Once the coach was fixed we continued on our way, but within three days of our scheduled week's holiday, Angelo went missing again. This time he'd managed to get out of the caravan unnoticed – it didn't take a second – and off he went.

As soon as we realised he had gone, Sean whizzed off like a madman in the Sunshine coach to look for Angelo while Coral and I wandered around the site hoping to find him. I was worried sick because the site was situated near to a steep cliff. My heart felt as if it were coming out of my chest and I was hardly calmed when I heard a driver telling another that 'some f***ing nutter driving a Sunshine coach' had just cut him up.

It transpired that Angelo had decided to walk into someone else's caravan but, as luck would have it, the caravan was occupied by a lady who just happened to be a special-needs teacher who taught children with autism! Angelo, it seems, just wandered in and sat down in front of the television and declared, 'I want to watch Bambi.' The lady contacted the site's information desk and then sat with Angelo until we arrived to collect him two to three hours after he had disappeared. 'That's it,' declared Sean. 'Pack the cases. We're going home!' That was the end of that holiday.

I crave for Angelo to initiate a conversation with me. I'd love him to be able to tell me what he'd like for his birthday or for Christmas, the way other kids do. But it wasn't until he was 10 years old that he ever showed any interest in his birthday or the Christmas festivities.

Prior to that Christmas I'd search his face for any expression of emotion or even just a smile, but each year there had been nothing of the kind. This used to make my heart ache and often

I found myself making an excuse – usually that I was going to make the beds – in order to get upstairs on my own for a little cry. Why couldn't Angelo be more like Patrick, who was always excited and had often written out his Christmas wish list way back in August? Patrick was always thrilled to open his presents and would often be keen to help Angelo open his.

But, at Christmas 2003, I was elated when Angelo suddenly became excited when he saw his presents and even wanted to open Patrick's presents too. It was as if a light had been switched on in his head. The previous January, Angelo had managed to blow out the candles on his birthday cake and these two incidents, which probably seem like very small steps to most parents, were very significant milestones for Angelo and our family. I cannot describe the feelings I experienced at these times, but they were very precious moments that truly lifted our spirits.

Angelo has a fascination for climbing. When he was 11 he scaled the fence at the bottom of our garden and jumped down into the garden of a neighbour, who became annoyed with him and called out, 'What do you think you're doing in my garden?' Stressed out, I called over to him, 'Why are you talking to my son like that? He's autistic!'

'Oh, I'm so sorry,' he replied.

But, at the end of the day, how was he to know? Since then we've heightened the fence between the gardens to avoid a repeat of the incident.

Shortly afterwards, we had a particularly frightening incident when our neighbours, who were planning to sell up, had scaffolding erected in order to have their house reroofed. I became concerned as soon as I saw the scaffolding. Because of Angelo's love of climbing, I was worried the structure would prove to be just too big a temptation for him. I asked the neighbour if he would consider putting a tarpaulin around the scaffolding so that Angelo couldn't get at it. Our neighbour agreed, but we had not reckoned on Angelo's powers of determination.

Work commenced and a number of tiles were lifted from the roof and stacked in piles, leaving only the wooden slats that had previously lain underneath them. Angelo was in our garden playing on his trampoline. Obviously I cannot watch him every second of the day, although I do keep a very regular check on him through the back window.

However, on this occasion, I quickly became concerned when I couldn't see or hear him. I hurried outside and called out to him but there was no response. At this time Angelo had been going through a ritual of clapping his hands but I couldn't even hear him clapping at all. I became very worried and continued to call out to him. Suddenly I heard three claps, but, hard as I looked, I could see no sign of him.

I hurried to the front of our house. Patrick was already there. When we looked up to follow the sound of the clapping, there was Angelo sitting inside our neighbour's chimney!

'Look at him! What's he doing? He's going to get killed!' screamed Patrick, who, by now, was going completely berserk. I was absolutely terrified that if Angelo moved again he could slip and fall further down into the chimney and I was wondering how he'd managed to get up there in the first place. Thank God he hadn't tried to step on the piles of roof tiles. If he had he would certainly have fallen from the roof.

'Good sitting!' I called out to Angelo, a simplistic phrase we often use with autistic children in our care when we want them to continue sitting still. 'Good sitting, Angelo!' I was desperate not to say or do anything to panic him into moving suddenly and equally anxious to calm Patrick down. Suddenly, all the neighbours appeared – some carrying cameras – while I frantically called the fire brigade, who swiftly arrived.

A fireman asked me how Angelo had managed to get up there in the first instance and, on learning he was autistic, asked me how best to deal with him. I told the firemen not to speak to Angelo in long sentences because he wouldn't be able to cope with that. 'Just be concise in whatever you say to him and he'll understand you.'

Meanwhile, Angelo had climbed out of the chimney and was now sitting quite happily on top, dangling his legs down the side of it, as he observed all the goings-on down below and watched excitedly as two firemen scaled the roof, managing to avoid the piles of tiles as they made their way towards the chimney.

While one neighbour tried to keep me calm by rubbing my back and comforting me, I telephoned Sean, who drove the short distance home with his mum and aunt just as fast as he could.

'Angelo, out of the chimney,' called the firemen when they got near him.

'No, thank you,' Angelo cheerily replied.

'Angelo, out of the chimney.'

'No, thank you!'

'Get hold of his arm,' I shouted to the fireman nearest to

Angelo, 'and he'll follow you.' It worked and, slowly but surely, the firemen carried him down to ground level. What a relief!

However, this experience did little to put Angelo off his love of climbing. As far as he's concerned, it's the higher, the better, and I was very relieved to be able to stop him from repeating his escapade the following day.

A couple of years later, when he was 13, Angelo found his way onto our flat roof. I was working for Health Call at the time and, as usual, I rang Sean just to check everything was OK back at home. This time, however, there was no answer. I tried ringing again, but still no answer. On the third attempt, a breathless Sean picked up the telephone. 'What's going on?' I asked.

'Your son has just climbed out of the window and got onto the flat roof,' he replied. 'He's jumping up and down on the edge and I'm trying to get him in but he won't come!'

Eventually, Sean outwitted Angelo by showing him his *Thomas the Tank Engine* model. 'Thomas wants you to come back inside,' he said. It worked and Angelo climbed back indoors through the window.

Living with an autistic child is difficult for the carer, but it's not too good noise-wise for neighbours, either – and particularly if your neighbours' kid ends up sitting in your chimney! However, we have been fortunate in that respect, since the lady living in the adjoining house is sympathetic – in fact she now works with us – and, on the other side, there's a lady who is often up in the night to tend to her own crying baby.

I find it difficult to speak about Angelo without getting

emotional because he needs so much help to cope with life. He'll need support for the rest of his life and I worry about who will care for him when I die. No one knows Angelo as I do – he comes to me for everything and I find that so worrying when I look to the future.

Do I have any feelings of hope for Angelo in the future? Not really, more like feelings of despair, to be honest. The only way I can get a reaction from him is when, sometimes, if he says a word and I repeat it, I may get a fleeting moment of eye contact, so I say it again and he repeats it. It's not a conversation, just a word here and there. He'll throw his arms towards me when he wants something. I say, 'What does Angelo want?' Then he'll do it again. I repeat, 'What does Angelo want?'

Then I'll say, 'I... ', he'll say, 'I... ' before I add 'want'. He'll then say, 'I want... ' and, after a pause, he'll say, 'cake, please, Mummy.'

Often, when I give him what he wants, he gets muddled and says something like, 'Thank you, good boy.'

You can almost see Angelo's brain ticking over as he attempts to communicate. I think it's important to encourage him and praise him whenever possible. If he wants to see inside a bag he'll say, 'Open box.'

'No, Angelo, try again.'

'...bag.'

'Well done, Angelo, good speaking.' And I'll give him a big smile and the thumbs-up sign. If he looks at me when he talks I say, 'Good looking, Angelo, well done!'

At the moment the conflict we have is over an old pair of socks. He wants to wear them every day. If I try to wash them there's a tantrum and they're becoming threadbare. He'll stand in front of the washing machine watching them go round and round and will often stop the machine early so he can retrieve them and put them in the drier. But he'll rarely wait longer than five minutes. After that he'll get them out and put them on. Now, whenever a hole appears in them, he'll bring them to me, then come back with a needle and cotton expecting me to mend them, which I do.

He's a much bigger boy now, but fortunately, his frequent frustrations are not expressed physically, although sometimes he'll tap my leg with his hand to show how upset he is. However, as soon as he's done it, he wants to pull his hand back. When he's really cross he'll just jump up and down, up and down, gritting his teeth and squeezing his hands together as his frustration increases.

Because he acts in a manner that would normally be associated with a much younger child, I sometimes find myself talking to him as if he were years younger and I have to remind myself not to. A recent psychologist's assessment tells us that Angelo's speech is equivalent to that of a three and a half year-old child, though I'm convinced it's more than that. It's just that he didn't really know her when they met and he was not at all interested in cooperating with her. I sometimes wonder if I'm trying to cover up for him in my own mind.

Angelo's very loving but, at the present time, still has absolutely no sense of danger. He's still into climbing, which is a worry. He's become a big, stocky lad like Patrick. With Sean being a big man, I've become the titch in the family. Angelo is sensitive in his own way and he hates to see me upset. If he sees me cry he'll come up to me and wipe my tears and give me a kiss on the cheek, so he's certainly much more in tune with my feelings – probably more so than anyone else.

His relationship with Sean is much improved and they often go out in the car or to the park together. But I still can't enjoy a conversation with Angelo, which is so frustrating. I'd love to know what he's thinking. If he's quiet I know he's up to something. When I suspect he's too quiet, I look for him and could find he's taken a dozen yoghurts out of the fridge and eaten them all, or he's emptied all the bags of crisps. One day recently he found a birthday cake and peeled all the icing off it so he could get at the sponge. Another time he emptied a box of washing powder all over the floor in the kitchen and I found him lying in it, shouting out, 'Snow! Snow!'

That's when he's really hard work. Recently Angelo was diagnosed as having attention-deficit hyperactivity disorder. The diagnosis was made in less than 15 minutes and the central-nervous-system stimulant Ritalin, which is used to calm the recipient down, was prescribed. I could hardly believe the condition could have been detected in such a short examination. Nevertheless, I administered the Ritalin but it gave him really bad heart palpitations. He began screaming and shouting and waving his arms around, so I took the decision to discontinue the medication.

I have to say, I cannot really believe Angelo ever had ADHD in the first place. I believe it's just that now he's in his mid-teens he's going through puberty and his hormones are going all over the place. ADHD is often cited as an excuse for bad behaviour but I cannot agree. The condition has a definite diagnosis and its severity is calculated on what is known as the Connor Rating Scale (CRS), which we use at our school. Although some of the questions were difficult to answer, we used the scale on both Patrick and Angelo, but felt it didn't really apply to them.

Now, even though Angelo's in his teens, we have only a slightly better routine in the evenings. We usually try to get Angelo to bed at around 11 p.m. We could get him to sleep at 8 p.m. but, if we did, he'd be awake again by 11 p.m., and that's no good for Sean or me. So, at 10.30 p.m., we start the process of getting him to bed. We take him upstairs to his room, though quite often he'll just follow us downstairs. Again, we take him upstairs until he decides to stay there to watch either TV or a video, or perhaps to look at his books.

The trouble is, when he puts on his TV he likes to put it on at full volume and we are often awoken by a *Thomas the Tank Engine* video blasting out in the wee small hours! It's amazing how many children with autism are hooked on Thomas. Back in 2002, the National Autistic Society commissioned a small research project to understand better the special relationship between children with autism or Asperger Syndrome and this programme. It seems Thomas has, for some children, been a vital point of entry into the world of communication and play – so much so that the National Autistic Society has seen fit to launch a larger-scale research study to investigate this special connection.

Even now, Angelo still loves jumping on trampolines – they are a very good stress-buster for him. We have a large one in our garden and it has saved us a fortune in beds and sofas. We first purchased a trampoline because Angelo had been constantly jumping up and down on our bed. In fact, he'd broken several beds by then. We'd even bought a metal bed, but he broke that on the day it was delivered. Eventually, my brother made up a plinth out of strong wood and we bought a couple of mattresses and now we sleep on those instead.

We've had more than a few sofas, thanks to Angelo's jumping exploits, and he has often damaged furniture with his inappropriate behaviour. One day I came downstairs after having made up the beds to find that Angelo had cut the nylon base of a chair with a pair of scissors and had slid into the hole he had made. The only part of him visible was his head!

Even now his behaviour goes through phases. He's currently resumed an earlier pastime of throwing things over the fence into our neighbour's garden. Fortunately, our neighbour Bernie works at the school, so he fully understands the situation, but, most weeks, he comes around with a carrier bag full of items that he's found in his garden. Sean had bought me a brand-new pair of binoculars prior to a George Michael concert at the new Wembley Stadium. It would be our first night out together in months, but the binoculars disappeared and reappeared only when Bernie knocked on our door. Other items thrown over into his garden have included a £20 note, videos, CDs, balls, toys, bras and knickers.

The reasons behind some aspects of Angelo's behaviour remain a mystery to me to this day. I recall a shopping trip to a local Aldi supermarket when he was four years old. He refused to go past the entrance of the store. As we approached the doorway he began to scream and throw himself around in his pushchair. I tried to calm him down, but he was having none of it. Each time I tried to go through the doorway he began screaming again. I decided to give up and to try and visit the store at a later date. When we returned, Angelo began to scream and wail. What was it about this doorway that triggered this response?

Later we visited Whipsnade Zoo and we experienced the same response from Angelo as we approached the entrance gate. It's so difficult when a child has such limited speech as Angelo to get to the bottom of what it is that's making him react in such an extreme manner.

Sometimes visiting friends triggered the same problem – we just could not get past their front doors without a screaming session. Nowadays, however, he's fine when we visit friends or relatives. He just makes for their bedroom to lie on their bed. It seems this is a familiar setting for him and it helps him to feel at ease.

There are all sorts of therapies available designed to help people like Angelo – some, obviously, being much better than others. At Hillingdon Manor we have always been open to fresh approaches, which brings me back to November 1999, two months after the school first opened.

An educational employment agency contacted a teacher, Richard Walker, to inform him of our need for a Key Stage 2 teacher to cover a week-long period. Although there is normally a calm aura around the school, over the first few days after Richard arrived, the normally tranquil atmosphere was not apparent, with several youngsters either screaming or running around upset for one reason or another. Worse still, some members of staff had been bitten, urinated on or scratched – which was worrying, to say the least. Fortunately, this experience did not scare Richard off and he remained to work his way through the week and, indeed, ever since.

In September 2000 Richard had the opportunity to attend an introductory weekend at the Institute of Craniosacral Studies, where he learned about working with patterns of resistance in the primary respiratory system – a name given to the core of the human body–mind system. It is believed the core of the system, the fluctuating movement of the cerebrospinal fluid, carries a healing potency that is taken up by all the fluids and tissues of the body to maintain health and order.

As the website of the Craniosacral Therapy Association of the UK explains, the therapy is:

a subtle and profound healing form which assists the body's natural capacity for self-repair. In a typical craniosacral session, you will usually lie (or sometimes sit) fully-clothed on a treatment couch. The therapist will make contact by placing their hands lightly on your body and tuning in to what is happening by 'listening' with their hands. Contact is made carefully so that you will feel at ease with what is happening. The first thing you will probably notice is a sense of deep relaxation, which will generally last throughout the session. With subsequent treatments this release of tension often extends into everyday life. The work can address physical aches and pains, acute and chronic disease, emotional or psychological disturbances, or simply help to develop well-being, health and vitality.

Craniosacral therapy is so gentle that it is suitable for

*babies, children, and the elderly, as well as adults and
people in fragile or acutely painful conditions. Treatment
can aid almost any condition, raising vitality and
improving the body's capacity for self-repair.*

Because the nature of the condition of autism and Asperger
Syndrome is often apparent as a huge pattern of resistance,
Richard became fascinated by the topic and was very keen to
find out more about how the primary respiratory system
worked, convinced it would make a contribution to the
children and staff at the school.

Over the following years, he has used craniosacral therapy at
Hillingdon Manor. Richard observed how the triad of
impairment was apparent among the pupils at the school.
Some, when they were upset, were perceiving stress that was
not really there and had a psychological perception of danger
rather than being in a situation where there was danger. Stress,
when perceived, is transduced into soft tissue contraction and,
when sustained over a period of time, leads to the activation of
the fight-or-flight mechanism in the nervous system.

The mind and body of an autistic person are upset together.
Richard noted that new arrivals at the school were constantly
on the alert, their brains and bodies becoming unconsciously
adapted to higher levels of stress, which, in turn, tended to lead
to overstimulation of the immune system, which created a
struggle between it and the nervous system, resulting in
susceptibility to immune suppression and hyperactive
disorders. From a soft-tissue point of view, this involves
depressogenic responses and resignation. In other words, it

results in upset individuals constantly being on the edge of a fight/flight response who, over a period of years, may show hyperactive disorders.

Being able to predict what is going to happen plays a large part in reducing anxiety levels. Teaching pupils how to relax on a daily basis obviously helps and this, coupled with Richard's craniosacral therapies, has enabled pupils to demonstrate an emerging ability of clearing up upsets with decreasing levels of support from members of staff, which also helps the pupils to repair and maintain relationships with others in their lives.

In a nutshell, the Craniosacral Therapy Association – a member of the British Complementary Medicine Association – states,

In response to physical knocks or emotional stress, the body's tissues contract. Sometimes, particularly when the shock is severe or occurs within an emotional situation, the tissues stay contracted. Any stresses, strains, tensions or traumas which have been 'stored' in the body in this way will restrict the body's functioning and may give rise to problems over the years.

Richard felt the above probably applied to Angelo and, together with Angela, he suggested the possibility of a pilot project that consisted of six craniosacral sessions between April and July 2004. In his resultant notes, Richard recalled Angelo's behaviour and responses over this period of time. He recorded how, at first, Angelo would not allow him to hold his head and rarely made eye contact, other than asking Richard's name.

Later sessions saw minute breakthroughs, with Angelo cooperating at times and occasionally making contact, and even placing Richard's hands on his head and allowing him to cradle him.

A year later, in July 2005, Richard approached me to suggest the possibility of further sessions with Angelo. Not only was this for Angelo's benefit but for Richard's, too, as he wanted to use the sessions as part of his coursework for his craniosacral practitioner training.

His notes over a nine-month period recalled several aspects of Angelo's behaviour and life as it was at the time. It took a while for Angelo to accept Richard in his space but, over time, this improved and he allowed Richard to cradle him on several occasions or rock him back and forth. He reported how, time and again, Angelo would hold his left ear and say, 'Help me.'

Angelo would repeatedly recite *Thomas the Tank Engine* stories loudly at night, often from around 4 a.m. to 7 a.m., but, by the second month of Richard's trial, I noted more clarity in his words rather than the gibberish I'd become accustomed to. Could this have been anything to do with the craniosacral sessions?

He became more responsive to verbal commands, for example, 'Angelo, please go upstairs and get yourself a clean shirt.' Nine times out of ten, he would do so – and put it on the right way round without any further prompting. On two consecutive Saturdays, he even used the toilet to have a poo. This was, indeed, progress, although he was still wetting his bed every night and even when he was awake.

After a period of not seeming too bothered about his ear, Angelo became very vocal and was again holding onto his ear.

He was in obvious discomfort. We wondered if this could have been an after-effect of the severe ear infection he had as a baby, but an X-ray revealed nothing of any significance.

December 2005. We'd had a total of just four hours' sleep over a 72-hour period but were pleased to note an improvement in eye contact. Angelo began practising his words in his bedroom. As we listened we heard him say, 'Hello, what's your name? My name is Angelo.'

January 2006 was a particularly challenging time. Angelo wet my bed seven times in a week; he just wouldn't go to the bathroom in time. He also defecated on his bedroom floor and then smeared the faeces on his body and the television.

However, his annual review at school the following month revealed some improvements. There were three main achievements, including an emerging ability of communicating effectively while using a computer; making better eye contact and focusing on tasks for longer periods of time; and a willingness to try more foods such as baked potatoes, tomato soup, tuna and chicken legs.

At home he was beginning to show more willingness to eat with the family at meal times and, after I'd been shopping, he would often help me to put the frozen food away in the freezer.

Over the period of the craniosacral therapy, Angelo's efforts at school had seen him make progress across the curriculum. His end-of-term reports indicated considerable progress in the activities he seemed to enjoy and those that had meaning for him.

After the final session, Richard had to decide whether or not there had been an observable connection between Angelo's academic progress, his social skills and the craniosacral sessions. Could these be quantitatively linked?

In his conclusion, Richard decided that there had been no obvious link but noted how Angelo's 'way of being' had shifted and evolved over the two-year period he had been involved with him.

So, the question remains as to whether or not craniosacral therapy is an effective way forward. To go into all the ins and outs of this therapy would require a book on its own, but the possibilities for its further use at the school are still being explored with a view to possibly utilising it again in the future.

All the time we've wondered what the problem has been with Angelo's ear, as he's often held it or asked for help, but could not explain what was wrong. Various consultants have failed to identify the problem but, when Richard did the craniosacral therapy with Angelo, he wondered if tinnitus could be the problem. We reckon he could be right – especially as it's a condition known to be in our family.

Chapter Fourteen

A Busy Schedule

Our lives are obviously mostly taken up with our commitments with the schools, Summacare, Autism Consultants, the college, the residential home and supporting HACS. Fitting in time for ourselves is often difficult and it seems I now live my life from one meeting to another. I have a very full diary.

Apart from being a director of Moorcroft Manor Ltd, Autism Consultants Ltd, Summacare and the college, I am also a volunteer at HACS Playscheme and a registered person at The Old Vicarage, and I'm also teaching dance and exercise.

As a marketing director, it's my responsibility to ensure that the Hillingdon Manor Group of the college, The Old Vicarage, Summacare and HACS have a good public profile and constantly to raise public awareness of autistic-spectrum disorders by attending open days and doing television, radio and newspaper interviews. I also attend fundraising events and functions throughout the year to promote all three companies, including the charity.

I need to keep up to date with all competitor activity and, wherever possible, to liaise with other service providers such as Partners in Autism, the National Autistic Society, the TreeHouse Trust and the All-Party Parliamentary Group on Autism to improve our own services wherever necessary. I also give five dance classes each week at Hillingdon Manor and at the college, and these require weekly planning and end-of-term reporting.

In my capacity as a registered person at The Old Vicarage, I support and oversee the registered manager and try to ensure that the high standards required in the running of the home are met and maintained through adherence to the home's policies and the Commission for Social Care Inspection regulations. I have to ensure that the Registered Homes Act 1984 and Care Standards Act 2000 are followed and have to attend weekly progress meetings. Further meetings are held to discuss and monitor the ongoing development plan for the home.

I have to be on hand to provide weekend and/or holiday on-call support and to provide monthly inspection reports to the Social and Care Standards Commission, and I manage the senior management team's supervision and their annual appraisal. In addition to this, I attend annual reviews for service users as and when required. I ensure there is adequate maintenance and I interview staff for the home. I liaise on a regular basis with the contracts manager for the home to acquire updates on prospective residents and I also liaise regularly with the human-resources manager on any up-to-date issues.

As one of the directors at the college, I support and oversee the principal. This is done on a weekly basis by email, telephone or personal visits. I attend monthly senior-manager progress meetings and liaise regularly with the contracts manager for updates on prospective students. Further liaison meetings are held with the human resources manager and the health and safety officer, and there are meetings to monitor and discuss the college's development plan.

Add to this the quarterly reviews of the senior management team and their annual appraisals and my involvement in monitoring quality at the college and contributing to the self-assessment report. I also attend bimonthly Hillingdon Safeguarding Committee meetings, where any relevant information over the serious safeguarding issues affecting the protection of vulnerable adults is disseminated, and, for the same reason, I attend Partners in Autism Committee meetings, and the All-Party Parliamentary Group on Autism committee meetings.

I am responsible for monitoring the safeguarding issues with the college's principal and I network with competitor activity and, where possible, liaise with them. I locate work placements for the students through existing and future employment contacts, and support and monitor the leadership team to ensure they fulfil the quality of education expected at the college and meet the standards demanded by the Learning and Skills Council and other national bodies. I attend open days for parents and business providers and ensure the college site and its resources are adequately maintained.

As a co-founder of HACS, I support its play scheme through

my role as a volunteer driver, and I attend monthly evening meetings, as well as supporting the charity director by attending presentations and functions to raise the charity's profile.

As a director of Summacare, I attend regular meetings and, as a director of Moorcroft Manor Ltd, I attend bimonthly meetings with the other directors to monitor the development and progress of the group and join them in reviewing our strategic development plan for all three companies. Other meetings include quarterly shareholders' meetings, quarterly meetings with National Autism Society Partners in Autism, bimonthly Metropolitan Police meetings, which raise the awareness of autism at police recruit and training stages, and quarterly safeguarding-adults meetings.

On top of all these meetings there are conferences and courses I need to attend to keep up to date with current issues, the following being just some attended within a 12-month period: Sensory Perceptual Issues in Autism; Living with Autism; Sexuality in Adults with Autism; Speech and Language in Autism; How to Write a Social Story; Dealing with Unacceptable Employee Behaviour; An Introduction to Autism; Disability Discrimination Act for Managers; Assertiveness in Management; Conflict Management Skills for Women; How to Do Effective Counselling; Diabetic Training; A Positive Approach to Autism; Understanding and Working with Autism; An Introduction to Adult Protection; Investigating Adult Abuse; Quality, Quality Everywhere; Non-abusive Psychological and Physical Intervention; The Importance of Consistency and Positive Behaviour Management; Understanding the Brain, Understanding Autism; Relationship Counselling for People with

Asperger Syndrome; Diagnosis of Autistic Spectrum Disorders; Positive Approaches in Managing Behaviour; and, finally, Sexuality and Individuals with Autistic Spectrum Disorders.

As with any business there are frustrations but it seems, in my world, someone, somewhere obviously feels I haven't got enough on my plate! While I accept that the authorities have a responsibility to ensure young people are properly protected from individuals who may not have their best interests at heart, recent events seem to show they have been taking these measures to extremes. Anyone working with children has to be scrutinised by the Criminal Records Bureau, and that makes perfect sense. If they consider you are fit to work with young people you are issued with a certificate to show the Bureau has approved you to do so.

I would have thought that, as the owner of one of these certificates, I would have been okay but that's just not the case. In a case of bureaucracy having gone bonkers, I've had to apply for Criminal Records Bureau checks on five occasions in the past two years! First of all I needed one for Hillingdon Manor, then I needed another for the college, then another for the residential home, another to cover my work as a volunteer, and yet one more for my roles as a director and proprietor. Now, I'm told that, as a mother who needs to accompany my own child to school, I need another Criminal Records Bureau check! It's barking mad.

While Patrick and Angelo had been receiving home tuition I benefited from three hours' respite every fortnight, thanks to a lovely man called Derek Jones, who later went on to work at Hillingdon Manor. However, once we'd opened the school and the boys began their education there, the powers that be saw fit to withdraw the respite care. As far as they were concerned, I didn't need it any more. Thankfully, though, through a private arrangement, Derek continues to care for the boys for a couple of hours a week after school and this enables me to work extra hours.

Fortunately, Zita regularly babysits for us, which, as you can imagine, is a true blessing. Sean's mum Coral and her sister Pam have now moved down this way and, with Coral, Pam and Zita's babysitting, Sean and I are able to attend a good number of meetings and to have just a little time to ourselves.

I still love to dance – that's my safety valve. If I didn't have that I'd probably end up in a psychiatric unit myself! Thursday nights are my nights for tap dancing from 8 p.m. to 10 p.m. and on Saturday mornings I dance for an hour. I actually went away for a tap-dancing weekend last year, staying overnight in a hotel. I felt really sick before leaving but my friends insisted they would drag me there if necessary because they felt I really needed the break.

Prior to leaving, I left Sean with a list – don't forget this, don't forget that – and I was really nervous on the way there but, once we'd arrived, I really enjoyed myself. However, I didn't sleep very well because I was worried about how Angelo was coping without me around. I was awoken at 6 a.m. by a telephone call from Patrick to tell me he couldn't sleep and wasn't it time I came home because he'd just had to change Angelo's bed? Thanks, Patrick!

HACS runs shopping trips for carers once or twice a year, which I really enjoy. Last time, we went to Brighton, but I always have to ring home about five or six times to make sure all is OK. I have to laugh at our situation sometimes because if I didn't I'm sure I'd go potty. Often I feel quite lonely living in a house with people with autism. I have to look after them, sort out all the bills, savings and finances, everything – though Sean now takes charge of all the shopping. I also get support from my sister even though she still lives in Middlesbrough. She reckons I couldn't have married and had a regular family because I would have been bored out of my head; that I've thrived on challenges, that I could do anything I put my mind to.

Do I ever think, Why me? Only for a second. The thing I crave most is just a little peace and quiet – and some sleep! When Angelo was much younger I felt as though I was on automatic pilot owing to the lack of sleep. I felt really weird. Drained. I was always exhausted, as though my shoulders were dragging on the floor. At first it was hard to function with day-to-day life.

Some mornings I still get up at four o'clock, having not gone to bed until past midnight, but I think my body's got used to it now. On the odd occasion that I do sleep well, I feel worse for it when I wake up – like a zombie, even more tired. Sometimes I feel like rolling up in a ball and hibernating for a few months to recharge my batteries.

Recently, I've been having weird dreams. I see myself holding a baby – a little girl, I think – and I keep putting her down but, when I turn around again, I can't see her and I get really stressed and cry. Then I find her again, hold her in my arms, then I put her down again and the process is repeated.

Sometimes I wake up sobbing. My sister is into dream analysis and she thinks there could be two reasons I have this recurring dream: first, I'm thinking about the baby I miscarried; second, it could be my 'other baby', the school – how I'm getting stressed out as we look towards securing its future.

We're still having a very difficult time with Angelo. He's been replicating what we believe is the sound he's hearing in his ear – a consistently high-pitched whining noise, and he's driving us all barmy going 'eeeeee' all the time. Even when he's at school Angelo constantly replicates the noise for hours on end. It goes right through you; it must drive everyone around him mad. One night I just couldn't sleep because of the noise, so I went downstairs, put cotton wool in my ears and tried settling down on the sofa – but I could still hear him. It must be so tiring for Angelo, too, and stressful.

There have been some encouraging signs though. We have recently acquired a little dog who we've called Chanel. Patrick had repeatedly asked Sean and I if he could have one and eventually we gave in. She's a little Jack Russell-Chihuahua cross and Patrick loves her to bits. Angelo, though, was not at all keen to be sharing his home with this four-legged interloper at first. If Chanel walked into a room, Angelo would walk out. Nevertheless, Chanel persistently followed Angelo around until eventually she won him over, which was lovely. Animals such as dogs can play a huge part in breaking down barriers with children on the autistic spectrum and it's wonderful to see Angelo now accepting Chanel, even to the point of allowing her to sit on his tummy while he gently strokes her ears.

I'm not a material person – although sometimes I feel as

though I'd love to have a Ferrari with a number plate that says 'BYE BYE' on it! That said, I feel I have grown as a person over the past few years. I always felt as though people such as doctors, psychologists, teachers and the like were all far superior to me – they were better educated and cleverer – but I've since realised they are just ordinary people and, nowadays, I am far more comfortable around them.

Sean will soon take up a post as a barrister, and they sometimes host barristers' dinners at Inns of Court. I would have found this quite intimidating a few years ago but now I feel really comfortable in their company and I get on well with them all.

As for friends of my own, well, I split them into two categories – my 'autistic' friends and my 'normal' friends. I can talk to my autistic friends about the problems I have been facing and experiencing, and I know they will understand where I'm coming from because they've been in similar situations. That's not meant to be disrespectful to my 'normal' friends, it's just that they can imagine only certain experiences.

Sometimes, even at home, things do get on top of me and I feel my head is about to explode. Once or twice it's gotten so bad I've got in the car and driven around a bit, then parked up and had a cry. Often it's just silly things that get on top of me. It's like a build-up of tiredness and frustration and a lack of sleep.

Occasionally, I feel I'm being taken for granted at home, and that's quite hard to cope with. On the last occasion, Sean and Patrick were having a bit of an argument. The trouble is, neither of them likes to give in and they were at loggerheads. Then Angelo started walking around on his hands and knees, making a wailing, droning sound, and I remember thinking, What the bloody hell's going on around here? I've just got to get a little peace!

I hopped into the car and drove off. Where shall I go? I wondered. I ended up in the rear car park at Hillingdon Manor School, just yards from our home. I parked up and tried to gather my thoughts – which would have been much easier had I not received a number of telephone calls from Sean asking me where I was and when I'd be back. 'I'm out – leave me alone!' I switched off my phone for a while, but when I switched it back on it listed around 30 missed calls from Sean and Patrick!

Other times when I've been too stressed to stay home I've driven to a nearby park, then telephoned my sister for a chat.

'You'll be all right,' she always tells me. 'After all, you wouldn't be able to cope with a normal life!'

Chapter Fifteen

Sean

It wasn't until 2003 that it was finally confirmed: Sean does have Asperger Syndrome. Although I'd never fancied telling him what I had suspected after talking to Christina Bertolucci, the subject was raised during some banter between Sean and me. I joked that, after one or two things he'd done, I wouldn't be surprised if he had Asperger Syndrome too. But I was surprised by his reaction, as he agreed it may be the case.

Grabbing the bull by the horns I suggested he meet up with Dr Fiona Scott, a chartered psychologist and honorary research associate at Cambridge University, who had become known to us through her dealings with Patrick and Angelo, and who was a member of the team behind the three-year study linking autistic-spectrum disorders to the MMR jab.

More surprisingly, Sean just said, 'OK, make an appointment for me.' Shortly afterwards we made the two-hour car journey to Cambridge. Dr Scott interviewed us both, then Sean was given some questionnaires to fill out and asked to give some information about his background. I suppose it was only around three or four hours later that the diagnosis was confirmed.

On hearing the news Sean went very quiet. Was he upset? Well, that's always rather hard to tell, since he does tend to bottle up his emotions. If he was, it didn't last. On the way home we actually had a laugh about it and, at least, a lot of pieces in the jigsaw of our relationship had now fallen into place. The only thing I noticed in particular was Sean's insistence on driving home – normally when we are together I'm the one who drives. We've not really spoken much about the diagnosis since. It doesn't really matter to me because he's still the same Sean I met all those years ago and fell in love with.

I like to grab whatever moments I can with Sean. I have to say, since his diagnosis, he seems to be so much more loving towards us. He's still not a touchy-feely sort of person. He finds that so hard to comprehend, but he's happy to give me a cuddle, just as long as it doesn't continue for too long! In spite of all the hurdles we've had to face in life, Sean and I are still really, really close. He has recently been diagnosed with an eye condition known as Stargardt's disease, which means his peripheral vision is good but his central vision is becoming progressively worse. Sadly, this is not a treatable condition and his sight is going downhill quite rapidly, although we've been told it will stabilise at some point.

Most things Sean says have to be right – it's black and white with no grey areas – which often gets people's backs up, although he doesn't mean to. He has strong, honestly-held views but sometimes these bring him into conflict with others who do not fully understand where he's coming from. He is so knowledgeable that some people see him as a threat. When he worked at Thames Water he was so good at his job in the IT department that he came over as being quite smug about it and this earned him the nickname 'God'.

Sometimes, I find it really frustrating when he seems to think I, or others, know what he's thinking. We had a meeting with a group of teachers recently, then we met up with some other teachers at a later meeting and, because Sean had told the first group certain things, he assumed the second group had already heard what he'd said to the first group.

Sean has little time for whingers and little tolerance of people who cannot give straight answers to straight questions, and looks back upon all we have achieved together as nothing particularly special at all.

I could theorise as to why he feels the way he does, how he feels he is treated by others, and what he thinks of society in general, but it would be far more relevant for him to do so himself. For that reason, the remainder of this chapter is in Sean's own words.

I wasn't at all bothered when I was first diagnosed with Asperger Syndrome. I didn't have any difficulties with it at all. I don't feel any different from the next man. It's just that, in my experience, some people just don't understand that I don't understand certain ways of behaviour. Rules and regulations don't always suit me, or sometimes I find it difficult to conform to them all the time.

To some people I may come across as a moody person

but I love being miserable. I wear black all the time, I like rain, I hate the summer, and I like Gothic-style material – I've even got tombstones on my screen saver! That makes me sound really sick, doesn't it?

I hate to hear people with Asperger Syndrome whining about their condition. Just get on with it! I just think that whining on about it creates an absolute negativity. For me it's really simple. People's difficulties, through careful analysis and willingness to assist, can be addressed. All this 'how they feel about things' really winds me up. What's that all about? In reality, is that really helping a person?

Anna's already mentioned how I'm not very tactile and how Angelo, particularly when he was younger, did not reciprocate her affection. Parents quite naturally want to be affectionate to their children but it's a fact that some children with Asperger Syndrome or autism just aren't that way inclined. They don't always have the same feelings as people who are not on the autistic spectrum.

People with autism don't worry about selfishness. They rarely see it as that. But everyone's selfish – not everyone is as considerate as they could be. The difference with a person with autism is the degree and frequency. If you look at how often it occurs, that's when you can analyse it.

People often ask me about the difference between Asperger Syndrome and autism. Very early on, in 1944, when it was first discovered, there were generally five differences. First of all, as far as Asperger Syndrome is concerned, there is minimal intellectual impairment, no language impairment, and sometimes difficulties over posture and gait.

People with autism usually have obsessions. People with Asperger Syndrome may have more intellectual obsessions, maybe with dinosaurs or astronomy, while a person with autism may have an obsession with an object such as a vacuum cleaner or a bus. And, finally, one that's rarely talked about is that some people with Asperger Syndrome may have slightly sociopathic tendencies. Sometimes things they say may not comply with the norm – they have a tendency to get attracted to some nutty ideals.

I often get shot down in flames when I mention this, but I've seen people get involved in right-wing ideals – neo-Nazism, for instance. That's not because they're neo-Nazis – far from it – it's just because extremists or those bearing militaristic views have very clear and defined ideals, a rigidity of lifestyle. Formulaic lifestyles often appeal to people with autism or Asperger Syndrome because they are so much easier to comprehend. The problem with this is that some may express racist views, for instance saying something like, 'I hate black people' or 'I hate foreigners'. Then you say to them, well what about Sally or Charles? – who just happens to be black or foreign – and they simply don't make that connection, they don't know how to reconcile such extreme views with people they may know and like.

That's why you shouldn't be too disturbed if someone with these conditions expresses such radical ideals – they may get really into such thought processes and then drop them just like that. Often our son Patrick will get a bee in his bonnet about something or other and go on and on about it for ages and then, suddenly one day, he'll forget all about it completely.

I believe society's attitude towards some disabilities needs to change. There needs to be more awareness of certain conditions if people with disabilities are to be given the opportunity to show what they can do in the workplace. I know there are plenty of disabilities out there but autism is reasonably well known in terms of numbers affected – supposedly one in a hundred people to some degree – but where would you go to find an employer who has a policy designed to assist somebody with autism?

I just don't see the infrastructure out there for people to succeed. Our life opportunities are restricted compared with an unimpaired person and people have an awful lot of potential that is either never utilised or underutilised. I think this makes their lives very difficult and frustrating.

I believe there's prejudice against people with Asperger Syndrome. There seems to be a lot of empathy when people are younger, but when they get older, particularly if they are more able, that's not the case. One person I once spoke to said he didn't mind helping people with autism, but it's just that some people with autism don't help themselves. I think that's the attitude of some people. They think there's nothing wrong with this person, it's all a pose – how can they be clever in this area and not in that area? Well, they may be very skilled and can manage a project, but their bedroom may be a mess.

Sometimes when you hear of someone with a high profile being reported in the media as having Asperger Syndrome tendencies, it's almost as if it's a criticism. We've seen it regarding a top, top politician in recent times, but it doesn't diminish his ability to do his job, so why point it out in the first place? Sometimes I've even seen it as a term of abuse.

That's the problem, though. I've seen people with Asperger Syndrome who are very eloquent and organised, discussing the issue at hand in an able and articulate way, but they could be picking their nose at the same time, not realising how socially unacceptable they appear.

When you get older, particularly if you want a conventional life, it doesn't take much to kick you out of the mainstream. That's why it's important for people with Asperger Syndrome to choose their careers very carefully. They're best placed in positions where they have a lot of autonomy and without so many pressures on them.

Some careers are much more suitable than others. Touchy-feely personal skills are not much good. If you need to work in a very tight-knit team for an organisation – and, personally, I can't think of anything worse – well, that would be dreadful. Careers with autonomy where you're reliant on your own skills are far better, the obvious being law, or teaching at the higher end of the scale (not necessarily in a school but in a college or university), computer programming, system engineers – jobs that may be intellectually demanding but have a certain predictability.

Even in law, you get yourself to a stage where the ideas are very complex but you can understand them because you are working in a framework that's very predictable. Strict rules. If you're taking a case to court, this has to be done by a certain day, and so on. It's almost modular.

If you look at the way the Disability Discrimination Act 1995 deals with autism and Asperger Syndrome, first of all there was a discussion as to whether the conditions were covered by the Act, but case law has settled that argument. That's fine, but the onus is on educational establishments and employers to make reasonable adjustments for a person's autism/Asperger Syndrome, but there just isn't the understanding. So many people, unable to discern a visible handicap, cannot comprehend why people with these conditions need to have any adjustments made.

So what sort of adjustments are necessary? A person with Asperger Syndrome in higher education may need a lot of clarity of expectations, of what's needed and when. They may, possibly, need help with organising their time so they can meet their deadlines. One of the big pitfalls for people with Asperger Syndrome is they can do only a certain number of things at a certain time, so they have to be very clear as to where their social life has to end so they have the time to do the work they need to do. The problem is that this doesn't happen, and that's why one-to-one support is very important.

I get annoyed when I hear that people with autistic disabilities are included in the workplace – that's just a load of nonsense. There's a whole range of attitudes ranging from 'this person hasn't got a problem' to 'we've all got problems, what makes you any different?' and even 'if you haven't got a physical disability, what's your problem?'

Some employers may say they're 100 per cent behind the Disability Act but then argue that it doesn't necessarily apply to them because of their 'special' circumstances. You still get that an awful lot – it's almost as if they're saying, 'Our job is so important we can't spend time faffing around on your behalf!' I recall an example of this attitude when I spoke to someone from the department that specialises in autism at the University of Birmingham. 'Why should you get any special treatment?' she asked. I was amazed this comment came from a woman who worked for an organisation that specialises in the subject.

The ideals behind the Disability Discrimination Acts of 1995 and 2005 are very good. I think inclusion means that the environment in which a person with a disability operates, for instance the workplace or a place of education, is modified such to take account of the effects of their disability. In a mainstream school the environment should be adapted to help that person.

What isn't inclusion is when that child goes to a specialist unit attached to that school. That's not inclusion, that's integration. Within schools, what the Disability Discrimination Act is designed to do is to extend that idea into higher education and then into the workplace. The burden is on the employer to make the necessary adjustments.

The emphasis is on 'reasonable' adjustment – an employer simply can't make adjustments that would undermine the practicalities of their business. So, for instance, a person with a physical disability – say they can't walk – couldn't be expected to find employment in a warehouse where they may be expected to move around a lot and carry boxes. However, the idea is to get people with disabilities included in society. The problem with autism and Asperger Syndrome is the lack of understanding of the conditions and knowing what adjustments might be necessary. There also seems to be a lack of willingness by some employers. In my opinion, however worthy the Act is, it has failed people with autism and particularly Asperger Syndrome and, if anyone can provide evidence to the contrary, I'd be more than willing to see it.

People need to recognise that employers have to comply with the Act. The benefit to society of doing so, having people with disabilities who are included, has to be a good thing. I think natural prejudices need to be addressed. Of course you could penalise employers – and the damages at employment tribunals are potentially unlimited. That's fine, but it doesn't always have the desired effect. More likely it encourages some employers to find a way around the situation. Ideally, employers would say we have to comply, we want to comply and it's good to comply.

The All-Party Parliamentary Group meetings on autism may have their weaknesses and failings, but nevertheless they're good for networking. In all honesty, our politicians are committed to addressing the difficulties people with disabilities have because, in this country, they've passed the Disability Discrimination Act 1995 and the Disability Discrimination Act 2005, and that's excellent.

But society in general is not prepared to take everything on board – so what can politicians really do about that? If the Prime Minister was to stand up and say we all have to be nice to people with disabilities, it wouldn't matter a hill of beans, would it? It's people's perceptions that matter. At least politicians of all persuasions have tried to do something about it and we should acknowledge that.

Money, of course, is a big factor and always will be. Some people argue that labelling someone with autism doesn't help their cause but, without the label, you don't get the funding – and sometimes a label is a passport to get things done. You're not labelling a person, you're labelling a disability, and that's not a negative approach.

Another thing that concerns me was a claim made many years ago that there's no such thing as autism – it's a social construct, it's all in people's minds. Then again, you still hear people say there's no such thing as dyslexia or ADHD – kids just need a good beating – and some so-called expert in America has claimed on the internet that it's the mother's fault if a child has autism because they're 'refrigerator mothers' – in other words children are not reciprocating affection or tactile responses because they haven't learned it from their mother. Does anyone really take such ludicrous claims even remotely seriously?

I personally think Asperger Syndrome is far too heavily diagnosed. I've heard of people being diagnosed after a *ten-minute examination. That's potentially disastrous. Someone may display certain traits, but it doesn't necessarily mean they have the condition. One so-called expert, a clinical psychologist, made a diagnosis at one of his seminars. The parents of a child came up to him for his opinion.*

The child's father appeared very rigid and stiff. When the psychologist said, 'I think your child has Asperger Syndrome,' the mother asked, 'Do you think one of us has Asperger Syndrome?' He told her, 'I think your husband may have' – simply because of the way he appeared. The whole thing was 'diagnosed' in the space of five or ten minutes. OK, the psychologist may well have been right, but he could have been wrong, and the point I'm making is, you shouldn't tell someone like that – far more care needs to be taken.

Normally, a diagnosis is likely to be fine, just as long as it's done properly. As long as good practice is applied, it shouldn't really be necessary to seek a second opinion. I wouldn't accept an informal diagnosis from anyone. How can they diagnose without a formal assessment? A good detailed background history is always vital.

There are a lot of people with high-functioning autism and Asperger Syndrome who could make a significant working contribution to society. I think that only around 16 per cent of people with Asperger Syndrome are in work. They have no learning disability or verbal impairment, so that should stand them in good stead – so why is it the other 84 per cent cannot get a job particularly when, in this country, unemployment stands at around six per cent?

The 'system' in Britain is designed to support people up to the age of 19. Maybe they'll go on for another three years but, after that, it's time to make their own way in life – but many need far more time and support. The trouble is, the system won't fund it.

Speaking personally, I never had any difficulties in my IT career, which benefited me considerably when Anna and I took on the Hillingdon Manor project. Never at any time did I feel we were taking on too much, because I was used to managing big projects through my work with Thames Water.

I still can't fathom why some people thought it was such a big deal, because the amount of money we needed to raise, £627,000, may sound a lot, but the amount I was dealing with at Thames Water was significantly more. When we took on the school project we had the right people in place, all of whom were committed to the cause. I didn't have a single sleepless night over it at all.

I just didn't see what the difficulty was.

And Finally...

After all the recent upheaval, life goes on at Hillingdon Manor and its associated facilities. Sadly, in July 2006, Angela Austin said goodbye and strolled off into the sunset to enjoy her well-earned retirement, while Sean Pavitt swapped his role as head teacher at the Upper School to replace her.

A year later, though, it was Sean's time to say farewell after he accepted a position as head teacher at an emotional behavioural disorder school in Dorset, not far from his parents' home. We were sad to say goodbye to Sean – and his wife Cheryl – after all his hard work at Hillingdon Manor and the Upper School, and knew we would find it tough to replace him, but we were very fortunate to find someone we considered to be the ideal person to take over the reins following an extensive internet search.

The staff and I were delighted, and not just a little relieved, to welcome Gail Pilling as the new principal at Hillingdon Manor in time for the following academic year, and we are confident that, under her stewardship, the work at the school can only continue to develop in a positive manner. Gail began her career at Hillingdon Manor initially working alongside Sean Pavitt for a short while prior to his departure. She is an educational psychologist, a speech-and-language therapist and an HMI (Her Majesty's Inspector) – all three roles being of great relevance and benefit to her new post. Gail was also able to back up her impressive qualifications with some considerable experience in supporting children with autism and Asperger Syndrome.

Also, I am so pleased and excited to report that all the uncertainty and distress leading to the take-over of Hillingdon Manor have finally been put to rest. After a really stressful year which had seen tensions between myself and some of the directors almost reaching breaking point – not to mention all the problems associated with the much publicised 'credit crunch' which made our ability to obtain loan finance much harder – we nevertheless strove to ensure that the developments needed to ensure the school could function appropriately were put in place.

Then, in the middle of 2008, we received an unsolicited approach from a company called Hillcrest Care Limited, one of the UK's leading independent providers of children's homes, foster care and learning disability services, who expressed an interest in teaming up with us. We already knew a certain amount about Hillcrest having been invited to one of their sites at Chipping Norton the previous summer. Without exception, we had all been very impressed by them. Coming through loud and clear during our visit was the fact that, although they were a successful private company, they were very client focused and had a proven track record. This was something we could all relate to.

After their approach I decided to try to find out more about them. My thorough investigations revealed that they were a large company with many interests, which I felt were complementary to our own. Without question they are a professional company run by very competent staff. Conversations with Roger Colvin, their chief executive, and managing director Richard Greenwell, made it clear to Sean and I that they shared the same vision with regards to the future as we did. Sean and I were not supportive of the idea of using venture capital to take the services forward and, for us, the fact that Hillcrest is a private company made them particularly well suited. Because of all these facts, we gave the Hillcrest partnership our full support and, eventually, after obtaining the support of the other parties involved, the merger was approved. The process of selling the company was obviously going to be long and expensive and proved to be very frustrating for Sean and me. Nevertheless in November 2008 the process was, at last, completed.

I shall be remaining in my role as a director of Hillingdon Manor School and the other adult provision which we provide at The Old Vicarage, Summercare and at West London Community College – the new name that has since been given to West Middlesex College. I am a significant shareholder of the new holding company, Hillcrest Autism Care Limited, and I will work closely with the Hillcrest management team as we build on top of the excellent achievements we have made to date.

Hillcrest's acquisition of Hillingdon Manor and its associated facilities added to the 500 staff and 6 schools that are part of the Hillcrest family. This was a huge burden lifted from my shoulders. At last, we could look positively towards the future by expanding and enhancing the services we already had to offer. In his press release after the partnership came to fruition, Hillcrest's Chairman and founder Barry Sampson said: 'We are delighted to be adding Hillingdon Manor School to the Hillcrest family. After our acquisition of Orange Grove foster care last year, which is going from strength to strength, we were keen to continue the strategic growth of Hillcrest into associated areas'.

Hillcrest is a well-established business. Founded in 1994, it currently has 10 specialist children's homes in England and Wales that cater for children with, amongst other things, emotional and behavioural difficulties. It is one of the largest childcare groups remaining in private hands. Hillcrests six fully registered DfES (the old name!) schools provide a full, rich and varied curriculum, which is delivered by qualified teachers and support staff.

The Learning and Disability Services wing of Hillcrest has created a number of exciting, pioneering and innovative projects which include residential homes for adults, and supported living with domiciliary care and residential children's homes that support children up to and during their transition to adult services. Barry Sampson, is also the chairman of Seaward Properties, which has been awarded one of the UK's top property awards, is the majority shareholder of Hillcrest Care, so we are more than satisfied with the high calibre of people we will now be working alongside.

Being part of the Hillcrest group will provide us with greater support and access to funds for expansion and development of the services we can offer. Hillcrest set to work immediately, adding an extra classroom block at the school to help accommodate the excess demand for places.

We have an exciting three-year development plan for Hillingdon Manor through which we will, hopefully, establish separate extended primary, secondary and Intensive Communication and Life Skills Department provision which is desperately needed due to the excess demand we have been facing. We also have plans to extend our admission criteria for our adult provision to include adults on the autistic continuum with more complex needs, and this will create a facility that will also benefit Angelo when he reaches 19 years of age.

Things have just been getting better and better, particularly at West London Community College, where work is still ongoing to meet the complex and specific needs of the students by way of a person centred approach. Each individual's programme is currently designed to promote the students' intellectual, psychological, cultural, physical and creative competencies. We offer courses in ICT, life skills, vocational training skills, stress management, assertiveness, and relationships with sex education. Among the more practical groups are a lunch enterprise scheme and a tuck shop. We offer choices of community-based physical activities such as swimming, football or working out in a gym.

The college was successful in securing a grant from the Football Association, which will run for the next three years. This has enabled us to form a seven-a-side football team in the West London Disabled Football League. As I write, the team are preparing for their second match, having won their first game quite magnificently!

Academic study at the college is available through a variety of routes. It is essential to plan, with the student, which option best meets their needs. This could be anything from attending university to a correspondence and distance-learning programme. Our staff work closely with colleagues from other services to form a multi-disciplinary team, providing a holistic approach to students' welfare and well being.

Weekly guidance counselling sessions are invaluable and provide students with the opportunity to raise any subject they choose in a private, safe and supportive forum. Students also have the option of an additional weekly session with a psychotherapist as this is particularly beneficial to those students who require Cognitive Behavioural Therapy (CBT).

I have to say that working with my new colleagues from Hillcrest, Barry Sampson, Roger Colvin, Richard Greenwell and others, has proven to be a real joy. As I have said earlier, we have formulated some very exciting plans to expand our services for people with autistic spectrum disorders, and there is no doubt in my mind that the future is now very positive indeed. My former colleagues have now moved on, and Sean is no longer involved in the company. Sean is one of the few people to successfully represent someone with Asperger's Syndrome in an Employment Tribunal, and he will continue his legal work; he will also be spending a lot more time developing his interests in financial markets.

Meanwhile, we have been further encouraged to learn of a potentially helpful Autism Bill which has been put forward by

Angela Browning MP who for many years has championed the rights of individuals with autistic spectrum disorders. If this Bill becomes an Act, it will be an extremely welcome piece of legislation. At the time of writing, the Bill is only at the second reading stage and, even if it gets the appropriate support in Parliament, will not come into force for quite some time. Nevertheless, I and the staff at West London Community College have been particularly pleased to read that the Bill appears to be focusing around independent living and daily life skills as these issues have, for the past year, been our main focus of learning. Our students have been thriving in a culture of independence and choice. Yes, academia is important but if choice is not made available, it is not a person centred or client led service.

We have been delighted that the Conservative and Liberal Democrat parties have both pledged their full support for the draft Bill should one of their MPs be selected in a Private Members Ballot. This makes it all the more important that people contact their MP to ask them to enter the ballot for Private Members Bills and to take on the Autism Bill if successful.

We've been urging organisations to pledge their support for the Bill which aims to strengthen information about the numbers of people with autism and their needs in order to improve local planning and commissioning of services. It aims to improve inter-agency working to ensure effective transition for disabled young people who are moving from child to adult services and, finally, it aims to ensure access and appropriate support and services for people with autism in adult life.

Readers will, by now, be fully aware that this is a major issue for Sean and me. Like other parents in our position, Sean and I are determined that everything possible is in place to help our children, Patrick and Angelo, cope with life, especially in the event of anything happening to us! The transition from school to adulthood for young people with autism demands a high degree of inter-agency cooperation, and this is where difficulties often arise.

Furthermore, eighty-six per cent of local authorities say that if they had more information on autism prevalence in their area it would help them with long-term planning. As things currently stand, adults with autism are often unable to access the right support and, consequently, become dependent on their families. Sixty-one per cent of adults with autism rely on their families for financial support, while forty per cent live at home with their parents.

Structural barriers prevent adults with autistic spectrum disorders from accessing the support they so desperately need. Local authorities tend to provide services via specific teams, with the teams categorised into client groups. People with autistic spectrum disorders will usually come into contact with the learning disability team and/or the mental health team. However, as autism is a developmental disorder, it is not appropriate to categorise autism as simply being a 'learning disability' or a 'mental health problem'. Failure to understand the needs of people with autism means that many individuals, particularly those with Asperger's Syndrome or high-functioning autism, find themselves falling through the gap between services that refuse to take responsibility for them.

A lack of understanding of, and training in, autism means

that the health and community care needs of a person with autism are not properly understood in an assessment; they are then unable to access the services they need, and the right types of support are also lacking.

The top three types of support that parents and carers believe their son or daughter with autism would most benefit from are, according to surveys, social skills training (sixty per cent), social groups (fifty-six per cent), and befriending (forty-nine per cent) and yet there is a clear shortage of these types of support.

If this Bill is passed through parliament it will make a difference to the lives of thousands of adults with an autistic spectrum disorder. Gaining the support of the Conservatives and the Liberal Democrats has been a major step forward.

We are committed to raising the awareness of autism and Asperger's Syndrome. Over recent months, three of our college students have developed a training package they can deliver to a variety of delegates, including social care professionals, company employers, parents and young people in transition. ASDAT – Autistic Spectrum Disorder Awareness Training – can be purchased by contacting the West London Community College.

Looking to the future, we have to recognise that our students, like everyone else, have emotional needs that have to be met, particularly when it comes to relationships. A group of students at the college devised and developed a friendship and dating agency which they called Friends 1st and, to date, there have been four successful events with up to thirty attendees at each. However, unbeknown to us, a Christian organisation also calls itself Friends First and they informed us that we should change the name of our dating agency as they had been using it for the past nine years. This came as a huge blow to the students who had really worked so hard on this project and had really established the name.

For those on the autistic spectrum, change doesn't come easily but I was impressed by the way the students decided to tackle the problem. Like true professionals, the students went back to the drawing board and announced a competition for all the members to come up with a new name for the group and offered a prize for the winning member. We await the result.

A parent and carer support group has now been established at the college where it is hosted every month. This is a free provision for any parents or carers of a person diagnosed as being on the autistic spectrum and 16 and over. We've made this service available to everyone, regardless of the borough in which they reside.

So, as you can see, since going into partnership with the Hillcrest family, we are going from strength to strength and the future of our centres is looking far rosier than it was a few months ago. I now feel that we are working as a cohesive team and there is hardly a limit to what we may achieve.

News of our work has been spreading worldwide. In recent weeks I have been approached by parents and professionals in the United Kingdom, USA, Canada, Japan and Barbados. I have been giving talks all over the country about our work; been featured on a breakfast show on Irish television; spoken at a national conference and have been invited to return to speak at next year's conference.

The fact that so many people are now sitting up and taking notice of what we have achieved, and that many of them wish to replicate our work, is immensely satisfying, but we do not intend to rest on our laurels.

Another initiative we are developing is a national website - AnnaKennedyOnline.com - which is due to be launched in 2009. This will be a charitable website with up-to-date information on autism research, parliamentary updates, places to visit for holidays that are autism child friendly, and Sean will have a legal section that will advise people visiting the site of any changes in education law, employment law etc. Basically, it is intended to be an all-singing, all dancing website concentrating on autism issues but with other interests as well.

Looking forward, our aim is to maintain the progress we have made as a family and with our work to date, and to ensure our boys and the students in our centres are equipped to live the rest of their lives as fully as possible.

It's been a long, hard struggle with many setbacks and obstacles along the way but, with the support of other dedicated parents, directors, shareholders, businesses and well-wishers, we have achieved an awful lot over the past ten years and I'd like to think that in another ten years I'll still be doing what I'm doing now – though, hopefully, without quite so much stress!

Sometimes, when I'm really exhausted I sit back and wonder why we've been doing all this, but then I only need to look at Patrick and Angelo to know the reason. They're unable to fight for themselves, so it's up to us to do it for them. However, we do not intend to rest on our laurels. There is still more to do and we will not rest until we have done it.

That much we owe our boys and others like them.

Acknowledgements

There are so many people who have helped us along the way who deserve our heartfelt thanks – and I'm sure there must be many more kind people and organisations who have contributed to Hillingdon Manor whom I may have forgotten and to whom I can only apologise.

Thanks, therefore, to the following individuals and organisations:

Esther Rantzen

Thank you, Esther, for agreeing to become patron of the school and HACS, for highlighting the issue of autism, and for your support. Also, congratulations on your participation on the ITV programme *I'm a Celebrity, Get Me Out of Here!* You proved that a 68-year-old woman can cope just as well as the younger generation in the jungle amongst all the spiders and snakes. You were brilliant and we're all very proud of you! I hope you were able to draw support from the pictures our pupils drew for you.

Sean, Patrick and Angelo

Thank you for introducing me to autism! It's been a roller-coaster ride!

Coral Kennedy and Pamela George

Thank you for moving down from Middlesbrough to help us through some tough times and for all the babysitting sessions.

Maria Luisa, Tony and Nico Davison

I'd like to thank my sister and her husband for listening to all my moaning over the telephone and for continually cheering me up. Thank you, Nico, for being a really great cousin to Patrick and Angelo. I'm sure Maria Luisa and Tony must have learned an awful lot about Asperger Syndrome when Patrick stayed with them for a week!

Maria and Tony Sammarone (Mam and Dad)

Thanks for supporting me and particularly to Mam for listening to me.

Tullio and Nikki Sammarone

I'd like to thank my brother and his wife for their support and all they've done for the boys, particularly Patrick, as he's always saying how much Tullio lifts him up when he's feeling miserable.

Aunty Anita and Uncle Ken

Thanks for putting me on the train to London all those years ago!

Acknowledgements

Norma

Norma looked after Patrick when he was placed in an incubator shortly after his birth. She has been my good friend ever since.

'Aunty' Zita and Ted Harrowing

Aunty Zita telephones me every single day without fail at 6.45 p.m. on the dot. She never judges me and is the nicest woman anyone could ever meet. She's Angelo's godmother and I feel as if I were the daughter she never had. Thanks, Ted, for your friendship.

Hillingdon Autistic Care and Support

HACS was the seed of all we have achieved. My thanks go to all involved.

Anne Robinson

Thanks for starting HACS with me.

Our Lady of Lourdes Church, Uxbridge

This is where we first set up our HACS meetings. Thank you for letting us have the use of the hall free of charge.

London Borough of Hillingdon

Thank you for giving us the keys to the school (eventually!). I have to be honest in admitting we have been very lucky to have dealt with you, as there are not many boroughs that would have done what you have done for us over the past few years.

Mary Milne, head of client services, Hillingdon Borough Council

You were one of the key people at Hillingdon Borough Council involved en route to our getting Hillingdon Manor. Thank you so much.

John Randall MP

John has been on our side even before Day One! Thanks for fighting our corner for us and for keeping in contact.

John McDonnell MP

Like John Randall, John has continually offered his support and has written many letters on our behalf to the council.

Councillor Ray Puddifoot

Ray has supported our projects at the school, the residential home and the college. Thank you for this consistent support.

Derek Jones

Thanks for giving me respite for a few hours a week when setting up the school and in the early days.

Christina Bertolucci

Thank you, Christina, for supporting Angelo and Patrick in the early days and for your invaluable workshops on autism.

Alex and Sally Honeysett

It's been a roller coaster, Alex! Thank you for supporting the project right from Day One. Thank you for your commitment to the cause.

Acknowledgements

Dave Clark

Thank you for your financial investment in Hillingdon Manor – even though you have not had children affected by an autistic-spectrum disorder. Thanks for believing in what we've been doing and for your continued support.

Barclays Bank plc

We went to a lot of banks and all of them except Barclays told us we had a nice project but to close the door on the way out. Barclays didn't, so thank you very much. Barclays was the bank that said 'yes'!

James Coombes

Formerly of Barclays Bank. Thank you for wording the letter paving the way for our loan to buy Hillingdon Manor in the way that you did.

Theran Dhatt

Our Barclays Bank manager. Thank you for your ongoing support.

Graham Reynolds

A solicitor with a son with autism, Graham was instrumental in the setting up of Hillingdon Manor School. It was Graham who put us on to Barclays Bank when all other banks were declining to help us purchase the school.

Nicholas Smith

Nicholas works for Barclays Bank. He has undertaken many fundraising activities for the school and HACS. A really nice guy for whom nothing is too much trouble.

Tony Kohn

The company secretary since Day One. Thank you for your support and your honest opinions.

Cliff Pearson

A parent of one of our pupils, Cliff can work magic. He is our maintenance man whom we just wind up and let go.

Beverley Williams

A very supportive parent of two children with autism. We've laughed and cried together, and shared scary stories about things our kids have got up to. I wish her all the best for the future.

Nigel Seagrove

After hearing me speak on the radio about Hillingdon Manor, Nigel got in touch and offered to supply us with all our signage requirements free of charge. Thank you. Let's hope you can make enough money to buy that Ferrari you're always going on about!

Bob Hillier

A parent of a child with autism, Bob was very supportive of our efforts to start up Hillingdon Manor School and became the treasurer of HACS. Such a likable man, Bob has since passed away. He is greatly missed.

Acknowledgements

Terry Crick

What a lovely man. A master of many trades who helped us so much to keep everything in good repair. Terry passed away a while back and, like the late Bob Hillier, he is sadly missed.

Graham Snoad

A former deputy head teacher at Hillingdon Manor School, Graham has a son with autism. Even before we opened the school he rolled up his sleeves to help with the painting. He has since moved on to work at a mainstream school but he has ensured Hillingdon Manor has links with his new school.

Councillors Catherine Dann and Peter Ryerson

Thank you, both, for speaking up for the school when we needed your support.

Hillingdon Rural Centre

The centre, run by people with learning disabilities, gave us lots of plants to make Hillingdon Manor School's gardens look so nice.

Humphrey Hawksley

A reporter on the BBC2 Newsnight programme, Humphrey has produced several really good television features on the school and frequently gets in touch for updates.

Hasbro

The toy manufacturers have donated lots of toys, games and puzzles and staff have held several fundraising events.

David Kamsler

David is a gem! He is from the Link charity and, through him, we obtained a lot of furniture when we set up Hillingdon Manor School and even more since then. A good friend.

Basingstoke Council

It was through Basingstoke Council that we were put in touch with David Kamsler from the Link. They helped to ensure we received a good amount of office furniture.

British Airways

The company staff did a lot of fundraising for us – things like wearing odd socks for the day and fun days.

British Airports Authority

Staff from BAA did a lot of work for us when we founded Hillingdon Manor School, including the fitting out of a kitchen as part of a team-building exercise. They did a very good job.

Thames Water

Sean's previous employers held a fundraising event for the school.

Acknowledgements

Community Services

Thank you for all those Saturdays when I would come in to Hillingdon Manor School to paint it in preparation for opening. It was so nice to see so many willing pairs of hands. Between them, your helpers saved us lots of money, which we were able to put towards other good uses at the school.

Jack and Jean Greiller

I met Jack and Jean through a wine club, which raised funds for the school. Afterwards they came to the school and, since then, have been on hand to offer their voluntary support.

Disney VoluntEARS, Hammersmith

The Disney toys, DVDs, CDs, and costumes donated and the work done in the sensory garden at Hillingdon Manor School are much appreciated.

Jonas Nilsson

Jonas has a daughter with autism. His help with the maintenance at Hillingdon Manor School has been invaluable.

Antoinette and Kevin Mullally

Thanks for your continued support throughout the years. You have both supported so many families along the way, far beyond your call of duty.

Heathermount School, Ascot

The help provided with establishing policies and procedures when we opened Hillingdon Manor was much appreciated.

Angela Austin

Thank you, Angela, for giving us the best opportunity to set up a centre of excellence for autism.

Sean and Cheryl Pavitt

Sean, it's been a pleasure to watch you bloom from starting off as a teacher, getting married, to starting a family. Thank you both for helping Patrick and Angelo through some difficult times.

Past and present staff

Past and present staff at Hillingdon Manor Schools, past and present staff at West London Community College, past and present staff at Summacare, past and present staff at The Old Vicarage – thank you, everyone, for all your dedication, not to mention all the extra hours you've all worked!

Sally and Chris Eaton

Thanks for your support and fundraising. Thanks also for your advice.

Brunel University

Your contributions from Rag Weeks and general support have been much appreciated. We've been very happy to have been able to take some of your work-placement individuals on as permanent staff.

Acknowledgements

United States Navy

Thanks for your efforts in helping us decorate at St Mary's Centre – even though one of the ceilings ended up being painted with gloss paint instead of emulsion!

Barbara Fisher

The community reporter and deputy editor of our local newspaper the Uxbridge Gazette, Barbara has consistently updated news of the school in the newspaper. She's become a friend and we appreciate her continued support.

National Autistic Society

How things have improved since we first contacted the society. It is now proved to be a really good resource – better information for parents, particularly when a child has just been diagnosed. We've since made several friends from the society and we would like to thank them for their support.

Ivan Sage

Thank you for helping me to write this book.

Julian Reader

It was Julian who gave me the idea to write this book and securing a successful publishing deal was thanks to him and his team.

Professor Uta Frith

Uta has given many talks on our behalf, free of charge. She worked in the field of autism for many years and we appreciate her valuable support and advice.

Dr Fiona Scott

Like Uta, Fiona has given many talks on our behalf. We met her when we first set up the school and it was she who diagnosed Sean as having Asperger Syndrome.

Hampshire Police Academy

I went to the academy with Alex, Patrick and Angelo to collect donated wardrobes, beds and chests of drawers when we were about to open The Old Vicarage residential home.

Ross Kemp

AKA EastEnders' Grant Mitchell. Thank you, Ross, for visiting the school and spending time with Patrick and the children.

Uxbridge police and firemen

Thank you for your fundraising efforts.

Botwell School, Hayes

Thanks to all concerned for raising funds with a sponsored silence.

Moorcroft School, Hillingdon

Thank you for your support in the early days.

Barry Sampson, Roger Colvin and Richard Greenwell from Hillcrest Autism Services Ltd

Thank you for your support in the early days.

Acknowledgements

Mencap

And, last but not least, thank you, Mencap, for the use of the swimming pool on site.

Judith Azzopardi

Thanks for taking on the challenge. I look forward to working with you.

Useful Contacts

Hillingdon Manor Lower & Middle School
For pupils from 3.5 years to 12–13 years
Intensive-skills pupils from 3.5 years to 14–19 years
Harlington Road
Hillingdon
Middlesex UB8 3HD
Tel: 01895 813679
Principal: Gail Pilling
Email: annakennedy1000@hotmail.com
www.autismconsultants.org
www.hillingdonmanorschool.org.uk

Hillingdon Manor Upper School

For pupils up to 19 years

Stables Courtyard

Church Road

Hayes

Middlesex UB3 2UH

Tel: 020 8573 7419

Email: annakennedy1000@hotmail.com

www.autismconsultants.org

www.hillingdonmanorschool.org.uk

West London Community College

(This college is for Social Services, Learning Disabilities funding and Direct Payments funded students)

Colne Lodge

Longbridge Way

Uxbridge

Middlesex

UB8 2YG

Tel: 01895 619700

Fax: 01895 619701

Email: annakennedy1000@hotmail.com

Web: www.autismconsultants.org

Acknowledgements

Hillcrest Care Ltd
Langstone Gate
Solent Road
Havant
Hampshire
PO9 1TR.
www.hillcrestcare.co.uk

Hillcrest Autism Services Ltd
Vine House
Harlington Road
Hillingdon
Middlesex
UB8 3HD
Tel: 01895 619734

The Old Vicarage Residence
For residents 18+ years
75 The Greenway
Uxbridge
Middlesex UB8 2PL
Tel: 01895 454710
Fax: 01895 619701
Email: annakennedy1000@hotmail.com
Registered Manager: Michelle Kelly
www.autismconsultants.org

Summacare Ltd

Offering provision to adults suffering from Asperger Syndrome
and high-functioning autism
Vine House
Harlington Road
Hillingdon
Middlesex UB8 3HD
Tel: 01895 436028
Fax: 01895 436025
Email: annakennedy1000@hotmail.com
Registered Manager: Lauren Whittingham
www.autismconsultants.org

Hillingdon Autistic Care and Support (HACS)

Registered Charity No: 1066859
A charitable support group for the parents and families of
children on the autistic spectrum.
The Vines
Harlington Road
Hillingdon
Middlesex UB8 3HD
Tel: 01895 271211
Director: Antoinette Mullally
Email: toni@hacs.org.uk
www.hacs.org.uk
All donations and enquiries welcome to HACS.

Acknowledgements

SPD Support

A non-profit internet-based support organisation run by a parent of a child with semantic-pragmatic disorder (SPD). www.spdsupport.org.uk

The National Autistic Society

393 City Road
London EC1V 1NG
Tel: 020 7833 2299
Autism Helpline: 0845 070 4004
www.nas.org.uk

Parent-to-Parent Helpline

A free 24-hour support line for parents of an adult
or child with an autistic-spectrum disorder
Tel: 0800 9 520 520
Fax: 020 7833 9666
Email: nas@nas.org.uk
www.nas.org.uk